colección **biografías y documentos**

THE MYTHS OF ARGENTINE HISTORY

Felipe Pigna

The Myths of Argentine History

The Construction of a Past
as a Justification of the Present

From the "Discovery" of America
to "Independence"

GRUPO
EDITORIAL
norma

Buenos Aires, Bogotá, Barcelona, Caracas, Guatemala,
Lima, México, Miami, Panamá, Quito, San José, San Juan,
Santiago de Chile, Santo Domingo

www.norma.com

Pigna, Felipe
The Myths of Argentine History - 1ª ed. -
Buenos Aires: Grupo Editorial Norma, 2005.
416 p.; 21 x 14 cm. - (Biografías y documentos)
ISBN 987-545-228-9

1. Historia Argentina - I. Título
CDD 982

©2005. De esta edición:
Grupo Editorial Norma
San José 831 (C1076AAQ) Buenos Aires
República Argentina
Empresa adherida a la Cámara Argentina de Publicaciones
Diseño de tapa: Ariana Jenik y Eduardo Rey
Imagen de tapa: Ilustración tomada del periódico
Don Quijote, agosto de 1897

Impreso en la Argentina
Printed in Argentina

Primera edición: junio de 2005

CC: 38007
ISBN: 987-545-228-9

Hecho el depósito que marca la ley 11.723
Libro de edición argentina

Contents

To all my beloved fellow countrymen who,
from Mariano Moreno on,
for the crime of dreaming a country
with more freedom and justice for all,
were cast into oceans, rivers and common graves,
in a vain attempt to make them disappear.

To Martín and Julián Pigna.

Our ruling classes have always attempted to deprive the workers of history, of doctrine, of heroes and martyrs. Every one of our struggles must start anew, separated from previous struggles; collective experience is lost and lessons are forgotten. History thus becomes a kind of private property, whose owners are also the owners of everything else.

RODOLFO WALSH

A working class hero is something to be.

JOHN LENNON

Introduction

Who controls the past controls the future:
who controls the present controls the past.

GEORGE ORWELL

Argentine society has, for the past 30 years, been living under the pressing demands of the struggle for daily survival, with little time or energy left to reflect on the origins and remote causes of the evils that afflict it. The process of political and social exclusion the majority of its population has been subjected to since 1976 has precluded their possibility of becoming citizens conscious of their rights, with a clear legal and referential framework to support their demands and assist them in their wishes for personal and social self-realization.

It is in such a context that the powers that be have managed to turn distant and recent history away from the interests of the majority, who have come to see in it but another subject in the school curriculum, and have been thus deprived of a useful tool to better understand their present and plan their future.

In spite of the ideological and methodological evolution of our historians and educators, the system has been able to instill in people's minds the idea that history belongs to the primary school alone. The struggle for independence or May Revolution, as it is known, is thus seen as something pertaining only to the primary school. The birth of our country as an independent entity has become the subject for a school play, and the events of that time have become for most Argentines hard to think about without the addition of black shoe-polish (for the negro makeup), burnt cork (for moustaches and sideburns), and the cries of street vendors peddling hot cakes.

These mechanisms have been alarmingly effective in depriving Argentine history of its political import and reducing it, in the social imagination, to nil. In this impoverished concept of history only the events of the distant past are considered historical, while others, such as the last dictatorship or the Menemist period, are branded as political rather than historical, as if both disciplines did not belong to one another and could be discussed separately.

This particular historical and political pedagogy has resulted in the idea that history and politics is what "the others" do, and that the common people lack the courage, the skills, the ability and – ultimately – the bravery, to make history. During the last dictatorship, ideas such as these prompted many to shrug off every victim of abduction or murder committed by state forces with the phrase "Well, they must have been up to something." In a country whose history has largely been one of dictatorships or bogus democracies, political commitment is hardly ever regarded in a positive light.

It is remarkable that one of the most widely addressed topics in our history or social sciences, the May Revolution, is hardly ever understood by the majority in all its social, economical and, above all, political dimensions. Some handbooks still repeat hackneyed phrases such as "Mariano Moreno was irascible and Cornelio Saavedra was temperamental." Of course, such qualifications could be exchanged and nothing much would change. Personal characteristics are used to cover up or blur the necessary distinctions about ideology, party politics and the interests each individual defended, the interests that explain why Moreno was eventually displaced and "mysteriously died at sea."

The national hero that stands apart from the rest of us mortals, the illustrious being whose supernatural endowments and virtues are such that none of us could ever hope to equal, is a useful creation of the powers that be. Such an example is a fabrication, and history is subsumed in the historical character. If there is an example to follow, it is that of the human being who in spite of his failings and defects chose to risk his life and overcome his limitations to fight for the future and the freedom of his or her country. Manuel Belgrano was such a one. A historical character can be taken as a role model, while the national hero cannot.

The process of cleansing politics out of history, thus depriving it of its social, economic and cultural basis, goes hand in hand with the tendency to either exalt or desecrate the protagonists of our past. The link between past and present being broken, history becomes something alien, subject to chance, and the new generations lose all interest in it.

For the young, history has become like one of those conversations you might overhear at a party, in which guests you don't know discuss topics you ignore. They feel excluded, they lack any sort of referential framework that might integrate them, and very soon they lose all interest. Inclusive referential frameworks are essential, and it is necessary to take the present as our starting-point to let them know that the country that came to being in 1810 is the same one we are seeing today, with many changes, with much progress and many reversals, but the same. And again and again we must return to the present day. The past-present relationship, the comparison of the events of the past and present events, resignifies historical facts and endows them with meaning.

On the other hand, prevailing conditions in our country make this connection rather easy to establish, and it has become a cliché to say that, among us, history repeats itself. Let me offer an example. We were giving some talks in Rafael Castillo, in the impoverished La Matanza party, in one of those schools labeled "high risk" by the very Ministry of Education. We were talking to a group of first to third-graders about conditions during the colonial period: dirt roads that flooded in heavy rain, no running water – which meant they depended on the water-carrier or *aguatero* – no electricity, few doctors, high infant mortality... And a little boy stood up and said "just like nowadays."

It has become a commonplace to say that we have turned our national history into a tale. But even that isn't true. All tales, especially those meant for children, begin with "Once upon a time" – that is, they provide context, a frame of reference for the reader to know where he or she stands. They tell us about a definite time and place, about specific people, their greatness and pettiness, their interests and ambitions, their power struggles, their love affairs. Few or none of these occur in the historical tales we tell our young.

No context whatsoever is given to them. The date "1810" might be mentioned and a bit of scenery thrown in, and that is all. What is the meaning of "1810" for a child of 8 or 10, or for a teenager at that? Something, surely, far more distant and unreal than the planet in which *Star Wars* takes place. These "historical stories" that are fed to us during our first years of primary school are devoid of passion, ambition or deeds. Why did our "national heroes" do what they did? The answer is always the same: "abnegation" we are told.

We cannot go on talking seriously about a history of which abnegation is the main drive. We must recover the much-abused concepts of "interest" and "ideology." San Martín crossed the Andes because it was in his interest to free Chile and move on to Perú, because he had revolutionary ideas which were part of a general process in the wider struggle to free America from Spanish domination.

History conceived as a dynamic process with strong continuities is inimical to the postulates of the "one-dimensional thought we have been subject to since the days of the last military dictatorship. In this respect, Eric Hobsbawm says: "The destruction of the past. or rather of the social mechanisms that link one's contemporary experience to that of earlier generations, is one of the most characteristic and eerie phenomena of the late twentieth century. Most young men and women at the century's end grow up in a sort of permanent present lacking any organic relation to the public past of the times they live in."[1]

But such views are still common today and many "social communicators" still accuse educators of "meddling in politics" when they refer to contemporary topics or events, or give their opinion on a certain historical process. But according to Catalan historian Joseph Fontana, "The historian's task is always political. Nobody can study the Inquisition as if he were investigating the life of, say, insects, in which he is not involved. If the historian's task

---

1 Eric Hobsbawm, *Historia del siglo XX*, Barcelona, Crítica, 1998. Eric Hobsbawm, *The Age of Extremes: A History of the World 1914-1991*. N.Y., Vintage, 1996.

is not useful to those outside the classroom as well as to those within, it is completely useless."[2]

One of the few positive consequences of the terminal crisis Argentina went through in 2001 has been a renewed interest in our history, that is, in the question of who we are, where we come from, why is it that we find ourselves in such a state, what we are and what we may come to be.

In a country that used to speak of its past as if it consisted only in the dates of battles and the disinterested (an unfelicitous word when we come to think of it) and abnegated deeds of our so-called national heroes, it is a good thing that men and women of different ages and classes have begun to take an interest in their most important patrimony: their identity. Because this is what it's all about: a country's history is its identity, it is everything that has happened to us from our birth to the present, our victories and defeats, our joys and sorrows, our glory and our miseries. As in a family album, we pass the pages feeling alternatively pride or shame, but always recognizing ourselves in them.

Suppression of identity was one of the greatest crimes committed by the last military dictatorship. The *desaparecido* ("disappeared one") was deprived of his name, which was replaced by a number assigned by his captors. His or her children were given new names, new identities and homes, often the very opposite of what their parents had dreamed for them. Something very similar has been done to our national history. They have also tried to suppress our national identity.

This book wants to help our people approach our history, so that they might learn to love it, to "reconquer" it, to enjoy this wonderful common heritage which, as most other

2 Joseph Fontana, *Clarín*, December 13, 1998, interviewed by Jorge Halperín.

goods in our beloved country, has been unequally distributed and unlawfully appropriated. History belongs to all of us by natural right, and the challenge is to write the history of all, of all those who have been or will be cast aside by those who believe they have the right to decide what is important and what is negligible. Those who fall outside history die forever, it is the ultimate despoilment the system subject us to: not even a memory remains of those who disobey due obedience, those who are honest come what may, those who rebel in the face of defeat; of those who like Túpac Amaru manage to keep their dignity in the most horrible torture and claims for the freedom of his brothers in a free America; of those like Manuel Belgrano, who spends sleepless nights putting down the project of a country impossible but just, who devotes his life to denouncing and attacking "those who make a party of themselves", who "use the privilege of office to their own benefit and condemn the other citizens to ignorance and misery"; or Castelli, who dreams a revolution and makes it in the region of South America were injustice most prevails; or Mariano Moreno, who burns out his life in six months of feverish activity, knowing power offers no truce and never forgives those who oppose it, knowing as well that if nobody opposes it everything will be much worse.

Knowledge about this past might help us reject the idea that "in this country things have always been amiss and will for ever continue to be so." Our history, richer in events than many, belies the idea that change is impossible, a conception in which even the possibility of dreaming of a better country is aborted.

This is part of the vacant heritage that has been bequeathed us. This pages purport to be an injunction to appropriate what belong to us by right.

The Spanish Invasions, also known as "The discovery of America"

From the moment of the discovery malice has had its sway,
persecuting men whose only crime was to have been born
in a land made by nature rich in opulence, men who have
preferred to leave their villages rather than suffer
the oppression and service of their masters,
their judges and their priests.

MARIANO MORENO
Legal Dissertation on the Personal
Service of Indians, 1802

America in 1492

America was not called America in 1492. It had been settled some 30,000 years ago. The first inhabitants of this vast continent arrived in successive waves, from Asia and Oceania, the former from the north and the latter from the south.

By 1492 they had developed varied forms of social organization. There were urban societies with many great and beautiful cities, such as that of the Aztecs, in the Mexican Central Valley, and that of the Incas, in the Central Andes. Maya culture, extended all over the Yucatán Peninsula, had by then mysteriously vanished.

The Mayas achieved a remarkable cultural development between the years 300 and 900 A.D. Their great city-states, adorned with wonderful artworks, were remarkable for their scientists and mathematicians, who had been able to establish the solar calendar of 365 days.

The Aztec civilization has reached its peak in the 13th century. Its people founded the greatest and most

21

populous city of its time: Tenochtitlán. The Aztecs lived from the spoils of war and the tribute the vanquished tribes were forced to pay. They were basically an agricultural people. As in the Maya cities, pyramids were prominent landmarks, their walls exhibiting, even nowadays, hundreds of hieroglyphs which bear testimony to the greatness of this culture. They followed two calendars, the lunar one, 260 days long, and the 365 days long solar one.

The Inca Empire encompassed a large portion of the present-day countries of Ecuador, Perú, Bolivia, Chile and Argentina. They were great warriors, farmers, artisans and architects, and they built for their cities elaborate systems of defense and irrigation.

As in Europe at the time, other American peoples had developed in differing degrees, according to their needs and the conditions of their regions, and were basically hunters and gatherers.

As a rule, these cultures respected all living creatures. Hunting was for food, not sport, and they took good care of their environment. Old men and children were in their societies the most respected, the former standing for memory and wisdom, for the future the latter. Amerigo Vespucci would say "These savages have neither laws nor faith and live in harmony with nature. They do not know private property, as all possessions are communal. They know neither frontiers, nor kingdoms, nor provinces, and they have no king! Nobody obeys anybody, every man being his own master. They are a very prolific people, but as property is unknown, so too are heirs." He concluded this description by saying that he no doubt had come to the borders of Earthly Paradise.[1]

1 Américo Vespucio, *El Nuevo Mundo*, Buenos Aires, Nova, 1951.

The inquisitorial eyes of the Spaniards were soon fixed on what they saw as the extreme sexual liberality of the original owners of the land. "Men and women walk around naked, in their pelts; in the weddings another man substitutes for the groom, as is their usual practice; if the groom be a chief, all of his guests will sample the bride before him and she will be praised for her toils. They will forsake their women for little cause, and they their men for none. Women walking around naked will sooner or later arouse the men, and much use of this nefarious sin makes these women bad."[2]

The language of the Arawaks, who lived in the lands where contact with the Europeans was first made, overflowed with poetry and was expressive of lives in permanent contact with nature. In conversation, they were never in any haste, never worried about getting rid of the other person as soon as possible, wishing rather to make contact, engage in conversation and get to know the other, share his or her joys and problems. So when naming things and persons, they always took their time. The rainbow was called "the serpent of collars," the sky was "the sea above." Lightning was for them "the radiance of the rain." A friend was called "my other heart" and the soul was "the sun in your chest." The owl was "the mistress of the dark night" Old men would call their walking stick their "ever-present grandchild." To signify "I forgive" they simply said "I forget."[3]

Columbus' language, when compared to that of these romantic Indians, was rather more neoliberal in nature. In

2 Gonzalo Fernández de Oviedo, *Historia general y natural de las Indias*, Madrid, Oriente, 1917.
3 Eduardo Galeano, *Memorias del fuego*, México, Siglo XXI, 1993.

the entries for the first two weeks of his famous *Journal*, a single word is repeated *seventy-five times: gold.*

Discoveries and Cover-ups

Contact between these lands and Europe brought about a great change both for European and American ways of life. It was, for the Europeans at least, a great discovery, and it became an endless source of economical resources and political power. Gonzalo Fernández de Oviedo said, in his *Historia general de las Indias,* that "the discovery of the Indies was the greatest event since the creation of the world, barring the incarnation and death of He who created it."

Adam Smith, one of the fathers of economic liberalism, would many years later, in 1776, agree with Oviedo, affirming, without the Catholic's qualms, that it was the single greatest event in the history of humanity.

The 15th century Europeans saw themselves as the center of the universe, and things came to existence only when they "discovered" them.

For the Americans it would bring about the tragic discovery that the days when they could decide over their life, their ideas, their mode of production and their religion, were gone forever.

Europe in 1492

With the decadence of Feudalism in Europe, the bourgeoisie consolidated its power. The word *bourgeoisie* comes from *burgh*, that is, the area outside the castle, gradually freed from the control of the feudal lord. The burghers were craftsmen and merchants, and it was they who consolidated the capitalist system of production, based on the circulation of money and labor in exchange for wages.

This slowly but inexorably brought about the ruin of the Feudal system, with its closed economy based on the unequal exchange of products and services. As the danger of invasions – which had led the people to crowd within city walls – diminished, kings gradually recovered their power and saw feudalism as an obstacle in the path of the national states, and the bourgeois as their allies in the task of putting an end to the old system. Within a few decades the Feudal system would be a memory, national states would be consolidated all over Europe and the kings would accept the bourgeois in their courts. In financing the luxuries and expenditures of the parasitic dynastic families, the bourgeoisie accumulated privileges and political power. Their loans on interest to the European nobility would result in considerable financial gain, the collecting of taxes would be placed in their hands and they would benefit from the enforcement of law, order and social discipline necessary for the development of their economic activities.

All of these changes would mould a bourgeois mentality which, attached to material objects and less prone to accept the medieval view that stated we should suffer the ills of this world to enjoy a better life in Heaven, would inexorably become hegemonic.

The perception that man – not God – is the center of the world would result in a cultural movement of great import, Humanism, the basis of the period known as Renaissance, one of the most brilliant in European history.

In Europe in 1492 most people lived in poverty and had little chance to enjoy works of art. Sanitation was very poor and diseases were rampant. The people had an average life expectancy of 35 and for the undernourished popular classes minor diseases might prove fatal. Most had no remedy and one out of every four children died in its first year of life.

People ate what they could and for this reason spices were necessary. These were used to preserve meat and to make meals tastier, and since the days of the Crusades they had been brought in from the East.

Chinese tales

European knowledge of Asia was made possible by two different events: the Crusades, between the 10th and 13th centuries, and the Mongolian invasions, between the 13th and 14th centuries. The Crusaders' declared intention was to recover Jerusalem and the Sacred Sepulcher for Christianity, but they also established trade posts along the Mediterranean and the Black seas. During the 13th century, Kubla Kahn's Mongols had conquered and unified most of Asia. This favored commerce between the West and the East, carried out mainly through Venice and Genoa, cities which managed to establish colonies in Asia and Africa.

By 1492 Europe had 60 million inhabitants, 20 million more than half a century earlier. The increase in the population and political stability augmented the value of human life. Life on earth was no longer seen as a mere stepping-stone to Heaven above. People wanted to enjoy their brief lives and the interest in riches and material goods grew.

In 1453 something happened that would have serious consequences for Europe: The Ottoman Turks invaded Constantinople. The commercial route between the West and the East was cut and the more powerful kingdoms began the search for alternative routes. Portugal opened the African route, that circled this continent to reach the Far East. Spain was ruled by Isabel of Castile and Ferdinand of Aragon, who had achieved political and religious unity by expelling the Muslims and Jews. After the reconquest, economic conditions allowed Spain to embark on a great maritime, commercial and military enterprise.

Out of curiosity, need and ambition, 15th century Europeans increasingly dreamed of ventures at sea. The Age was an adequate one. Technical improvements gave them navigation instruments such as the compass (brought from China), the astrolabe (invented by the Arabs) and the sextant. Shipbuilding ingenuity had also resulted in the invention of the caravel, which, combining square and triangular sails with a modern rudder, was more secure and efficient in the open sea.

But there also was a Venetian, Marco Polo[4] by name, who wanted to go further, to the very source of all these riches. He was lucky, and his luck soon turned into fortune. Marco reached the court of the Great Khan, establishing a commercial relationship together with a deep friendship, and had to take many oaths as to his return before the king would let him go.

With Marco, there came from the Far East, besides gunpowder, spaghetti and the rudiments of the printing press, a group of fantastic tales which, corrected and augmented by his fertile imagination, would be published in a book that would make him famous: *Il Millione*. In its pages, Polo told stories of China and its riches, going as far as to build great bridges of gold flanked by ruby walls.

---

4 Venetian merchants Matthew and Nicholas Polo traveled into the Mongolian Empire in 1254, to open new routes for commerce. In Cathay, as China was then called, they were brought to the presence of the Great Khan Kublah. Years later Nichols would return to Cathay with his son Marco, barely fifteen at the time. His fantastical accounts would encourage other travelers to reach these fantastic and legendary lands.

Polo opened a direct route into the land of spices and eastern products, as well as into the feverish imagination of adventurers all over the world, who dreamed of following in his steps.

The Admiral

In Genoa, a young merchant named Christopher Columbus, intent on increasing his wealth, took delight in Marco Polo's books and in the maps he worked with. He also read with passion the *Historia Rerum Ubique Gestarum* by Pope Pius II; the *Imago Mundi* by French Cardinal Pierre d'Ailly, published in 1410, and the map and letters that in 1474 the Florentine scholar Paolo del Pozzo Toscanelli had sent to the Portuguese king through his friend, the Lisboan clergyman Fernando Martins.

He devoted much attention to the two former, as his almost 1800 marginal notes reveal, and he extracted a number of references to Biblical lands located in the distant East, such as Earthly Paradise, the Garden of Eden, Tarshish and Ophir, the Kingdom of Sheba, Mount Sephar and the Island of the Amazons, places he would soon relocate in the Indies, which he thought were the far reaches of Asia. In Toscanelli, who followed Marco Polo, he read about the Great Khan and the Asian mainland: Cathay, Mangi and Cyamba (China) and Cipango (Japan) an island 1500 away from the mainland and famed for its riches.

Columbus had a very sensuous idea about the shape of the Earth. Rather than rounded, he saw it in the shape of the female breast. "The world is not round, but has the shape of a woman's breast and the nipple corresponds to the highest part, close to Heaven; below this is the Equinox and the far reaches of the East were all land and islands end."[5] If this was the case, by sailing west one could reach the East – and this was what most Europeans kings and the bourgeoisie desired.

Columbus' idea wasn't particularly original. Aristotle (384-322 B.C.) had already alluded to it by mentioning Antilia, an island between Europe and Asia. Saint Augustine, in his *Civitas Dei*, divided the world into Europe, Asia and Africa and held that only in these could be found the citizens of heaven, even if other possible lands existed on Earth; these were nevertheless excluded because not peopled by Adam's children.

Saint Isidore of Seville, in his *Book of Numbers,* holds that three is the perfect number because it includes beginning, middle and end, and is the number of the Three Magi, the sons of Noah and the parable of the yeast and the three measures of flour. "The World – this Sevillian would say – is, like the Trinity, one, though parted into three." In another book, *Etymologies*, Saint Isidore speaks of a mysterious land in the midst of the Ocean, perhaps the fourth part of the planet.[6]

The Highest Bidder

Columbus had an interview with King John II of Portugal in 1484. King John listened carefully but was dismayed by Columbus' economic and honorific pretensions – he would be named Great Admiral of the Ocean and demanded ten percent of all profit – and rejected his proposal.

5 Letter form Columbus to Queen Isabel.
6 Edmundo O'Gorman, *La invención de América*, México, FCE, 1958.

Columbus then went to Spain; walking it if his biographers are to be believed. He was lodged in La Rábida convent near the Port of Palos. He there met Friar Juan Pérez,[7] confessor to Queen Isabel. This prelate set up an appointment with the queen, at the time in the Andalusian city of Cordova.

To make the most of his time, while he waited, Columbus met Beatriz Enríquez de Arana, a girl "of humble birth" and on the 15th of August 1488 had a child by her: Hernando Columbus, who would later accompany his father in his voyages and become his apologetic historian.[8] Columbus would forsake the woman but not the child.

The Catholic sovereigns[9] were too busy parading what their name implied:[10] recovering the territory occupied by the

---

7 15th century Spanish Franciscan clergyman, probably the official accountant to Queen Isabel, and her confessor. He met Columbus at La Rábida Monastery soon after the latter's arrival in Spain. He talked the queen into supporting Columbus' enterprise and signs in his name the Santa Fe Agreements.

8 He would write paragraphs like this: "Columbus, which means pigeon, a sign that he was chosen to carry the olive bough and the baptismal oils across the Ocean, as Noah's pigeon signaling peace and the unification of the Gentiles with the Church, after darkness and error have vanished." Hernando Colón, *Historia del Almirante*, Buenos Aires, El Ateneo, 1944.

9 Towards the close of the Middle Ages two large reigns had been established in Spain: Castile and Aragon. In 1469 the two crowns were united through the marriage of Isabel of Castile, then 18 years of age, and Ferdinand of Aragon, of 17. In spite of the unification, each kingdom retained its peculiarities: Spanish was spoken in Castile and Catalan in Aragon. Aragon had interest in the Mediterranean, where the basis of its empire – the Catalan thalassocracy – was, while Castile was searching for new horizons beyond the Atlantic.

10 The Borgia Pope Alexander VI would give them the title of "Catholic" in 1496, together with the privilege of collecting the third

Muslims and expelling the Jews from their dominions, and were not too keen on destining energy or resources to other affairs.

But once they had taken the Muslim Kingdom of Granada, on the 2nd of January 1492, they decided to support Columbus' enterprise. Conditions were written down in a document known as the Santa Fe Agreements, signed April 17, 1492. In it, the Spanish crown agreed to finance the expedition and to give Columbus the following rights:

• He would be lifelong admiral of the isles and mains he discovered, and this title would be hereditary.

• He would be named viceroy and governor of all lands discovered.

• He would have right to ten percent of all maritime commerce.

The document was drawn by the royal notary Juan de Coloma, who included a clause to protect royal rights and that would lead to endless dispute between Columbus, his descendants and the Spanish crown. This clause stated that Columbus would obtain all the rights mentioned in this Agreement "provided that these would conform to precedent and that other Castilian admirals had in the past obtained the said privileges and rights."

The Search for Business Partners

Columbus needed partners in order to finance his foray into the East, into the lands Marco Polo had called Cathay (China) and Cipango (Japan).

---

part of all tithes in the parishes and bishopries of Castile and Aragon. Previous Spanish popes include, in the mid-8th century, Alonso I from Asturias, and Peter II of Aragon in the 13th.

Reluctant to provide for the expedition with her own jewels, Queen Isabel unearthed an old litigation with the town of Palos, which had been fined for smuggling and piracy: a royal letters patent signed April 30, 1492 changed the fine into the provision and equipment of two caravels named Pinta and Niña.

Columbus went to Palos de Noguer and set up a commercial partnership with the Pinzón Brothers and Luis the Santángel,[11] a local financer. To the two caravels provided by the town of Palos he would add the largest ship of the expedition, the Santa María, a hundred feet in length. La Gallega, renamed Santa María by the captain, would be the ensign ship. With its fifty feet, La Pinta would be commanded by Martín Alonzo Pinzón, and the similarly sized La Niña would sail under Vicente Yáñez Pinzón. Martín Alonzo had recently returned from Rome, where he had conversed with a Vatican cosmographer about the lands not yet discovered to the West; he also had copies of sea charts where these islands could be seen. In one of them, drawn in 1482 by a Roman named Benincasa, Pinzón could see, to the west of Africa, huge isles called Antilia and Salvaga.

The proclamation urging all to embark in the expedition was issued the 30th of April, and soon some eighty-five

11 Luis de Santángel came from a Jewish family of converts. He was born in Valencia in 1435 and had served King Ferdinand since 1478, as his counselor in financial matters. He was a friend of Columbus and his influence was instrumental in the approval of his project. As Treasurer of the Holy Brotherhood (the rural police in charge of controlling highway robbery) he managed to collect 140,000 maravedis to finance the expedition, to which he added 17,000 florins of his own. In spite of his services to the crown, his family, because of its Jewish origins, was prosecuted by the Inquisition.

men had signed up. Only four of these were convicts currently in jail.[12] The rest of the crew was made up of law officials, a notary, a surgeon ("barber and bloodletter"), a physicist, a pharmacist and a royal inspector who would look after the monarchs' interests. Unfortunately for those who like to justify the "Spiritual conquest" of the Americas, not a single priest was on board.

Masters and pilots would receive a monthly income of 2000 maravedis, sailors 1000, shipboys and pages 700. In those days a cow as worth 2000 maravedis and a *fanega* (1.6 bushels) of wheat would cost 73.

Ships were not easy to come by. Most were being charted by Jews who after the expulsion had to leave Spain in haste.

The First Spanish Invasion

The three ships, fully manned and equipped, were ready to sail by the 2nd of August 1492. The expedition set sail for the Canary Islands the following day, and reached them on the 9th. They repaired the ships, loaded further supplies and on the 6th of September they set off on their venture into the unknown.

Columbus had calculated they should have to sail some 700 leagues (about 2200 miles) to reach the lands of the Great Khan (China).

On the first days of October many grew impatient and started talking about the return. Columbus consulted

12 Bartolomé Torres, homicide – he had murdered the town crier of Palos – and his friends Juan de Moguer, Alonso Clavijo and Pero Izquierdo who had broken into the public prison of Palos to free their comrade. Back in Spain a royal decree of 1493 granted them their pardons as "they had gone in our service and put themselves in great danger to discover the isles of the Indies."

33

his captains and Martín Alonzo Pinzón suggested that those who did not want to continue should be hanged. He offered his services in case the Admiral didn't care to hang them himself, as "We will not return without good news."

On the night of October 11 and 12, Columbus affirmed he was the first to see the lights of what was thought to be the Asian coast, thus depriving the humble sailor of La Pinta, Juan Rodríguez Bermejo, a Sevilian born in Triana, of the honors and the 10.000 maravedis of the reward.[13]

Those who insist on celebrating Columbus Day on October 12 can run into some trouble if recent investigations confirm that the man known as Rodrigo de Triana uttered his cry not on the 12th but the 13th. But this last number was considered a bad luck omen, and as October 12 was the feast of Our Lady of Pilar, patroness of the Catholic sovereigns, and, in this year of 1492, a Friday, Day of the passion of Christ, to boot, the Admiral changed the date to better please his patrons.

So on October the 12th (or 13th) Columbus and his men were within sight of the island of Guanahani (in what is now the Bahamas) and called it San Salvador. Convinced he had reached Asia, Columbus was nevertheless nonplussed by the absence of the traditional Chinese merchants and the presence of a people so "beautiful and peace-loving," who in their ignorance of destructive weapons would hold a sword by its edge.

---

13 Oviedo tells us that this sailor from Triana, annoyed at Columbus' trickery, left Spain for Africa soon after their return, and converted to Islam.

The Best Folk in the World

Neither Columbus nor the kings had the faintest idea that they had reached a new continent. They believed they had reached Asia, but anyway felt entitled to take possession of the land and its inhabitants, about which Columbus had to say: "They are the best folk in the world, and certainly the most gentle. They know no evil – neither killing nor stealing – they love their neighbors as themselves and have the sweetest manner of speech in the world, laughing at every word. They would make good servants and fifty men would be enough to overpower them and force them do our will."

Exploitation of the natives began during this first of Columbus' four voyages. The Arawaks, original inhabitants of the lands first discovered by Columbus, did not know work, fire arms or power hierarchies. They didn't need to work in order to support themselves. A very generous nature satisfied all their needs.

There was no illness then,
Nor either sin,
We had in us a saintly devotion.
Healthy we were.
There was no illness then,
No pain in the bone,
No fever,
No smallpox.
This was not the stranger's way
When they came to our world.
They taught us fear,
And flowers withered at their step.
To make their flower live,

They sucked our own flower dry.
To castrate the sun!
That's what the strangers are here for.[14]

The admiral continued his exploration of the new lands and reached the great island of Cuba, which he called Juana, and Haiti, which he called Hispaniola. In it, with the remains of the shipwrecked Santa María, he built, on the 25th of December 1492, the Fort of Nativity. Thirty men were left to guard it. In a desperate attempt to confirm his hypothesis that Asia could be reached by sailing west, he had all his men swear an oath before the royal notary, to the purpose that this new coast could not be an island, as an island couldn't be that large, and had them sign a document stating that "A few leagues of navigation will take us to political peoples, with a knowledge of the world."

The return trip was eventful, plagued by drawbacks and storms. Columbus reached the Azores and headed for Lisbon. As an admiral he would be received by John II of Portugal, who tried to talk him into admitting that these newly discovered lands belonged to Portugal and tried to hold him back, but Columbus managed to sail the Niña to the port of Palos on the 15th of March 1493.

Yellow Fever

Columbus and his people brought to America all the intolerance of a Spain that needed to affirm its dubious unity and identity by destroying and eliminating the Other: after the Moors and the Jews they took on the "savages". The

---

14 "Poema maya del Chilam Balam", en *Poesía azteca y maya*, Buenos Aires, Eudeba, 1962.

Admiral makes this point in one of his letters to the sovereigns: "In this year of 1492, after ending the war with the Moors and expelling the Jews, you thought of sending me to the said regions of the Indies."[15]

Perhaps not fully recalling the famous laws of the *Siete Partidas* laid down by Alfonso the Wise, which stated: "freedom is the noblest thing on earth; while servitude is the vilest,"[16] Governor Columbus enslaved the natives and gave them order to bring as much gold as possible. Soon after, according to Harvard historian Eliot Morison, he started severing the hands of those who could not produce at least a nugget for their pains. Columbus' biographer states he is unable to praise him on this: "Columbus himself invented this horrific system of producing gold for the purpose of exportation. Those who fled to the mountains were hunted down with dogs, and those who remained were decimated by hunger and disease, while thousands of desperate creatures drank manioc poison to put and end to their misery."[17]

In this way the Europeans, in their greed for a quick profit in silver and gold, introduced the natives to forced labor and began the destruction of their original social organization.

Queen Isabel reacted with alarm to the news about the depopulation of her new lands in these first years of the conquest. In a royal provision dated December 20, 1503, this

15 Tzvetan Todorov, *La conquista de América, el problema del otro.* México, Siglo XXI, 1992. *The Conquest of America: The Question of the Other*, Oklahoma, University of Oklahoma Press, 1999.

16 Leyes de las Siete Partidas, part. 28, Ley 8, título 22, parte 4.

17 In Zinn, Howard, *La otra historia de los EE.UU.*, México, Siglo XXI, 1999. *A People's History of the United States: 1492-Present*, New York, Harper-Collins, 1995.

"protectress of the Indians" said: "The Christians living in the aforementioned Isle (Hispaniola) neither find laborers for their granges or farms, nor arms to dig for whatever gold might be found in the said island, and it is Our wish that the Indians receive the necessary instruction to farm the land and extract the gold for these my lands."[18] The Queen, affected by Columbus' disease, the "yellow fever" or obsession with gold, suggested the Indians should be paid a salary.

During the first two decades of the 16th century, some 15 tons of gold were extracted and the shipments corresponding to the *quinto real* (20%) tax were duly sent to Spain. This metal soon ran out and the Spaniards had to look around for other means of support.

Historian Carlo Cipolla says that "the gold appropriated by the conquerors was exclusively the product of robbery, looting, and booties. The drawback to every parasitical activity is that it can't go on forever. Sooner or later, depending on the reserves of treasure or the efficiency of the despoilers, the victims are bereft of all their goods and the thieves have nothing left to steal."[19]

Justifying Despoliation

Even today some texts try to justify what went on, invoking the "need" for expansion of European nations. Did these "needs" entitle them to commit genocide, to impose their culture and enforce different modes of production? It is rather interesting to observe that the same civilizations

18 Vicente Sierra, *Historia Argentina*, tomo 1, 1492-1600, Buenos Aires, UDEL, 1956.
19 Carlo Cipolla, *Conquistadores, piratas y mercaderes*, México, FCE, 1999.

that based their power and wealth on the imposition of private property will forget about respecting it when it belongs to "savages."

Even Ginés de Sepúlveda, one of the great ideologues of the conquest, asks, in one of the dialogues of his *Democrates alter:* "If a prince, not through avarice or hunger for empire, but only because of the poverty or scarcity of his realm, should do war on his neighbors to take hold of their fields, as in dire need of some prey, could that be called a just war?" He answers himself thus: "That would not be a just war but mere larceny."[20]

Gold for Baubles

To demean the Indians it is common to say that they willingly exchanged their gold ornaments for objects which for the Spaniards had no value, such as mirrors, bead necklaces or musical instruments. But what these arguments really reveal is the speaker's ignorance, as gold in America had no value of change, no value "in itself," as it had for Europeans. Here were no gold coins, and nobody waged wars for them. Gold was just a material natives used in their crafts. The objects the Europeans brought were interesting and new, and the natives longed to have them.

Friar Diego de Landa said: "The Indians have lost little and won much with the coming of the Spaniards. They now have the use of coin, without which they had lived adequately, but with which they become more like men."[21]

20 Ginés de Sepúlveda, *Democrates alter*, Buenos Aires, Indianas, 1927.

21 Fray Diego de Landa, *Relación de las cosas del Yucatán* (1576), México, Garibay, 1976.

In the Name of God

Columbus went before the king and queen in Barcelona and was granted an annuity of 10,000 maravedis and a prize of 335,000. The new lands would be called "Western Indies"[22] and Pope Alexander VI was asked to confirm their rights over these "Indies."

The spreading of the Catholic religion in America and the material benefits it promised would come to be seen as a spiritual and material compensation for all the losses the Catholic Church of the Old World had suffered as a result of the Protestant Reform, the dwindling of its parishioners and the expropriation of ecclesiastical properties.[23]

Pope Alexander VI was a Valencian, Rodrigo Borja (Italianized to Borgia) by name. His path to the Papal chair was paved by simony,[24] a great fortune amassed in his years before the Vatican Chancery, and the economic and political support of the Kingdom of Naples, which belonged to the Kingdom of Aragon and was ruled by King Ferdinand, one of the two rulers on which Machiavelli based his study of unscrupulous rulers in *The Prince*. The other one would be Alexander's son, Cesare Borgia. About Ferdinand, Machiavelli wrote: "Always

22 For the Europeans, the Indies comprised the East part of Asia, including present – day countries of China, Korea, Burma, Japan and the Moluccas. Japan was then called Cipango and China, Cathay and Mangi.

23 Silvio Zavala, *Historia de América en la época colonial*, México, Instituto Mexicano de Geografía e Historia, 1961.

24 *Simony* was the sin of buying or selling ecclesiastical preferments, benefices, etc. The word is derived from Simon Magus, who offered to pay St. John and St. Peter to be taught how to perform miracles (*Acts* 8:18).

making use of religion, he turned his hand to a pious work of cruelty when carrying out his great exploits."

In this same book, Machiavelli writes: "Alexander VI was always, and he thought only of, deceiving people; and he always found victims for his deceptions. There never was a man capable of such convincing asseverations, or so ready to swear to the truth of something, who would honor his word less. He is an example of how far a Pope can prevail with money and power in his hands."[25]

Pope Alexander is considered one of the most corrupt popes in history.[26] All charity destined to the poor he spent in lavish orgies in which he "caroused with youth of both sexes and, opinion in his day had it, even with his own daughter, the famous poisoner Lucrezia,[27] as well. It is also rumored that he had a child – both son and grandson – by her.[28] Lucrezia was named Governor of the town of Spoleto and plenipotentiary regent of the Vatican in her father's absence.

---

25 Nicolás Maquiavelo, *El príncipe*, Madrid, Sarpe, 1983, pp. 108-109. Niccolò Machiavelli, *The Prince*, London, Penguin Books, 1979, p. 100.

26 In 1498 Alexander had rebellious Dominican friar Girolamo Savonarola burn for having denounced the corruption and dirty dealings of the Church.

27 Italian humanist Sannazo wrote an epitaph in verse which read: "Here lies Lucrezia Borgia, who was to Alexander VI daughter, wife and daughter-in-law."

28 This was the famous "Roman child" and two papal bulls were issued for his sake. In the public one, the Pope legitimated Juan and acknowledged him as son of Cesare and an unmarried woman. In the second, and secret, one, he acknowledged he was the Pope's and Lucrezia's son and bestowed a hereditary dukedom upon him. This secret bull was deemed necessary to prevent Cesare Borgia form appropriating the domains of his brother-nephew.

No less than eighteen cardinalships were created in Spain during Alexander's period as pope, five of which went to the Borgia family and the rest, according to Guicciardini, were sold in auction. "Ten papacies would not be enough to satiate this family's voracity," Giannandrea Boccaccio would write to the Duke of Ferrara.

Alexander's reputation was so bad that verses like these were not uncommon in Rome: "Alexander sells Peter's keys, / Christ and his altars / And why shouldn't he / When he paid good money for them?"

This Alexander who, according to conservative historian Paul Johnson, was "the worst pope of them all,"[29] laid on the shoulders of the no less Catholic sovereigns of Spain the task of spiritual conquest of the new lands. Monogamy should be forcibly imposed and sodomy, incest and idolatry razed out.

The Pope himself wrote to the Catholic Kings: "Once having completed, please God, the reconquest of the Kingdom of Granada, and desirous to crown your hopes, you sent, with great toil, dangers and expenditure, our beloved son Christopher Columbus with ships and willing men, in search of these distant and hidden lands, across a sea never before plowed by any prow. (...) And they discovered some very remote isles and mains, peopled by numberless folk who walk about naked (...) and appear to be apt and willing to embrace our Catholic faith and learn good manners. We might hope that, if properly indoctrinated, the name of Our Lord Jesus Christ might enter these lands with great ease." And he determined: "Not by your asking

---

29 Paul Johnson, *Historia del cristianismo*, Buenos Aires, Javier Vergara, 1989. *History of Christianity*, New York, Touchstone, 1979.

but out of our pure liberality, proper knowledge and full apostolic authority, we grant you and your successors the sovereigns of Castille and Leon and to all posterity, every one of the aforementioned lands and islands discovered so far and to be discovered in the future, so long as they are not already subject to some Christian lord, in the name of the authority of Almighty God, descended to us through St. Peter and of the vicarship of Jesus Christ, which we hold on Earth. It is to be understood, on the other hand, that this grant does not entitle you to grab the land or holdings of any Christian prince."

We might, in this case at least, cast a doubt upon papal infallibility, as it is obvious that the Catholic sovereigns appealed before the pope to obtain this grant. In a letter to Columbus dated August 4, 1493, they say "You know that we have sent for Rome for a bull about all these isles and lands you have discovered or are about to; we have it in our power at present and are sending you a copy with the authorization to make it public in those lands, for everybody to know it is not possible to go to those lands without our permission; carry it with you, so that in all other lands you add to our possessions you might show it."[30]

In another letter to the admiral they leave no doubt as to the close relationship between Pope Alexander and themselves: "As we know that your knowledge of these matters is greater than anybody else's, we beseech you to send us your views on the subject, to have the bull modified accordingly."[31]

We might wince at the "pure liberality" of a pope who generously bestows on others what does not belong to him,

30 Silvio Zavala, *op. cit.*
31 *Ibid.*

as long as it did not belong to any other Christian prince. If we follow Jesus Christ's injunction to "Render to Caesar the things that are Caesar's" we might infer that the new lands and mainland had their owners, not precisely Christian princes: they were the American "Caesars." Why were these "savages" denied the right of property so zealously protected when it pertained to Christian princes, that is, the King of Portugal or Prester John, the only other rulers with lands outside Europe?

Such liberality was not kindly regarded by the Portuguese, particularly by their king, John II, who managed to produce other bulls, as brilliant and valid as those issued by the Borgias. The first one had been granted by Martin V and authorized the Portuguese to discover al lands to the east of an imaginary line going through Cape Bojador; the second, granted by Calixtus II, uncle to Alexander VI, in 1456, awarded Portugal all lands discovered or to be discovered as far as the Indies.

This new evidence prompted Pope Borgia to issue, on May 4, 1493, the *Intercaetera* bull, dividing the Earth in two. A line was traced 100 leagues west of the Cape Verde Islands; to the east of this line everything belonged to Portugal; to the west, to Spain. But as America had no existence as yet, this meant the Spaniards were being given all the lands of Asia where the Portuguese had already established their colonies. Things came to a head and the Portuguese threatened with war, a situation which eventually led to the signing by Spain and Portugal of the secular Treatise of Tordesillas, by which the line was moved 370 leagues to the west of the Azores. Thanks to this agreement Portugal would eventually obtain Brazil.

This treatise, which in God's name generously gave so much land away, made the French king Francis I exclaim:

"Let me see the clause in Adam's will that says that France must be deprived of its share of the New World." As this will couldn't be produced, Francis upheld the doctrine according to which possession was determined by effective occupation of the territories, and sent many expeditions equipped with letters of marque to the new lands. European expansion was under way. Soon, England and Holland would follow the French.

The Second Invasion

With increased enthusiasm the Catholic sovereigns approved and financed Columbus' second voyage. Fourteen caravels and three larger vessels manned by a crew of 1500 sailed for the new lands on September 1493.

Greed and enthusiasm led their majesties to empty the prisons of their inmates: "To use of our pity and clemency with these our subjects, we hereby desire and will that whatsoever persons who have until the day of publication of this our letter committed any murder or injuries, or any other crimes of whatever kind or quality, save heresy, to do service in Hispaniola." This was a queer way of honoring the agreement with Pope Borgia, as these men were hardly the ideal people to spread the Gospel among the "savages". As Germán Arciniegas would later put it, "in this way, their majesties had the devil bake their hosts."[32]

The Admiral had not given up his search for Cathay and left his brother Bartholomew in charge of Isabela.

Columbus returned to Spain taking 500 natives in chains. These were the first slaves to cross the Atlantic. Barely 200

32 Germán Arciniegas, *Biografía del Caribe*, Buenos Aires, Sudamericana, 1973.

would make it to Europe: the rest died of hunger, the plague, and the cold they experienced during the journey.

In Columbus's absence the Spaniards quarreled and the Indians were mistreated.

The Heroic Resistance

Very soon the natives switched from astonishment to active resistance against their aggressors. "The Christians, with their horses and swords and lances started massacring them and committing all sorts of cruelties. They would storm their villages and neither young nor old, nor women pregnant, or delivered, they would shrink from disembowelling. They would set up grill broilers of stakes on forks, over which they would barbecue their captives. And this is why the Indians began looking around for ways to expel the Christians from their lands and strongholds."[33]

According to Oviedo, before committing themselves to the struggle, the invaded peoples took the following precaution: "The lords of the island thought it meet to betake themselves to the following experiment to ascertain if these Christians were or were not mortal men. Accordingly, they took one of them and drowned him, and once he was dead they told him to rise, and as after three days he wouldn't and began proffering an offensive odor, they took their mortality as a proven thing and began their rebellion with uprisings and killing of Christians."[34]

One of the authors of this experiment was chief Caonabó, who had led a peaceful life in his lands until Bartholomew

---

[33] Fray Bartolomé de las Casas, *Historia general de las Indias*, México, FCE, 1951.

[34] Gonzalo Fernández de Oviedo, *op. cit.*

Columbus attacked his village and enslaved its dwellers. Caonabó and his wife Anacaona got their warriors ready, attacked the fort of Natividad, burned it to a cinder and massacred most of its inhabitants. Their resistance lasted for two years, and the Spaniards began fearing Caonabó and his men.

Alonso de Ojeda, an old veteran from the wars of the reconquest of Spain, visited the chief, smilingly invited him to mount his horse and when he did he fettered him and informed him he was now an offering for the Castilian monarchs. Caonabó realized he had become a prisoner of war, and died on the ship carrying him to Spain, some say out of the cold, some out of chagrin. His wife continued the resistance for a few months until she was captured and murdered.

Years later, jurist Ginés de Sepúlveda would pronounce this doctrine of "fair war" official by claiming "that inhuman and uncultured barbarians are by nature meant to be servants, and should be forced to admit the domination of those who are more prudent, powerful and perfect than they, as according to natural law matter should obey form, the body the soul, appetite reason, the wife the husband, the children their father and what is imperfect that what is perfect, in order to banish nefarious blunders and the portentous crime of eating human flesh, and to spread the Christian faith in all the corners of the globe."

It is important to state that very few of the American cultures practiced anthropophagy, while the Spaniards often did. Speaking about the conquest of Veragua, Oviedo tell us "Diego Gómez and Juan de Ampudia ate one of the Indians they had killed and after that joined a few others in the killing and eating of Hernán Darias of Seville, who was infirm."[35]

---

35 Gonzalo Fernández de Oviedo, *op. cit.*

To this we should add the well known episodes of anthropophagy in the Buenos Aires of 1536.

Sepúlveda's theories, based on Aristotle,[36] were very successful among the Spanish nobility, who in their unlimited arrogance offended the God they claimed they worshipped by believing themselves to be All powerful, as He was. But the French, the English and other European princes did not share their views.

By 1535 these official views the crown had about the Indians, as expressed by Oviedo, had modified the early opinions of the Admiral. The Indians were no longer the best folk in the world but "inclined to vices rather than to work, melancholy, cowardly, vile and prone to mischief, of big lies, little memory and no constancy whatsoever." But of course we can imagine these characteristics to be the result of 43 years of Spanish oppression, massacre and "pedagogy."

But the whole conception of war, the superiority of their firearms and the diseases against which the natives had no defenses determined the victory of the invaders. They imposed their culture, their religion and a manner of labor based on the exploitation of the natives' labor force. In a few years the Caribbean islands were depopulated.

According to the latest estimations of the ethnographers, about 300,000 natives lived in Hispaniola by 1492. One third of them died between 1494 and 1496. According to a census conducted in 1514 by Miguel de Pasamonte and Rodrigo

---

36 "Humanity is divided into two classes: owners and slaves (...) The first have the right to order, the second are made to obey. Against these war is always legitimate, as it is in a manner a hunting down of men who have been born to serve but will not accept their fate." Aristotle, *Politics*, 1-I, C-III, 8.

de Albuquerque, Hispaniola housed some 5000 Spaniards, scattered in 14 villages, and 26,300 Indians. In 1548, Oviedo would write: "Of the more than three hundred thousand inhabitants of that island alone, not 500 are left. Some were killed by the cold, some by the work, others by smallpox. Many took manioc juice or swallowed poisonous herbs; others hanged themselves from trees. The women would follow their husbands, and rather than bear children to be the servants of strangers, they miscarried through art or potions. All of this was God's punishment for their sins, but the latter were also responsible, as they mistreated them, and loved gold better than their neighbor."[37]

Mortality was also increased by the decline of agriculture, as the Spaniards deemed it unworthy of them to work the soil unless in search of gold, and the natives refused to sow, determined to kill both themselves and these voracious oppressors who, according to friar De las Casas, "would each one consume in one day what might support three families of Indians."[38]

Pedro Mártir de Anglería said that "the men the Admiral brought with him on his first voyage were mostly unruly, lazy and without quality, all they desired was their freedom at any cost and could not withhold from any kind of outrage, taking the women of these islands before the eyes of their fathers, brothers and husbands, given to rapine and rape."[39]

37 Francisco López de Gomara, *Historia general de las Indias*, Madrid, Oriente, 1902.
38 Fray Bartolomé de las Casas, *op. cit.*
39 Pedro Mártir de Anglería, *Décadas*, libro IV, cap. I, pp. 43-44.

The Traffic of Human Beings

As the work force virtually disappeared, the crown started importing African slaves. In 1442 Pope Nicholas V had granted the Portuguese king Alfonso V the right to subject and enslave "the infidels," i.e. all non-Catholic Africans. Thus began the terrible history of the slave trade, which would cost the African continent the loss of 30 million persons between the 15th and 19th centuries, torn from their homes to be sold as things.

The Third Invasion

The signing of the Treatise of Tordesillas only increased competition between the Spaniards and the Portuguese. The King of Portugal sent an expedition under Vasco da Gama, and the Catholic Monarchs faced a serious dilemma. Columbus' fellow voyagers were spreading stories about the Admiral's improper treatment of the natives and of the very Spaniards. And the versions about the extraordinary riches of "the Indies" were being held in doubt.

But because of Portuguese expansion, the monarchs consented to finance a third expedition, more modest in scope, with eight caravels and 220 men, ten of which had been convicted for murder.

This expedition left on the 30th of May 1498 from San Lúcar de Barrameda, with six ships. Columbus had decided to divide the fleet and sent three ships to Hispaniola. The remaining three, commanded by the Admiral himself, sailed to the southwest, reaching Venezuela and the mouth of the Orinoco River.

While Columbus continued his search for the Great Khan, Bartholomew governed with an iron hand, putting both Indians and Spaniards against him. In Hispaniola, to the south of Isabela, he founded Santo Domingo, which would become one of the bases for the conquest of the whole continent.

Bartholomew – who had been appointed *adelantado* by his brother in 1494, two years after the so-called discovery – behaved so villainously that the monarchs had to send Francisco de Bobadilla as governor and judge of Hispaniola during royal pleasure. He reached Santo Domingo in August 1500 and, finding out Bartholomew's crimes to be true, concluded his brother could not have been but an accomplice, and forthwith both were put in chains and sent to Spain. They thus tasted a drop of their own.

The queen believed Bobadilla to have exceeded his command and absolved Columbus – only withdrawing his salary and the titles of governor and viceroy – and backed him in his next enterprise.

The Other Church

Those who are wont to justify the unjustifiable with the old singsong about "understanding the mentality of the times" should consider how members of the clergy and freethinkers contemporary to the events fully condemned the conquest and the ensuing massacre. Together with unscrupulous brigands like Columbus and his associates, we find Spaniards who opposed the massacre perpetrated in the name of God and the King. Most noteworthy among them was a man who came to America with Columbus, became an *encomendero*, was a direct eyewitness of the genocide and, ashamed and thoroughly disgusted, joined the order of the Dominicans and became the Indian's most radical advocate, under the name of friar Bartolomé de las Casas. The issue was for him crystal-clear, with little room for debate: "The only reason why so many and such an infinite number of souls have been killed and destroyed by the Christians is and is only their ultimate lust for gold, their wish to become rich in no time and climb to the highest ranks of society, out of all proportion to their birth."[40]

Many noteworthy men accompanied De las Casas, as friar Antonio de Córdoba, Francisco de Vitoria, Domingo de Soto, Vázquez Menchaca and friar Antonio de Montesinos. Montesinos read out, in the Advent[41] of 1511, in the Cathedral of Santo Domingo, a homily that shocked the *encomenderos* and slave-traffickers and would make history: "You are all in mortal sin and in it you live and die, for the great tyranny that you use with these innocent people. Tell me, what right and what justice have allowed you to keep them in such horrible bondage? Under whose authority have you waged detestable war on people who lived in their lands peacefully and in ease, and have consumed infinite numbers of them in as yet unheard of devastation and slaughter? How come you keep them in oppression and exhaustion, barely feeding them and never curing their ailments, so that they die, or rather are murdered, while toiling night and day to fetch you gold? And when have you cared about their souls, who takes care they know about God their creator, go to mass, are baptized and observe holidays and the Sabbath? Are they not men? Have they not rational souls? Isn't it your duty to love them as you do yourselves? Is this so hard to understand? Are you devoid of feeling? How have you sunk to such depths of lethargy

40 Fray Bartolomé de las Casas, *op. cit.*
41 In the Catholic calendar, the period beginning four Sundays before Christmas.

and sleep? Believe me when I say that in such a state as you are in, you have as much chance of salvation as the Moors and Turks that lack and reject the holy faith of Our Lord Jesus."[42]

The immediate result of Montesinos' ardent political allegation were the Laws of Burgos, sanctioned by the Catholic sovereigns in 1512. These tried to mitigate the indiscriminate exploitation of the natives, granting them – at least in theory – festivities, wages, proper treatment and indoctrination. But these laws were never applied, as the conquistadors made use of the royal seal of Castile that read "to be accepted but not applied." The exploitation and death rate of the indigenous people not only continued but considerably increased.

Another response of the crown to this debate over the Indians was to have official jurist Palacios Rubios draw up a document called *Requerimiento*, through which the natives were informed of their new status of subjects of the kingdoms of Castile and Aragon. This bulky bundle read as follows: "God made Heaven and Earth and a human couple called Adam and Eve, from whom we all descend, and left Saint Peter to rule over the human race." It went on to say that the pope, who lived in Rome, was the descendant of this Saint Peter and had granted the Indies to the Catholic sovereigns in certain documents which "you are entitled to see if you so choose." The men sent by the crown had been received by other natives who had allowed them to proceed

---

42 The autograph text of the sermons has not been preserved. What we have has survived in friar Bartolomé de las Casas' *Historia general de Indias*.

to their indoctrination. The Indians were exhorted to take their time in digesting this information. "I thus request and require of you to understand what I have told you and take as much time as is fair to understand and debate it." If, on the other hand, they still refused to accept the Spanish rights in spite of everything that had been explained to them, "I guarantee that with God's help I will proceed with vigor against you and will wage war in all parts and means I can summon, and I will yoke you to the obedience of Church and Throne, and I will take your persons and those of your wives and children and make you slaves and as such sell you."

This absurd document ended by saying that the blame for whatever misfortune might ensue would fall on the Indians, not on the Spaniard's, heads "and I protest that for all deaths and damage that ensue, you, and not His Majesty, nor myself, nor any of the gentlemen that here accompany me, will be held responsible."

This *Requerimiento* was duly read to all the as yet unconquered Indians who of course, because of their unconquered status, could not understand a word of Spanish let alone Latin, the language it was written in. It frequently occurred that the Indians, unable to bear the reading of this unintelligible gibberish to the last, would leap into combat, giving the Spaniards the very opportunity they had been waiting for, of hunting them down in a "fair war as a fair punishment for refusing to accept the generous conditions of the Castilian monarchs."

López de Gomara wrote down the answer of a certain chieftain from the South American Cenú region to the conquistador who had read the *Requerimiento* to him: "As to the Spaniards coming in peace, their attitude disclaimed it; as to their kings, in the face of all they asked, it could only be concluded that they were paupers, and as to this individual who had given out the land, he must be crazy and was looking for trouble, in that he gave away to a third party what didn't belong to him in the first place, and in wanting to stir up trouble with those who had possession of them since the dawn of times. That he was willing to give them supplies, but as to gold they had but little, and esteemed it even less, as having no use for daily life. As to their worshipping an only God, they heartily congratulated them, but had as yet no desire to change their own religion. As to their threats, they might do well in leaving their territories as soon as possible, as they didn't take to demonstrations of foreign brute force and might be tempted to treat them in the same manner they had treated the owners of the hanging heads that decorated their village right then."

De las Casas tells us the story of chief Hathuci, who had escaped captivity in Hispaniola and fought the invaders with heroism. On being captured, and before being burned at the stake, a Franciscan friar gave him the chance to convert "so that he could ascend to Heaven where peace and harmony reign." He also warned him that, should he choose to decline, his soul would descend to hell to suffer eternal torment. The rebellious chieftain asked. "Do Spaniards go to Heaven as well?" "Of course," the friar replied. "Then," the chieftain answered, "I'd rather go to hell."

Lonely and Final

After Columbus published, in 1502, his *Book of Prophecies*, the monarchs began worrying about his mental health. In it, Columbus pointed to the need and urgency of embarking on the conquest of the Holy Sepulcher, and claimed he was the man who, according to Scripture, "would champion faith to the furthermost regions of the world." He stated that the mission of reaching the Indies by sailing west had been entrusted to him by God and announced that the world would come to an end in 1657.

Blandishing such hypothesis, Columbus tried to persuade Ferdinand and Isabel to support his Fourth voyage and devote the earnings to the conquest of the Holy Sepulcher. Unconvinced, and unsure of his sanity, they gave him permission, four ships and a crew of 140 men. He was forbidden to touch Hispaniola, and all earnings would go to the Royal Treasury. Notary Diego de Porras would be in charge of enforcing these conditions.

Columbus, together with his brother Bartholomew and his son Hernando, then 13 years of age, set out from Cadiz on the 11th of May, 1502. He attempted to land in Santo Domingo but Ovando, the governor, in ordinance to the royal decrees, didn't allow him to. Columbus sailed to Jamaica, later to Honduras and Costa Rica. What he saw of the land convinced him that the Ganges River could not be very far. He didn't understand where he was and decided to sail back for Spain.

He arrived on the 4th of November 1504, only a few days before his protectress, Queen Isabel, died. Columbus' letter to Their Catholic sovereigns reads like mournful tango lyrics: "I was at your service for twenty-eight years and now there remains not a single hair in my head that is not white. My body is ill and wasted (…) Alone in this pain of mine, ill and awaiting death every day, let he whom charity, truth and justice assist cry for me. I haven't undertaken this voyage to gain honor or wealth, as my hope of both was already dead. I have approached your Highnesses with the best intentions and the proper zeal, let the truth be told."[43]

But there are times when crime does pay, and on his return to Europe Columbus, seriously ill by then, took good care that Ferdinand would acknowledge his rights and the percentages due to him. The Catholic king refused to see him and Columbus had to chase him all over the realm. In 1506 the king was in Valladolid to hand down the crown to his daughter Joan "the Mad" and Philip of Habsburg, "the Beautiful." And there was the Admiral as well, hoping to be received by the new monarchs. The only reply he received was a letter in which Ferdinand suggested he should come before the *Junta de Descargos* and offered him, should he renounce all of his rights to these "discovered" lands, a seigniory in Leon. Columbus does not give up, and writes to Ferdinand. "As Your Highness is not ready to uphold what he has promised in word and seal, together with the queen, for a ploughman like myself to contest all this would be like to sow the wind; let that be then, since I have done what I could and will now let God do the rest, as he has always been altogether prosperous and attending towards my needs."

Christopher Columbus died in Valladolid on the 21st of May 1506, without realizing he had "discovered America," without any glory and with his good name and honor seriously affected.

The Admiral had apparently been forgotten by all. He wouldn't even be rewarded with the opportunity to name the new continent. America would get its name from

---

43 Cristóbal Colón, *Los cuatro viajes del Almirante y su testamento*, Madrid, Espasa-Calpe, 1977.

Florentine navigator Amerigo Vespucci[44] who had visited the new lands in 1499 and 1502. On returning he wrote two famous letters: one, written in 1503 and published in 1504, to Lorenzo Piero de Medici, and the other one to his schoolmate Pietro Soderini. This one was translated into Latin and included in the appendix of *Cosmographie Introductio* by Martin Waldesmüller, Professor of Geography in Lorraine.

The account of Columbus' third voyage, the one in which he reached the mainland, was published in 1508, while the account of Vespucci's voyages was already known in 1504 and 1507.

In his introduction to Waldesmüller's work, French geographer Jean Basin de Sandocourt suggested: "In truth now that three of the parts of the world, Europe, Asia and Africa, have been amply described, and that a fourth has been discovered by Amerigo Vespucci, we don't see why his discoverer, a man of sundry wit, should be denied the right to call his America, as if to say, Amerigo's land; just as Europe and Asia took their name from women."

Years later Waldesmüller and Basin acknowledged their mistake, and in the map they published in 1513 they gave the name Terra Incognita, and not America, to the new world. But it was already too late.

---

44 Born in Florence in 1454, Vespucci went into commerce as a clerk of the Medici family. In 1492 he was a commercial agent based in Florence and had a close acquaintance with a number of seamen of the time. In 1508 he became a member of the Burgos Junta and was named master pilot of the realm.

The Motherland

We have long heard that Spain is our Motherland. But what kind of a mother is she? Everything seems to suggest that she is an adoptive mother who has appropriated her children: we know nothing about her giving birth but we know a lot about her kidnappings, her thefts, her acts of suppression of identity.

Moctezuma and Atahualpa, for example, were kidnapped and held for ransom, and the tons of gold and silver paid for them weren't enough to prevent their death and torture at the hands of Cortés and Pizarro respectively, who to top their feats melted the priceless works of art of the two greatest empires of the Americas into uniform ingots. The Spaniards also suppressed the identity, the religion and the language of the people they had conquered. A royal decree of King Charles V stated: "We have cognizance that even the most highly developed of the languages of the native inhabitants is incapable of expressing the mysteries of Our Holy Catholic faith." The Spanish state decreed that "polygamy be suppressed and they be instructed in the alphabet, good manners, arts and cusotms in order to lead better lives. All of this is worth much more than the feathers, pearls and gold we took from them, particularly because they did not give these metals their proper and adequate use as coin, the only valid manner of use." These are the words of López de Gomara, one of the spokesmen of the Motherland, in his *Historia general de Indias*.

After many a debate, the Spanish crown finally admitted, in the *Leyes Nuevas* (New Laws) of 1542, that its new children were human beings, only minors, and so had to be committed to the guardianship or *encomienda* of the Spanish residents in America, who would instruct them in the Catholic Faith and in return make them work from sunrise to sundown and pay tribute. In this way the *encomienda*, a cruel system of forced labor and exploitation, came into being.

These were the beginnings of this our "Motherland," and her appropriated children were subsequently treated in very much the same manner by her.

As is common in the case of the children whose parents have kept the real facts of their origins and birth from them, these American children of Spain began to have misgivings about the bonds of kinship uniting them to this distant, authoritarian and castrating mother. In 1809, one of her most unruly of her offspring, born in Tucumán province, Argentina, said: "Up to this point we have tolerated a manner of banishment in our own land; we have seen, for more than three centuries, our primitive liberty subjected to the despotism of the unfair usurper, who degrading us from the human level has called us savages and treated us like slaves. (...) It is time to cast off this fatidic yoke, it is time to raise the banner of freedom in these unhappy colonies they have acquired without rights or deeds and kept with the greatest tyranny and injustice." This is how Bernardo de Monteagudo, future secretary to San Martín, expressed himself.

The mother would take her time to recognize her children's independence. In June 22, 1860, forty-four years after the United Provinces declared their independence from Spain and all foreign domination, Queen Isabel II of Bourbon deemed it wise to accept reality.

The adoptive sons prospered and multiplied, while the mother was not even able to take care of her own and started expelling the native Spaniards from the country to the cities and from these to the lands of their brothers and sisters on the far side of the ocean. The Argentines, as they had begun to call themselves by then, received them generously, without asking too many questions. Way from the clutches of such a mother, the newcomers began to prosper as well.

In this way, friendship and solidarity between Spaniards and Argentines began to grow and grow, in spite of kings, presidents and dictators.

In 1936, a child of the Inquisition began to take over Spain, and Argentina, then undergoing the period known as Infamous Decade, raised through raffles, festivals and theatrical plays millions of pesos for the arms and stomachs of the Spanish Republic. And Spaniards and Argentines went over to defend such universal values as freedom, solidarity and dignity. One of them, Raúl González Tuñón, was received by his "brother" Antonio Machado with these words: "You have come from so far away to live in the threat of Fascist bullets and howitzers. Please receive our thanks." In this manner Machado thanked the Argentine poet who has suggested that "We, so close to dawn should form poetry's brigades."

There they sang, fought and wrote history and lost the battle together, these Argentines and Spaniards who would rather be the sons and daughters of the people, as an Anarchist hymn would say, rather than any Motherland's. This is how they dreamt themselves in the mid-30s.

Some would remain in those lands forever, to become a part of history. Others chose Argentina as their fate, the native born and the exiles as well. Here they opened publishing houses that could publish their Federico García Lorca, their Miguel Hernández, as well as many of our local talents, unknown until then.

The years passed and with them the dreams of these men, to be reborn in their grandchildren, in the 70s. In their record players, vinyl records of the songs of the Spanish Civil War told of the days when the tables would be turned for the poor to eat their fill, and Our Holy Father was sorely questioned about the Fifth Commandment. It wasn't the choir of the Spanish CNT singing these songs, it was local groups such as Quilapayún or singers like Daniel Viglietti with many, many other young enthusiasts joining in. Until darkness came back again, and the military dictatorships of South America began their hunt, following the example of that very same Inquisitor and Generalísimo our Motherland had spawned.

And thus it came to pass that the road of exile was reversed and gratitude became hospitality as thousands of artists, psychologists, journalists, writers and people whose only occupation had been their political commitment were granted, thanks to the Spanish people, a place in the world.

History had decreed that just when Argentina was entering its darkest night Spain would recover its freedom, its poetry, its vitality, after forty years of obscurantism under a regime that bethought itself the heir of the imperial and conquering Spain of yore.

But while Spain emerged from its period of dictatorship in a relatively prosperous state, Argentina emerged bankrupt from its own horror, with economic, and thus political, power concentrated into a few hands. The social and economical model imposed during the reign of terror of dictator Jorge Rafael Videla and his minister of economy José Alfredo Martínez de Hoz survived the return of democracy. The state was unconcerned about welfare and during the 90s, under president Menem, it put all business into the hands of a few powerful groups, who immediately saw the advantages of turning the corrupt members of the political class of Argentina into business partners.

The Argentine state was sold in auction and the main buyers were the corporations of the Motherland. Having as their godfather no less than the lobbyists of the – in name at least – Socialist Spanish government, firms such as Repsol, Telefónica, Endesa, Aguas de Barcelona, Gas Natural, BBVA, HSBC and Iberia began to control key areas of Argentine economy and communication, making profits so fabulous that the bribes paid to Argentine government negotiators paled in comparison.

Between 1991 and 2001, Argentina took 27.7% of Spanish investments abroad. The profits were even more fabulous than the investments, and even more astounding was the paltriness of the reinvestments in the local market: for every dollar the Spanish firms made, barely 20 cents were invested in local maintenance, the rest was wired to the main office in Spain. These recovered, in eight years, 55% of the capital they had invested. The case of Telefónica is particularly illustrative: the Spanish company paid 625 million dollars for the state-owned Argentine telephone company Entel, and in its first four years made a profit of 2.6 million dollars, significantly increasing the cost of service with the aid of the local Supreme Court.

Spanish business in America only grew and grew, and dollars began to pour into Madrid just as gold and silver had done in the old colonial days. Once again America was feeding the Motherland which had exhibited its opulence while hiding the corpses of the Potosi miners that made it possible, and now looked away from the misery of a continent that was once again making her rich.

And once again, we have the people on one side and governments on the other. While the people of Spain organize collections of foodstuffs and medication for the people of the country that was once one the granary of the world, the very same country that in their times of need had sent them Evita Perón with tons of wheat, the Spanish government bars the entry of, or deports, the Argentine youth who flee no longer the bayonets of the military but the economic disaster of which Spanish holdings and banks are in a great measure responsible.

We have always known there are two Spains: the deeply felt *Spain of the Heart* of poet Raúl González Tuñón, the Spain that gave us friar Bartolomé de las Casas; and the other one, the Spain of Pizarro, Franco, José María Aznar an his bankers. The latter one is the appropriating mother Machado warned us about: "Of these two Spains, one will chill your heart."

Santa María of Good Hungers

Absurdities have a tendency to pass unquestioned from one generation to the next. One of these is the story of the great hunger suffered in the first settlement of Buenos Aires, founded by Don Pedro de Mendoza and his associates. The starting point is so false that all conclusions cannot but bear the same stamp of falsity.

As told by the conquistadors and as repeated for five hundred years after them, the story seems to assume that the natives, legitimate owners of the land according to natural law, had the duty to indefinitely supply an army of parasites who had come to take over nothing less than their "lives and holdings."

These romantic chronicles portray the Spaniards as victims of a hunger that appears as an implacable natural phenomenon, when the truth is that they were a bunch of greedy invaders prone to constant bickering among themselves. Our Pampas were devoid of palaces and kings to kidnap and ask ransom for. It could only breed riches for those who knew how to work its soil, as the Querandí Indians – who do not appear to have been undernourished at all – had been doing for generations before the invaders came.

The "nobles" that came with Don Pedro, and the vassals accompanying them, all shared the Spanish philosophy about work, clearly expressed in the Middle Ages by Alfonso X, also known as The Wise, in his Laws of the *Siete Partidas*. In them, workers and artisans were called "little people." The royal ordinances of Castile stated that gentlemen, "as is publicly known do not make a living as tailors, carpenters, jewelers, barbers, spice merchants, retailers, shoemakers, or any other base or vile occupation. And if the said gentlemen do not keep to these rules, as videlicet, to keep a horse, and bear arms, and refrain from the practice of the aforementioned base and vile occupations, they are not to be granted the title of gentlemen." The common people were thus offered the choice of becoming beggars or joining one of the many religious orders, where they could enjoy salary, a roof and a square meal. Those who worked were punished, both economically and morally, and on their shoulders fell the whole burden of taxation, of which royal officers, nobles and gentlemen were excluded.

The Origins if Charrúa Gumption

Rivalry between Spain and Portugal had only increased after the generosity of the papal bulls and the Treaty of Tordesillas. Neither side had been placated, and both courts were teeming with spies only too eager to tell one king about the transoceanic plans of the other. It was in this context that, around 1515, the Spanish king learned of the plans of his Portuguese counterpart to beat him to the lands lying south of Brazil.

If we are to trust the royal letters patent of Doña Juana, dated in Burgos the 2nd of July, 1512, the Spanish pilots were not to be trusted, as they "do not know how to hold the quadrant nor the astrolabe nor the altitude dial, do not know the points of the compass, and every day make so many navigational mistakes they do great disservice both to the crown and the merchants."[1]

With these considerations in mind, the Spanish crown set its eyes on Juan Díaz de Solís,[2] en experienced seaman with much experience in navigating the Americas, and named him master pilot, entrusting him with a secret mission because "in this there must be great secret kept, as nobody must know that I have given money for this or have in any way participated in the making of this voyage." Ferdinand "the Catholic," then sixty-four years of age, had not lost his wiles and sent with Solís "a person trustworthy and of great precaution, secretly bearing powers exceeding those which We have entrusted unto Solís himself."

The *Casa de Contratación* gave the king a bad report on Solís. The King asked this to be sent to him forthwith and said he would imprison the man if the charges were to prove serious. Evidently Solís did not surpass the ordinary level of blackguardism necessary to command an American expedition, as his fleet sailed off with no greater ado from Bonanza anchorage on the 8th of October 1515.

The new mission brought Solís to our shores, so that he could taste of the sweet waters of the River Plate and the Charrúa Indians could taste of him. Early in 1516 he came

1 Agustín Zapata Gollán, *Los precursores*, Santa Fe, Colmegna, 1980.

2 Solís had worked until 1505 as a Cartographer for the *Casa da India* for the King of Portugal. In 1508 he was in the *Junta de Burgos* with Amerigo Vespucci and Vicente Yáñez Pinzón, when it was decided to send an expedition to search for the transoceanic pass through the Central American isthmus, to reach the Spice Islands. This voyage turned out a failure and had to return to Spain in 1509.

to a huge estuary which he believed to be the sought-after pass to the Pacific Ocean. Something must have caught his attention, because he asked one of his men to taste the waters, which were pronounced not salty but sweet (i.e. fresh). With enviable creativity, Don Juan Díaz decided to call this river "Sweet Sea."

A few days later the fleet had to land on an island to bury the steward, who had recently died, apparently of natural causes. He was called Martín García and to this day that island bears his name.

Curiosity, together with the desire to imitate those colleagues of his who kneeled on the ground and, in the name of God, the King and Everything Else, took possession of what was not theirs, led him to his ruin. He managed to land, perhaps to kneel, but was presently struck by a flight of arrows and died, together with eight of his men. The Charrúas did not take to uninvited guests.

The sole survivor was a boy, the youngest in the expedition, called Francisco del Puerto. The Charrúas granted him his life and took him with them. He lived amongst them for ten years, marrying and Indian woman who bore him two children.

The Charrúa Indians lived in what is now Uruguay, the South of Brazil and the Argentine province of Entre Ríos. They were and would continue to be a warrior people, and it would take the Spaniards more than a century to establish any kind of settlement in their lands. This would be Santo Domingo de Soriano, in 1624. As from 1811, the Charrúa people would join the forces of José Gervasio Artigas, the Uruguayan rural leader and patriot, who greeted them as his brothers.

It is not certain if the locals lunched on Solís and his men. One of the chroniclers, a certain Herrera, states that "the Indians dragged the dead away from the coast, and still in sight of the ships, cut off their heads, arms and legs, roasting the bodies whole and eating them." But Fernández de Oviedo merely states that they took the boat and, breaking it, set it on fire. Naturalist Félix de Azara, on the other hand, substantiates his disbelief in the banquet in which Solís served as main course, in the fact that "custom is what most endures among these barbarians, and had they done it then, they would still do so now, but they neither do it, nor conserve memory of having ever done." But our own Jorge Luis Borges seems to credit this gastronomical account:

> *And was it across this muddy river of dreams*
> *That the prows came to make me a motherland?*
> *The painted ships must have bobbed up and down*
> *Among the water hyacinths and the tawny waves.*
> *On second thoughts, we must suppose the river was*
> *Of bluish hue, as made out of fallen sky,*
> *With a tiny red star to mark the place*
> *Where Juan Díaz fasted and the Indians fed.*[3]

What it all amounts to is that the invading Castilians had "discovered" – as they were wont to put it in their Castilian language – the famous river they called "Solís River" and the Portuguese "River Plate." This was more than a semantic distinction. As the discoverers used to attach their names to their discoveries, calling it "Solís River" meant accepting Spanish rights over the area, whereas the more neutral "River Pate" said nothing whatsoever about the Spanish claims.

---

3 Jorge Luis Borges, "Mythical Foundation of Buenos Aires".

Magellan in Dire Straits

The Spanish crown was nevertheless obsessed with the inter-oceanic pass, and afraid the Portuguese would beat them to it. They thus came up with the idea of hiring a Portuguese pilot to search for it, and the task fell on Ferdinand Magellan. As was usual practice when the Spanish crown was concerned, explorers had to see about the financing of their own expeditions, and Magellan found his in Cristóbal de Haro, a rich merchant and his financial partner in the enterprise.

Magellan's expedition reached Bahía San Julián, in what is today Santa Cruz province, Argentina, in March 1520. He decided to winter in the area and sail again in spring. His sailors were amazed at what they saw, as the Italian chronicler Antonio Pigafetta's account well shows: "One day we were unexpectedly faced with a man of gigantic stature, singing and dancing almost naked on the beach and covering his head with sand. Our commander sent a man ashore, instructed to repeat the very same gestures as a token of peace and friendship, all of which was appreciated by the giant, who let himself be tamely led to a small island our commander had landed on. On seeing us, the giant pointed his finger skywards, as if to suggest we had come down from the sky. He was so tall our heads barely reached his waist; beautifully proportioned, his features broad and painted red, his eyes circled in yellow and two heart-shaped spots on each cheek. His scant hair had been whitened by some kind of powder. (...) Our commander offered him food, drink and a large steel mirror, on seeing which the giant, never having seen such an object nor, in all possibility, his own figure, retreated so hastily that four of our men standing behind him fell. We gave him silver bells, a small mirror, a comb and some beads, after which he was returned to the shore, escorted by four well-armed men."

Some say that it was this encounter that gave the whole region its name of Patagonia, as Magellan's men dubbed these original inhabitants "Patagons" after the giant Patagon, a popular hero of chivalric romances such as *Amadís de Gaula*, parodied in Cervantes' *Don Quixote*.

As soon as Magellan observed the first signs of climatic change he ordered the expedition to proceed, but some of his men, fearing that by going further south they would fall off the map, organized a violent mutiny. Magellan dealt with it by taking the drastic measures of executing Captains Luis de Mendoza and Gaspar Quesada and abandoning Juan de Cartagena and Friar Pedro Sánchez de Reina to a lingering death in the desolate coast. Another mutiny was awaiting him further on, and this time he lost a whole ship, which returned to Spain with its rebels on board.

Magellan was finally granted his wish to name the famous inter-oceanic pass but, as Solís, he would not live to enjoy the glory thus obtained. He died on the way to Spain and was replaced by his deputy Juan Sebastián Elcano, who barely made it to Seville with eighteen survivors and let King Charles V know about al the interesting business possibilities the new voyage had opened for his empire. Among these were the Molucca Islands, bursting with more varieties of spices than had been imagined possible.

But somebody else would reap the profits: the English-educated Venetian navigator Sebastian Cabot, named master pilot of the realm after Solis' death. Cabot presented the king with a minutely detailed plan to seize the Moluccas and immediately turn them into a spice-producing territory. King Charles heartily approved the project, albeit warning through a royal letters patent, against sexual license on board:

"To avoid the scandal and inconvenience which proceed from the presence of women in such armadas, it is our will and decree that in the aforementioned armada no woman of any kind whatsoever should be allowed, and you are entrusted with the task of visiting those ships before they sail off to ensure this be so."

Cabot set sail for the Magellan Strait in 1526, but en route he made a brief stop at the Canary Islands, where, at a safe distance from the king's scrutiny, a few "women in love" (the name prostitutes where known by in those days) were invited on board. On reaching Santa Catarina, near what is today the City of Florianópolis, he heard for the first time the legend that would change his life. It told of a Great White King who lived in a silver-walled palace laden with treasure. Due obedience was not a highly prized value in those days, and Solís swapped the Moluccas mission for the River Plate adventure. Coming down the Atlantic he was surprised to meet a man in European clothes: this was Francisco del Puerto, the sole survivor of the Solís expedition. Del Puerto had lived with the Charrúa and Guaraní Indians and during this sojourn the legend had become a certainty inside his head. He joined Cabot and they sailed together up the river the natives called Paraná and the Spaniards, for want of a better name, had to learn how to pronounce. In the meeting of this river with the Carcarañá they founded the Fort of Sancti Spiritu, the first Spanish settlement in Argentine territory.

But Cabot had an *idée fixe* and no time to fix bronze plaques to commemorate the event. Having learned from Solís' mistakes, he left thirty heavily armed men in charge and sailed on towards his rendezvous with the White King.

Charles V, waxing impatient, sent a "rescue" expedition commanded by Diego García, former companion to Solís, which reached our shores in November 1527. The world was small in those days, and Cabot and García soon met. At first they quarreled bitterly, but García soon understood that it was better to bury the hatchet and, in exchange for a share of the profits, become Cabot's friend and let the Moluccas go hang. The two expeditions merged into one and off they went up the Paraguay River, in search of the Great King.

The First "Legend"

The men of Sancti Spiritu Fort, for want of anything better to do, started to mistreat and enslave the Indians who, commanded by chiefs Siripo and Marangoré, reciprocated by defending their own and eventually attacked the fort on September 2, 1529, torching it down.

Many years later Captain Monasterio, gunsmith to Argentine patriot Manuel Belgrano, would baptize one of his cannon with the name of Marangoré, in homage to the chief's resistance to the invaders.

In an ingenious effort to demonize the original inhabitants, Chronicler Ruy Díaz de Guzmán invented the legend of Lucía Miranda, the beautiful wife of invading officer Sebastián Hurtado, one of the leaders of the *razzias* that regularly issued from Sancti Spiritu to hunt the locals down.

The story, copied from at least ten similar episodes in *The Iliad* and *The Odyssey*, tells of how "evil chief" Marangoré and his brother attacked the fort and massacred all its inhabitants, except Lucía, five other women and the children. But Marangoré and his brother Siripo fell in love with Lucía, and Hurtado, who had not been present when the attack took place, let himself be caught to attempt the rescue of his wife, and was condemned to death. Lucía convinced

Siripo she no longer desired her husband and obtained his pardon. But the Spanish couple was caught in the act, after which Lucía was burned on the stake and Hurtado lanced.

Historian Vicente Fidel López dismisses the whole potboiler as "a story, that does not even merit the name of legend."

But legends, and ashes, were all that remained of Sancti Spiritu itself. Cabot and García on hearing the news hurried back, but it was too late, and barely twenty of Cabot's men, out of the original two hundred, made it back to Seville, on July 22, 1530. Soon after their arrival Cabot and García began to quarrel about their rights over the newly "discovered" territories and over the prerogative of organizing an expedition who would take one of them to the mythical lands of the White King. Eventually, Cabot would tire of the constant bickering and leave for England, where he served the new king Edward VI.[4]

Don Pedro

In 1533 Charles V returned to Spain after two years in Germany. Good news, together with a few tons of gold and silver, had arrived from Perú. The booty was in part the product of the abduction and murder of Inca Atahualpa by Francisco Pizarro and his gang. The Inca ruler had thoroughly complied with his kidnappers' demands, handing over to them two rooms filled with silver and two with gold, but

4 Cabot explored what today is Canada, Labrador and Newfoundland. As president and chief counselor of the Royal North Seas Company he negotiated business agreements with Russia. At his death he left a very important collection of notes and maps, which Queen Mary Tudor handed over to her husband, King Philip II of Spain.

he would nevertheless be cruelly tortured by these paragons of Western Civilization. The rest of the booty came from the looting of temples, and from priceless works of art which the conquistadors saw as "devilish symbols of idolatry" and promptly turned into ingots.

Not that the emperor was worried by any of this, as the illegitimate increase of his treasure made him happy enough and the prerogatives of Absolutism allowed him to cheerfully confuse the riches of the state with his own.

Those who enjoy curses and prophecies and like to repeat that "crime doesn't pay" and such other sayings whose wisdom historical studies hardly ever confirm, might in this case be happy to learn how little Charles V would profit from these ill-gotten gains, as Spain continued to be a poor, backward country, with hardly any industries worth the name; as 80 percent of the capital America had provided was squandered by the successive Spanish regimes in the so-called "wars of religion." The origin of these conflicts was, truly enough, the Lutheran Reform and its subsequent European expansion, but the ruling passion was economical. One of the principles of the Lutheran Reform stated that the Church should give away, like it or not, all of its property. The German princes, wishing to seize on the papal lands, enthusiastically supported Luther and his followers.

Charles, who was after all the grandson of the Catholic sovereigns, had to take an interest in defense of papal rights, particularly when considering how Alexander VI, the Borgia pope, had furthered Spain's interests and claims.

These unending "Holy Wars" bled the Spanish treasure dry and forced the country into an implacable and unremitting policy of exploration and expansion, needed to finance the Habsburg's imperial adventures. Already in 1529 Charles had been forced to sell the Moluccas to Portugal for a paltry 350,000 ducats.

The emperor was also conscious that his attempts to stop the Portuguese had barely been successful, as Admiral Martín Alfonso de Sousa had navigated up the River Plate in 1532, dotting its shores with monoliths representing the Portuguese crown and writing in his diary: "This is the most beautiful land men have ever seen and one of the mildest. I had with me Frenchmen and Italians and Germans and men who had been to India; but the beauty of the land held them in awe and we were so transfixed that none could think of going back... One cannot say or write about the beauty of this river, of its blessings, and the land's." This report, which would be confirmed by his spies, led the emperor to send an *adelantado* to take possession of the land, conquer it and establish villages and forts.

The man on whom the emperor's choice would be bestowed was far from being a nobody, as many of his *adelantado* colleagues had been. He was a Grenadian nobleman with family ties to the Archbishop of Toledo, the richest and most important diocese in Spain. He had been educated at court, first as page to the heir to the crown, later as an "Emperor's gentleman." He had participated in the Italian campaign and the sacking of Rome.[5] Gossip has it that he

5 The sacking of Rome took place in May 6, 1527. It was led by Lord High Constable Charles III, eighth duke of Bourbon. The soldiers had mutinied after not receiving their pay, and Charles III led them into Rome to force the Pope to pay the 300,000 ducats he owed them for their services. Pope Clement VII refused to pay and the imperial troops, forgetting their Catholicism for once, spent eight days in sacking the city, including St. Peter's and the papal palace.

became rich through sacrilegious thefts he passed off as booty obtained from the prelates he had defeated.

Don Pedro signed, in 1534, a *capitulación* (agreement) in which the emperor called him "my servant and gentleman of my house (...) who has offered to conquer and settle the lands and provinces of the Solís River, also called River Plate."[6] He was, as was usual practice, induced to kidnapping "if in your task of conquest or government you should chance upon a chieftain or lord, seize upon him and turn over to the crown one-sixth of all treasure, gold, silver, pearls or stone his ransom might bring in; the rest can be distributed among the conquistadors."

In the same, Mendoza was granted a salary of 2000 ducats in gold per annum and 2000 additional ducats "to help him in the costs of the aforesaid settlement and conquest," but it was made very clear that "these four thousand ducats are to be obtained from the resulting revenues and benefits of those lands, which it is Our right to perceive."

And it certainly wasn't enough, as don Pedro had to seek foreign aid. He signed private agreements with the Weslers

---

According to historian Blanco Villalta "Mendoza took part in the sacking, which was accompanied by all the excesses a rapacious, lustful and undisciplined mob can carry out." Blanco Villalta, *Historia de la conquista del Río de la Plata*, Buenos Aires, Atlántida, 1946.

6 The *capitulación* was an agreement signed by *adelantado* and king. The king authorized the *adelantado* and his heirs to govern a part of the territory and exploit its riches. They had to found cities and forts, levy taxes and convert the Indians. In such a manner they advanced the frontiers and occupied the lands without risking or investing those capitals of its own the Crown needed for its European wars. These *adelantados* made an advance of their expenses in return for the hypothetical profits.

and the Neitharts, powerful German and Flemish bankers who were close to the Spanish emperor and who had already made neat profits out of the conquest of Venezuela without risking their own hides.

A few months later, the Spanish crown would decree a somewhat curious division of South America into four parallel zones, 200 leagues – some 700 miles – wide, running from north to south. The first one, starting in what is now Ecuador, was called New Castile and went to Francisco Pizarro; the second one went from south Perú to north Argentina, was called New Toledo and went to Diego de Almagro; the third, New Andalusia, spanned the northern half of Argentina and went to Pedro de Mendoza; the fourth and last had no name and went from the present-day city of Mar del Plata to the province of Santa Cruz. It would have gone to Simón de Alcazaba had he not died before he could take possession.

Mendoza put master Juan de Osorio in charge of the recruiting of the men for the expedition; a rather easy task, as all believed they were about to participate in the conquest of an empire where gold and silver ingots were used as bricks.

By the time all preparations were over, Don Pedro was almost over as well. The syphilis he had contracted during the Roman ravishings was in its terminal state and for a year he hadn't been able to leave his bed. His sores and the anxiety of all involved in his expedition multiplied at a similar rate, and when the Emperor was thinking of replacing him he decided to sail.

His expedition set sail from San Lúcar de Barrameda on August 24, 1535. Its fourteen ships, fifteen women and 1200 men made it the most powerful conquering expedition ever seen.

Mendoza was accompanied by his brother Diego, his nephew Gonzalo, Juan de Ayolas, Domingo Martínez de

Irala, a few clergymen and his master Juan Osorio. Fernández de Oviedo states that when they set off, everybody expected the *adelantado* "would make the sea his grave."

His sores and the excruciating pain forced Mendoza to delegate command on his second, Osorio. Having reached Rio de Janeiro, the deputy was emboldened into conspiring to achieve full command. Juan de Ayolas denounced him after hearing him say: "Why should the people of this armada obey Don Pedro, who knows nothing of the art of war and gives orders without consulting any of us?" Mendoza gave Ayolas the task of fulfilling his orders: "That wherever and in whichever place the said master Osorio be seized, he shall be put to the knife or the sword or any other manner of death, until his soul from his flesh take leave."

Father Lozano, an eyewitness, gives an account of this, the first crime in the Mendoza expedition: "A certain evening, while Juan de Osorio was walking along the shore, Ayolas turned to his mates and giving them the sign they all fell upon him and let daylight through him. Mendoza then emerged from his tent and seeing Osorio's corpse, said: 'His insolence and arrogance have now received their just desert.' Soon after his brother, Admiral Don Diego de Mendoza, reached the camp and, on hearing of what had been done, said: 'Pray God this fault and this gentleman's death bring not perdition upon all our heads.'"[7]

Don Diego had the foresight to seek culprits for the impending disaster.

---

7 P. Lozana, *Historia del Paraguay*, tomo II, Buenos Aires, Ediciones Porteñas, 1916, p. 74.

The Landowners

The fleet reached the area of present day Buenos Aires early in 1536. According to shipman Antonio Rodríguez, the beginnings were not very promising, as the first six Spaniards to land were promptly devoured by tigers. Deciding, perhaps, to make the most of the time they needed to digest this repast, Pedro de Mendoza left the Magadalena, his ensign ship, and covered the basic formalities of the foundation of Santa María de los Buenos Aires, in all probability in the area where Parque Lezama stands today. They built four churches, a house for the *adelantado* and a few mud and straw huts, and disembarked the surviving horses and mares, 72 out of the original 100.

About this, historian José Luis Romero rightly says: "Where culture and population are concerned, the Europeans saw America as a veritable emptiness. This was the cast of their conquering mentality. Their foundations proceeded *ex nihilo*. Over a nature they knew nothing about, over a society they crushed and annihilated, over a culture they chose to ignore. Their cities were European enclaves in the midst of a wilderness. Within them, the social norms, the religion and, above all, the designs they had brought from beyond the seas were zealously preserved. The acme of their mentality can be reduced to a single idea: To create a new Europe were nothing had ever been."[8]

Mendoza, following in the other *adelantado's* footsteps, created the *Cabildo* or town hall, named mayors and aldermen, chosen among the wealthier or most respectable – hardly the same thing – and followed the time-honored Castilian

8 José Luis Romero, *Las ciudades y las ideas*, Buenos Aires, FCE, 1971.

practice of giving away what did not belong to him. But this time the true proprietors would not take a kind view of his deeds.

Because the land had its legitimate owners. These were the tribes later known as Pampas, called, because they fed on the fat of guanacos and fish, Querandíes, or "men of fat," by the Guaraní Indians from up north.

The Querandíes were hunters and fishers and formed small family groups with common ancestors, governed by chiefs. As they believed in virtue and leadership rather than heredity, their chieftains were elected according to their deserts. Some of these, called head chiefs, governed larger communities, and confederacies were not uncommon. Chiefs had to consult important decisions with an assembly or parliament called *traun*. The conjugal union was formalized by the groom giving presents to the bride's family. A man was entitled to as many women as he could buy.

They believed in a supreme deity called Chao, "father" who was in fact four persons in one: an old man, an old woman, a young man and a young woman. These four persons watched over the conduct of all human beings: if they strayed from the right path, Chao withdrew his protection and they were helpless before the *gualichos* or demons who could then harm them or lead them to their deaths. On rising they prayed to Chao while facing east, where the sun rose and life originated.

The Querandí Indians believed in the afterlife, and in their tombs they placed food and implements the departed might need in his new life beyond the great mountain ranges.

They were never hungry, as they were amply supplied with venison and the meat of the guanaco, the coipu and the ñandú. The thistle, fish, the fruit of the algarrobo tree, together with maize they got through exchange with other peoples, supplemented their diet.

The Heroic Resistance

The initial reaction of the Querandí Indians was one of curiosity mingled with friendliness, as the chronicler of the expedition Ulrico Schmidl, an overseer sent by the Wesler bankers, relates: "These Querandí Indians brought to our settlement and shared with us their pilfers of fish and meat for a full fortnight until one day they failed to come, upon which our general Pedro de Mendoza sent 300 lancers and 30 horsemen fully armed. I was one of them and our orders were clear: we should kill or seize as many Querandí Indians as we could and take their settlements."[9]

Dean Gregorio Funes, ideologue and supporter of the conservative Saavedra faction in the early days of Argentine independence, and an ardent defender of the conquest and its ways, would later give a curious view that contradicts the eyewitness report: "The *adelantado* sent his men with words of friendship and of peace, to exhort them to continue rendering a service he was much obliged to receive."

But patience did not seem to run high among Don Pedro and his men, as that single slackening in the daily delivery for 1200 was enough to driving "noble" Don Pedro to order in "friendly words" the massacre of the locals.

And the Querandí Indians lost their patience in turn: they summoned the great council of confederate tribes and got together a 4000-strong army: "The said Querandí Indians –

9 Ulrico Schmidl, *Viaje al Río de la Plata*, Buenos Aires, Emecé, 2000, p. 150.

Schmidl relates – fight with bows and darts shaped like short spears with a flint edge. They also whirl a long cord with a stone ball tied to its end, such as the lead ones which in Germany are used. The horse's or deer's legs hit by this ball are entangled by the cord, making them stumble and fall, and with such a ball they also caused he death of our captain and *hidalgos*, and our infantrymen with the aforementioned darts have been killed as well."

This Battle of Corpus Christi was an imposing one and had serious consequences for both sides involved. The Indians awaited the invaders beside a river and let them draw near. "And when we attacked they set up a defense so fierce that they gave us great harm: our captain Don Diego Mendoza and six *hidalgos* on horseback and around twenty infantrymen met their deaths. They lost at least 1000 men, and fought very bravely, as we will never forget."

It is said that a certain Diego Luján died in battle, dragged by his horse into the river that to this day bears his name.

And this was but the beginning to the invaders' woes. Indian reinforcements poured on as the messages sent by the different chiefs reached their destinations, and the tribes besieged the city sending showers of incendiary arrows to burn out the roofs of the shacks. A small group of Querandí Indians in canoes managed to set fire to one third of Mendoza's fleet. And the siege had serious consequences for the invaders, who were strong in the idea that working for sustenance was beneath their dignity.

"After the Querandí Indians laid siege to our city – Schmidl relates – misery was so great that many died of starvation; horses being few and cats, mice, snakes and other vermin running out, they resorted to eating shoes and other leather goods. At this point three Spaniards stole and ate a horse, which after receiving torment they confessed to having done, upon which they were hanged. That night, three other Spaniards stole upon their corpses and cut from their thighs and other parts pieces of flesh, to sustain themselves."[10]

Such was the life in the village of Buenos Aires in those days. Not that everybody went hungry in the same way, as Bartolomé García tells: "He sent me, with six mates, to hunt for him, and every day he would be served a dozen and a half partridges and quails he and those who were closest to him fed on."

Added to his gluttony and selfishness, his disease advanced and ravaged his being with anger, deliriums and madness. He never left his cabin in the flagship Magdalena, stationed near the shore, and deep ulcers had eaten into his hands, back and head. He was afraid of the dark and was driving his constant companion, María Davila, crazy with his demands that she never leave his side. His doctor, Hernando de Zamora, daily increased the dose of mercuric chloride at his request, and the patient almost died of the ensuing intoxication. He would awaken from his nightmares screaming "You Jews killed our master and now are dying off like fleas! Poor Osorio, how have you unmade me, and all." The *adelantado* was right in one thing: his men were dying off like fleas. Only 650 out of the original 1200 were left.

In 1537 one of the survivors, Luis de Miranda, wrote the first romance[11] of the River Plate, which said:

Dung and feces
Which some could not digest
Many would sadly ingest

10 Schmidl, *op. cit.*, p. 154.

11 A romance is a brief epic or lyric tale, written in octosyllables, apt for singing and dancing.

Causing dread.
To such a point things came
That men's flesh they also ate
As was done in Jerusalem.[12]
The things that we have seen
Have never in Scripture been read:
To eat the roasted flesh
Of your own brother.
The stronger, the lamer.
The wiser the more lost,
The bravest but hungry and fallen.
Our general[13] *has caused these ills*
through lack of self-government
And his disease as well
has brought these evils on our head.[14]

Among the few "decent" women who had arrived with Mendoza was Isabel de Guevara. This is what she wrote to the Queen about the weakness of the men and the courage and the willpower of the women of this first Buenos Aires:

Most High and Mighty Lady:

To this province of the River Plate, accompanying its first governor, Don Pedro de Mendoza, a few women have come, one of which, as her fortune would have it,

12 A reference to the siege of Jerusalem, led by emperor Titus in 70 A.D., well-known in Spain through the eyewitness account of historian Flavius Joseph.

13 An unequivocal reference to Pedro de Mendoza.

14 Transcribed form the paleographic edition of the romance by José Torre Revello, based on the copy of the original manuscript by Gaspar García Viñas.

is this your humble servant. The armada brought 1500 men to the port of Buenos Aires, but through lack of supplies and the great famine thereof, by the end of three months 1000 had died. (...) And men had grown so weak that they loaded on the women all the work, such as washing their clothes, ministering to their wounds, cooking what little there was, washing them, taking the guard, tending the fires, loading the crossbows and, whenever the Indians gave us war, we also had to fill our verses with fire, raise the soldiers who were fit for rising, raising the alarm and bullying the soldiers and marshalling the field. Because by then, as we women need less nourishment than men, we had not fallen to such great weakness. I have written this and brought it to the attention of Your Highness to let you know what great ingratitude has been used on me, because at this point most of what there is has been given out, both to the ancient and the modern, with no notice taken nor memory kept of my tasks and toils. No Indians have I received, nor any other service or compensation. (...) I thereby humbly beseech you to grant me my *repartimiento* on a perpetual basis and, as fit reward for my services, let my husband be appointed to a post fit for the quality of his person and (...) the merit of his service.

In many years Our Lord lengthen your most Royal life and state. In the City of Asunción, the 2nd of July of the year 1556.

Kissing your most royal hands, I remain,
Your Highness' servant.[15]

---

15 Letter from Isabel de Guevara to the governing queen, dated in Asunción the 2nd of July 1556. In Jorge Caldas Villar, *Nueva historia argentina*, Buenos Aires, Juan C. Granda, 1980.

The lack of resources, hunger, internal strife and the hostility of the Indians soon had the Spaniards on the run. Some left for the recently founded city of Asunción; others, among them Mendoza himself, returned to Spain. Before leaving, Don Pedro signed over his *adelantazgo* to Juan de Ayolas, making it clear at the same time that Ruiz Galán would govern in his absence.

He also left a sealed letter dated April 20, 1537, with some practical recommendations as to the administration of justice, which bring to memory the Osorio case: "If justice be applied to any, let it be with much right, and if you can let it pass, do so, thus serving God; and if not, let it not be without due process, but should it so pass that treason be out, known by you to be certain and true, but no sufficient witnesses can be found, secretly push him into a well by night."[16]

In the last of his sealed letters he said: "As you know, in Spain I can but eat from the sale of my estate and all my hopes are placed in God and in you, because being my son and having received such honorable position you should not forget me, leaving as I am with six or seven sores on my body, four on the head and one in my hand that won't let me write or even sign (...) And should you obtain through God's grace some jewel or other valuable stone, do not forget to send it to me so that I might have some remedy for my toils and my sores."[17] In another paragraph he said that he was taking accountant Felipe Cáceres with him, as the repeated

16 Vicente Sierra, *Historia de la Argentina*, Buenos Aires, UDEL, 1957.

17 Gustavo Gabriel Levene, *Breve historia de la independencia argentina*, Buenos Aires, Eudeba, 1966.

accusations of embezzlement and theft didn't recommend "leaving with you this quarrelsome man." He also advised his men that, should they "go much further up" and meet Pizarro or Almagro, they should make friends with them, and Almagro offer 105,000 ducats for that part of his *gobernación* bounded by the Southern Sea, or even 100,000, he should have it." And finally begging "and whatever else in my benefit you might get, do so, as I do not wish to starve to death."

He didn't get any of this, an died at sea, on his flagship Magdalena, the 23rd of June of 1537. Dean Funes wrote about him. "Mendoza's age-long credit has been due more to the goods of fortune than those of nature. When the former abandoned him, the hero vanished as well, and only his weaknesses were left. Without any genius, talent or valor worthy of the name, and even worse, prey to that pettiness of passions that soil the reputations of the ultimate people of earth, he had not been born for great exploits."

Mendoza's expedition, like no other by the emperor himself, had been an absolute failure. Buenos Aires was completely abandoned in 1541. It had been the greatest defeat suffered by the "universal Empire" of Charles V in the Indies, and it had been inflicted – in the words of one of the chroniclers – by "savages who ignore the most basic norms pertaining to private property, as having no habit of appropriating their own or other people's things."

Industry Day
(September 2, 1587)

And if all Spaniards who come to these lands were friars,
or interested in the conversion of these peoples,
I truly believe conversation between both parties would be
fruitful in the extreme; but as the opposite is the case,
exactly the opposite will be the effect; as it is obvious
that most Spaniards who come to these parts are among
the lowest, and strong in varied forms of sin and vice.
Were people as these given leave to walk around
the Indian villages, for our sins, the former would be
converted to the vices of the latter, rather than attracting
them to any virtue.

HERNÁN CORTÉS
Letter to Charles V

Industry Day has been celebrated on the 2nd of September ever since 1941. It commemorates an event that, if closely scrutinized, has much to say about our national identity, as well as about the state of affairs resulting from the de-industrialization program started by the military government that came to power on the 24th of March 1976, and continued by the Horsemen of the Apocalypse of our recent past, president Carlos Menem and his minister of economy Domingo Cavallo, as well as president Fernando De la Rúa & Co., from 1989 to 2001.

Surely few countries in the world – not to say none, and thus contribute to inflate our national ego with yet another example of our uniqueness and originality – must have chosen, to do homage to their national industry, to celebrate a crime – smuggling, in this case. It happened on September 2,

1587 in the territory known today as the Argentine Republic and at the time belonging to the Viceroyalty of Perú.

On that day, a caravel called the San Antonio, commanded by a certain Antonio Pereyra, set sail for Brazil from the Riachuelo anchorage, which then served as port to the city of Buenos Aires.

The San Antonio carried in its holds cargo originating in the province of Tucumán and shipped by bishop Francisco de Vitoria. It consisted of cloths, and bags of flour produced by the – in those days – prosperous province of Santiago del Estero. But the governor of Tucumán, Ramírez de Velasco, denounced that the innocent-looking flour bags concealed silver ingots from Potosí, each one weighing several pounds. Its exportation was strictly forbidden, so this "very first of Argentine exports" was really a cover for a case of smuggling and illicit commerce.

Business in Tucumán

Bishop Francisco de Vitoria had, while serving a Charcas merchant, been able to establish commercial ties with prominent members of the *Audiencia*, thereby obtaining a permit to import slaves from the River Plate.

Not a single slave had entered America through the port of Buenos Aires yet, so Vitoria can be considered the pioneer of the African slave trade. The *Consejo de Indias* (India House) had nevertheless recommended him "as he is a great preacher and a learned one" and also as his former post as counselor of the Inquisition in Spain recommended him excellently well.

In 1586, Juan Ramírez de Velasco was appointed Governor of Tucumán. Among his first measures were a condemnation of common law marriages (illicit cohabitation), sodomy and rape. Bishop Vitoria and his partners of the *Audiencia* of Charcas were his sworn enemies. Governor Ramírez de Velasco kept denouncing bishop Vitoria's systematic practice of contraband, but the members of the *Audiencia*, too busy calculating their own profits in the enterprise, gave him not their "audition."

In his notes, Ramírez de Velasco said that "in the Cathedral of this our city is bishop the Dominican friar Don Francisco de Vitoria (...) and if there is sore lack of priests it is not because of the unfruitfulness of the land but because of the bishop's ill treatment. So far I have been excommunicated twice. All his business is dealing and double-dealing."

As Ramírez de Velasco couldn't get rid of the bishop, he took it out on his followers. A certain García de Jara, who had killed some eleven Indians "and forcibly violated nine Indian girls, six of which, being of tender age, died in consequence; and he has soiled the name of many, being of those who like to rinse their tongues in the virtue of honest women," had, on Velasco's orders, his tongue cut off and nailed to a post and what remained of him hanged "until he die of natural death."

The bishop, who held an *encomienda* of more than 20.000 Indians, had never paid much attention to what St. Jerome (347?-420), anticipating Karl Marx by a few centuries, had said: "As the merchant adds nothing to the merchandise he sells, if he gets more than what he paid for it, his gain implies the other's loss; and in any case, commerce is bad for his soul, as it is past belief that, given the opportunity, a merchant won't cheat." He must have also overlooked Saint Ambrose's (340-397) condemnation of private property: "Whatever above your necessities you get, through violence you take. Was God unfair enough to unequally distribute the means, to have you wallowing in abundance while others pine in need? Whatever bread you hoard, to the hungry belongs; whatever cloth, to the naked, what money you hide away would have rescued the unfortunate."[1]

The governor wrote to King Philip II in these terms: "Bishop Vitoria has cowed your vassals with his continuous excommunications, and he sets an example not of what a prelate but of what a merchant should be. (...) He does not fulfill his duty nor go to church, and as to the conversion of the natives, he couldn't care less (...) While the processions were in the streets he was indoors tying his bundles to send to Brazil (...) Sixty Africans the English sent him have arrived (...) he brought them to our city (...) he leaves his tasks as shepherd unfulfilled to attend to those of the merchant, and forgets about his poor fold (...) And whenever he gets wind of scandal or sin, he starts a cause, and the accused, rather than fall into his hands, give him everything they own (...) So far we know the bishop has sent to Brazil one thousand and fifteen marks of white silver and thirty-nine 8-oz. marks of gold and three hundred and sixty 22-carat gold pesos and two chains weighing one hundred and ninety-five pesos each and fifteen marks in wrought silver he sent in the said ship to Manuel Tellez Barreto, governor of Bahía."

The "Industry Day ship" sailed back with a hundred and twenty unwilling passengers (black slaves for the Potosi mines, as well as pans and bells) but was boarded by the English pirate Thomas Cavendish and his men. This pirate, unaccustomed to sermons and prayer, and unheeding of the bishop's presence, took the ship with all its merchandise and half its slaves. Thus forced into an unwilling poverty vote, Vitoria had to walk half-naked all the way to Buenos

1 Juan Agustín García, *La ciudad indiana*, Buenos Aires, Claridad, 1923.

Aires, where he was rescued and, to Velasco's immense chagrin, restored to his diocese. The following year he was back on his feet, selling 60 slaves in Potosi and collecting enough capital to pursue his trade with his own ship and passengers, who carried some 40,000 to 45,000 pesos among the lot. This time, a strong storm assailed them, sending them "to the other side of the river" – as the governor of Tucumán informed in December 1588. The castaways buried their silver and dodged the Indians as best they could, waiting for the expedition sent to rescue them from Buenos Aires. The bishop managed to recover 15,000 pesos the natives held from him; according to the governor "because God decided to overlook the offenses this man's unbridled tongue had given Him." But perhaps the All-Powerful had second thoughts, because once they were back – but, as will be seen, not safe – in Buenos Aires, governor Torres de Navarrete, acting on the maxim that "He that hath pity upon the poor lendeth unto the Lord," seized upon their silver, took 5000 pesos for himself and the rest distributed among the neighbors; and Vitoria and his men had to walk it back to Tucumán. Some heretics have suggested that this voyage made the bishop of Tucumán the precursor of our country pedestrian pilgrimages.

The *cabildos* of the area rallied against this bishop whose "faith" was solely in business. Ramírez de Velasco's successor, Hernando de Lerma, went as far as banishing dean Francisco de Salcedo, who had been appointed by Vitoria, to the city of Talavera del Esteco. Salcedo proceeded to incense the population and turned the Mercedarian convent "either into a barracks or a brothel, depending on the time of day." Apparently, as soon as the prayers were over, a back door opened into the temple through which shrouded women entered in stealth. Talavera became "a city of lechery" and Salcedo as its overlord, challenging the authority of Tucumán.

All of this would eventually lead to he bishop's removal from his diocese. The governor of Tucumán accused him of having expelled all the priests under his jurisdiction and – what was for the time an even greater fault – of being a "new Christian", i.e. a Jew. In a state that had used religion as its anvil and mold, all those who could not prove the purity of their blood were discriminated. Accusing somebody of being a *marrano* – a convert who had kept his Jewish faith – or merely of being a "new Christian" was as effective a weapon as any.

But what bishop Vitoria surely never imagined was that his creativity would earn him a place in the whimsical official ephemerides of Argentina.

And those who like to link Argentina's industrial development with Spanish colonization, in whose practices they see a precedent for "policies protective of industrial development," would do well to remember the real order of November 28, 1800, which prohibited manufactures in the colonies. It would be ratified by another on October 30, 1801, which read: "About the excess of manufacturing establishments contrary to those that prosper in Spain and are meant to supply our Americas.

"His Majesty will not allow their development or increase or even permanence as they are contrary to the good and happiness of his vassals and dominions and as he suspects that, getting used to the heat and labor of the said establishments, his vassals will refuse to do work in the gold and silver mines, or cultivate those precious fruits and goods that are sorely need in Spain.

"So it is His Majesty's will that Your Excellency will seize upon all these establishments found in the district under your command, and destroy them through the means you find most convenient."

The First Infamous Decades:
Fraud, Corruption and Shady Deals
in Argentina during the Colonial Period

The corrupt are greater and more insolent sinners
than thieves, as these steal in fear, while the former
do it openly and securely. The thief fears the law's whip,
while they want to turn their deeds, no matter how noxious,
into the pillars of the law. The thief might cower
under the threats of the law and refrain from doing
what is forbidden; but corrupt rulers shape the laws
to whatever illicit advantages their malice and
cowardice might lead them to.

JUAN DE SOLÓRZANO PEREYRA
Política indiana, 1647

In the colonial period, the least studied in our school curriculum, can be found a number of keys for the interpretation of Argentina's present. This was the time when the same elites that would remain in power through the many cycles in our history took shape. This was the time when large tracts of land, commercial concessions and permits for the practice of the nefarious slave trade, stepping-stone of many a fortune of our "patrician families," were handed out.

It is also during those centuries that saw the establishment of a model for our present corrupt state. And under its wing, a society that would empirically learn that laws are flexible, norms can be ignored and, in general, that the law goes one way and people go the other.

The main responsibility for such pedagogy of illegality lies on the rulers we had to suffer during that prolonged period, the longest in our history so far. To get started on the facts, all of the colonial governors, except Hernandarias, were excommunicated by the different River Plate bishops. In most cases this was a moral punishment for the way they went about their jobs, in others, they stemmed from disagreement on commercial matters and power conflicts between bishops and governors, another constant trait of the period.

A very small number of these viceroys and governors successfully passed the *juicios de residencia* which evaluated their performance. The rest were arrested and underwent confiscations and imprisonment.

It is certain that those who like to paint the colonial period in bucolic colors, as a supposed "age of innocence" have never taken the trouble of going through the archives where judicial processes on theft, contraband and other crimes pile up. In all of these cases it was always the state that promoted and furthered corruption. This leads us to reflect on the ways history not so much repeats itself (a much repeated commonplace, usually uttered in resignation) but to give its due importance to the merely historical assertion that states that, if conditions are not changed, opportunities for ill-gotten gains continue and the culprits walk around in impunity: that is, that equal causes will produce equal effects. Rather than repeat itself, history will continue.

Buenos Aires, the Capital of Brazil

In 1578, King Sebastian of Portugal set sail for Morocco on a rather risky expedition and died in the battle of Al Kasr al Kebir. As he had no direct heirs, the crown went to his ageing uncle Don Enrique.

King Philip II of Spain, being the nephew to the Portuguese king Emanuel I "The Fortunate" (1469-1521)[1] claimed a throne he considered vacant. The Portuguese nobility opposed his claim and proclaimed the prior of Crato king. But Philip II had quick reflexes and sent a fleet and an army under the Duke of Alba, who defeated the Portuguese and negotiated with their nobility the proclamation of Philip as king. This unification, that would give rise to the greatest empire the world had ever known, was consummated in the Cortes of Thomar in 1581.

The terms of this successful negotiation can be summed up in the following phrase: "The Crown in exchange of the right to share the American wealth with the Portuguese courtiers."[2] But this unity would only be apparent, and under its surface a sordid economic war was waged between the Portuguese and Spanish ruling classes. This war, expressive of intense mutual mistrust, would find its ways into the remotest recesses of the huge empire.

It is in such a context that Juan de Garay founded Buenos Aires for the second time on the 11th of June 1580. The new settlement would provide an Atlantic outlet for Peruvian riches and also a wedge driven into the Portuguese domains in America and their seat, the increasingly prosperous Brazil.

The insignificant hamlet that gave the Peruvians their outlet to the Atlantic would also become the beachhead

---

1 Emanuel I married, in succession, the two daughters of the Catholic sovereigns: Isabel (1495) and María (1500). He later wedded Leonor (1518), daughter to Joan I of Castille and Philip II's grandmother.

2 Enrique Larriqueta, *La Argentina renegada,* Buenos Aires, Sudamericana, 1992.

through which the Portuguese would try to advance on Perú. "Peruvian born," Larriqueta says, "Buenos Aires would soon start turning Portuguese."

When the Kingdom of Portugal became dependent of the Spanish crown, the Portuguese and Brazilian *cristianos novos* (new Christians) began to worry. Philip II was a religious fundamentalist and under him the Portuguese Inquisition acquired added vigor, both in Portugal and in its colonies. In Brazil, the officers of the Holy Order heard accusations and made business: they would turn in the converts that were "Judaizing" Lisbon and seized all their goods.

This prompted thousands of Jews to emigrate from Portugal and Brazil to the Spanish colonies where they wouldn't be known. In the face of such difficulties, the fragile unity of both crowns and the relaxation of customs controls stemming from it offered new opportunities. Business, whether legal or illegal, began to flourish.

In a veritable exodus, the new Christians fled to Bayonne, Bordeaux, Amsterdam, Antwerp and Hamburg. They also came to the main commercial capitals of America, such as Havana, Cartagena, Portobello, Lima, Charcas and Buenos Aires. Their activity, towards the close of the 16th century and all trough the17th, was of great importance to the population of Buenos Aires, as it awarded them an escape valve to palliate the "scarcity of supplies" at a time when an absurd and severe legislation condemned Buenos Aires to choose between illegal commerce or a slow but inexorable death.

Many Spaniards of the day became rich by smuggling Jews into America through the slave ships. The *Revista del Instituto Argentino de Ciencias Genealógicas* published an interesting document on the subject: "Don Bernabé González

Filiano, born in Tenerife, accused of being a passenger to have come without His Majesty's license, and of unknown occupation, is sentenced to be punished for his crime and reembarked. As, however, he has married a Castilian female, well known in these parts and descending from conquistadors (she was Irala's granddaughter) he is pardoned, as the laws protect him."

No More Than a Hamlet

Garay's map reveals a city that stretched fifteen blocks S to N and nine E to W. Its layout stretched from Avenida Independencia to Viamonte and from Balcarce-25 de Mayo to Salta-Libertad, using the names the streets bear today. Barely forty blocks around the Plaza were meant for building sites – "solares," they were called. Garay also handed to each settler a block in the suburbs, in which he could "take care of his Indians, his services and his needs." These "distant" blocks were but a few feet away from the corner of the present-day streets of Viamonte and Maipú.[3]

Juan de Garay reserved for himself the plot where the Banco Nación stands today. He doesn't seem to have much valued it, as well into the 19th century the place it was known as "wraith cove," so unkempt and forlorn it looked.

The *Riachuelo de los navíos* (boats' rivulet) was the city's natural port, located in the vicinity of Humberto I street. The commercial port could be found at the present day site of the "Vuelta de Rocha" in La Boca district.

A letter written by a Franciscan friar to Philip II gives us some insight into the conditions of these early *porteños*:

3 Raquel Prestigiacomo y Fabián Uccello, *La pequeña aldea,* Buenos Aires, Eudeba, 1999.

"These unfruitful lands would have been a paradise for the English Puritans, who are used to manual and mechanical labors; but for people of quality and nobility such as we are, they are a veritable curse, as we lack Jews and Moors to serve us, tame Indians are nowhere in sight, and we are forced to till and dig the land with our own hands."

A royal letters patent issued by Philip II seems to have been issued in answer to this priest: "Information reaching me from the Indies has it that many that in these my lands were wont to work and provide for themselves by their own labor, on arriving at the Indies and coming into some possession, refuse to work and prefer to loiter all day long, and of these there are many; so that I hereby command the governor to urge such men to work their land."[4]

As said before, Buenos Aires was a vast province that also included Santa Fe, Corrientes, Paraguay and Uruguay. But the administrative seat of this vast territory was deficient in many ways.

In the years following its foundation, Buenos Aires was a hamlet comprised by some hundred shacks buried in misery and mud. The dispositions in Philip's Population Ordinance were still far from being fulfilled: "Large buildings should be built so that the Indians understand that the Spaniards are there to stay and learn to fear and respect them and desire their friendship and give them not offense."

The first habitations surrounded the fortress by the river, where the people would take refuge in case of danger. Three convents flanked it; beyond that were the straw and adobe houses where the families protected by the fortress' soldiers

---

4 Juan Agustín García, *La ciudad indiana*, Buenos Aires, Jackson, 1957.

lived. The poorer inhabitants had to take care of their farms and protect their livestock as best they could from the rapacity of bandoliers who stole their animals and threatened their lives and property with complete impunity.

Juan Agustín García tells us that "larceny became a habit," to such an extent that a governor had to issue the following edict: "As the lack order and moderation that is to be found in these parts is so great, and horses, oxen, mules and other livestock are stolen as a matter of course, and those who do allege they but follow prevailing use around these parts and commit no crime; and because the said practice is harmful and detrimental to the common good, and is forbidden by the laws of the realm and subject to grave penalties, I hereby decree that no person whatsoever, of whatever state, condition or kind, be it negroes, mulattoes, Indians, half-breeds or Spaniards, dare take or steal or in any other manner dispose of the aforesaid goods without proper permission and will of their legitimate owners, on pain of death and other penalties subject to law."[5]

Mud and adobe soon gave way to mortar and brick, and the cane of the primitive cane structures was replaced by the wood of the *urundai* and the pine tree.

Travelers who visited the Buenos Aires of those days agree about the simplicity and even paltriness of its architecture. They also talk about the amplitude of private homes, organized around large patios and, when bricks began to be used, sporting many rooms and servant's quarters. The availability of land allowed them to include vegetable plots and orchards. It was not the façade of the house that indicated rank or social position, but rather

5 Juan Agustín García, *op. cit.*

its location – the distance from the city center – its furniture, crockery and the number of servants.

The virtual blockade the court had imposed made daily difficult in extreme: "There is at present in this city neither wax nor wine, nor oil to light the Holy Sacrament; no taffeta, silk nor holland, nor any other cloth to dress the altars and ornament the church with; no steel or iron for the artillery in the port, none for the plowshares and sickles to harvest wheat, none for axes to cut down trees and carve wood, for hoes to dig, or to erect a wall; no goatskin or any other stuff for breeches; no cloth for shirts, no holland or cotton fabric for collars, nor any soap to wash them with, nor any material to clothe oneself; and all of this to such an extent that nowhere in this city can be found ribbons for one's shoes and all things necessary for the well-being and the clothing of a human being are lacking."

The Plaza Mayor (today's Plaza de Mayo) was the center of commercial, political, social and religious activity. The Riachuelo area, the natural port, was where the common people lived.

What is today Defensa street linked the port to the city, and along it the altos de San Pedro Telmo developed, concentrating all business related to the port and its activities. It also included brick and tile kilns, modest dwellings and warehouses for exports and imports. Only in 1653 a regular ferry crossing of the Riachuelo started operating.

The French traveler Acarate du Biscay[6] said, about these first *porteños* and *porteñas*: "They love their leisure and the

---

6 Acarete du Biscay was a French traveler who lived in Cádiz, learned Spanish and in 1657 set sail for Buenos Aires on a ship the captain of which allowed him to use his name and passed him off as a nephew of his, as foreigners were not allowed in the Indies. After

pleasures and are Venus' ardent devotees. I confess that in this they are to be excused, as the women are beautiful, of good shape and fair complexions. There are more women than men, and besides the Spaniards, there are French, Dutch and Genovese, but they all pass as Spaniards, as otherwise they wouldn't be allowed to stay, particularly those who are not of the Roman Catholic faith, as the Inquisition keeps a vigilant eye on all."[7]

Under Potosi's Shadow

Buenos Aires made no sense without the mines of Potosi, the one and only reason for the foundation of our city. During the last third of the 16th century, owing to the introduction of the new technique of silver refining through mercury amalgamation, originated in Huancavelica, both the amount of silver recovered from the ore and the exploitation and death rate of the Indians doubled. The "imperial village" was wealthier than it had ever been.

At its peak, the population of Potosi reached 160,000 inhabitants, greater than in some of the most important cities in Europe at the time. Because of its size as a market, it soon became the leading consumer of goods in Spanish

---

the River Plate area he visited Perú by way of Córdoba. He spent some time in Potosí, where he engaged in commerce. He later returned to Buenos Aires and on May 1659 returned to Europe in a Dutch ship. In 1698 the account of his trip was published in London.

7 "An Account of a Voyage up the River de la Plata, And thence over Land to Perú. With Observations on the Inhabitants, as well Indians and Spaniards; the Cities, Commerce, Fertility, and Riches of that Part of America," translated into Spanish for the *Revista de Buenos Aires*, vol. XIII, by Daniel Maxwell, Buenos Aires, 1867.

America. In a context of generalized poverty, its ruling class flaunted the highest buying power in the continent.

As a consequence of the exhaustion of Indian labor and the disastrous decline of the population, Potosi also became the largest centre of demand for black slaves in the Spanish Empire.

The Dirtiest Business

Potosi was a man-eating machine. The insatiable greed of the Spanish ruling classes and their European neighbors had managed to depopulate almost all of the surrounding areas. The American sources of manpower dried up, as the Indians died away at an alarming rate in the mine shafts of the Cerro de Plata. But the demand was greater than the production capacity, and so involuntary immigrants had to be shipped from Africa.

"The decrease of the naturals," writes jurist Antonio de Leon Pinelo, in his defense of the slave trade, "is so remarkable in all the Indies that the slaves brought from Guinea are not only useful but essential for the survival of the Indies."[8]

Millions were thus forced away from their homes, torn from their families and culture.

It appears that only the Portuguese observed the Church's regulations about baptising black slaves before shipping them. Some priests – particularly the Jesuits – were outraged at the manner in which this sacrament was administered, and asked permission from the Crown to baptize these men anew. "Neighbors from Córdoba report

8 Florencia Guzmán, "Vida de esclavos en el antiguo Tucumán", en *Todo es Historia* N° 393, Buenos Aires, 2000.

that the priests in Angola, rushed by the urgency of the trade, line up as many as 300 or 400 Negroes, at the Church, the *Quibangas*, the plaza or the beach, the day before they are to be shipped. Keeping them in chains to prevent their escape, and without any catechism whatsoever, so that they do not even know who God is, the priest will go about telling each one: 'Your name will be Pedro, yours Juan, etc.', writing down the names for them to remember. When this is over, they go over the line once again, tossing salt into everyone's mouth, and, in their third round, they sprinkle them with water, sometimes hurriedly, with a sprinkler, and there the baptism ends. Then, before leaving, with the aid of an interpreter, they say one or two things to them."[9]

Fray Tomas Mercado, a witness in Sevilla to this "nefarious traffic," recalls the nightmarish journey: "They travel so closely packed together, so filthy and battered, that those who bring them have assured me that they travel in groups of six, yoked and shackled in pairs, so that they are chained from head to toes, transported below deck, locked from the outside, where neither the moon nor the sun will ever shine, where no Spaniard dare poke his head in unless forced to, nor remain longer than an hour without a serious risk to his health, such is the stench, the crowding and misery of the place. And their only solace is what they are given to eat only once a day, not more than an average bowl of corn flour or raw millet, which is to them like our rice, with a small jar of water; that and the regular beatings, whippings and cursing. This is the usual procedure."[10]

9 Maud de Ridder de Zemborain, "Cuando en Buenos Aires se remataban negros", en *Todo es Historia* N° 393, Buenos Aires, 2000.
10 Florencia Guzmán, *op. cit.*

During the first part of the trip, some slaves, still in possession of their natural dignity and rebellious spirit, refused to eat, but the sailors, chosen amongst the cruellest, stuck funnels into their mouths and force-fed them so that they would not lose weight and could be sold at a higher price. There was not the slightest tolerance on board. As soon as an outbreak of any epidemic was detected, the sick were thrown into the sea, chains and all.

Once a day they were brought up on deck and bathed in sea water, and their bodies were covered with oil.

Those who tried to escape were punished in such manner that the rest would dismiss the idea of freedom forever. Some were burned alive, others were killed after being forced to eat their shipmates' hearts. Flayings followed by death were frequent, and other such some atrocities, devised, in this as in other cases, by the standard-bearers of the "most advanced culture of the time," that is to say, the English, who vied with the Portuguese and the Dutch for the monopoly of this traffic of human flesh.

But the misfortunes of the Africans did not end on landing. According to the letter of a Jesuit dated in 1635, illegal traders in Buenos Aires would often drown the slaves when in danger of getting caught: "We had to fight in no small degree with the greed of their masters, who exploited them cruelly. The former know how to conceal these miserable slaves, and in danger of being caught with them, they suffocate them in water to avoid the penalty issued against introducing African slaves into Perú through Paraguay."

Those who survived these tragedies had yet to be sold and reach their final destination: the Cerro de Plata in Potosí. In this way their "safe arrival" spelled not the end but the beginning of their torment and misery. Years later, the main slave traders of the River Plate and surrounding areas would be the well-known Martín de Alzaga and his partner, José Martínez de Hoz.

Lima and Seville versus Buenos Aires

In accordance to the regulations of the Spanish crown, the sum-total of the wealth produced at the bloody Cerro de Plata could only be shipped from the port of Lima, taken to Portobello and from there to Seville. This system had been worked out for the virtually exclusive economic benefit of the merchants of this Spanish city and their partners from Lima, both of which contributed bountiful "commissions" to the Crown.

There had to be a scapegoat and Buenos Aires was assigned the task of watching the back of the Lima route. The procedure could hardly be any more cumbersome or Kafkaesque: merchandise was shipped from Spain to the Isthmus of Panama, from where it was sent to Lima to be transported overland to the far-away consumer markets of the South. By the time the products reached their destination, the various intermediaries along the way had extraordinarily inflated the prices, which were high enough to begin with. Those who dwelled in the River Plate area were thus chronically short of money and could not even cover their bare necessities.

"In the whole of this *gobernación*, it is not possible to sell anything except in this port, and by this is commerce obstructed, as also by the difficulty foreigners have in finding enough Indians, or anyone else for that matter, to serve them for their money, because there are only a few Indians and these, with their wives and children, serve the *encomenderos* alone, and Christians are so scarce that very soon they will disappear, and so will the haciendas in the countryside and the livelihood of the Spaniards, who are and have always been so poor that cannot even afford to buy Negroes. There is a very large number of mares and wild horses which the Indians have learned how to ride and use, having become in this so dexterous they do not need saddle or harness. The Christian Indians and Indians fit for service total (…) eight thousand and fifty souls, and the pagan one hundred ninety-nine thousand and two hundred, not including their wives and children. No priest is there to tend to the pagans, except for two discalced ones, one of them a good interpreter and a devoted servant of God, and six Jesuits, also interpreters, for three provinces."[11]

In such a context, contraband[12] was the only way out, and it thus became our first national industry.

The First Argentine Invention

In those days, a CV was very much like a criminal record, and when in 1592 the viceroy of Perú had to appoint a governor for the River Plate, he chose his friend and partner, the Charcas *encomendero* Don Fernando de Zárate.

In spite of royal regulations, a sizable part of the silver from Upper Perú kept being shipped to Spain from the port

11 "Carta a S. M. del gobernador del Río de la Plata", Buenos Aires, 25 de abril de 1611, en Archivo General de Indias, Sevilla, Charcas, 10.

12 The word "band" (*bando*, in Spanish) means ordinance, decree, law or any legal resolution; so that "contraband" refers to everything that is done against the law. But general use has limited the scope of the word and "contraband" has come to mean the act of evading taxes by introducing or taking out merchandise in violation of the laws and procedures regulating foreign commerce.

of Buenos Aires, so the Crown decided to apply stricter measures and issued the royal letters patent of 28th of January 1594, by means of which it ratified the prohibition against trading, applicable to all the ports of America that had not been authorized for that purpose:

"(…) that through the River Plate neither people nor merchandise from Brazil, Angola, Guinea, or any other possession of the Portuguese Crown may be introduced into the provinces of Perú if they come not from Seville; that the route and passage be closely watched and that neither natural nor foreign people be allowed to enter without our leave or command."

Complying with this order would have spelled the death of the city-port, and since no one commits suicide unwillingly, the Porteños began to seek out ways of corroborating the Spanish saying "Every law has a loophole."

The charming nephews of governor Zárate, known as the "mad lads," were so fervently and overtly devoted to smuggling that complaints reached the *Audiencia* of Charcas. In January 1595 the court sent the royal accountant Hernando de Vargas to investigate the offenses perpetrated with the tacit approval of Uncle Fernando. Vargas received so little support from the local authorities that he decided to send the king a letter reporting the irregularities, stating also that there was nothing he could do, and returned to Charcas.

Free to act as they pleased, uncle and nephews inaugurated the much celebrated "native cunning" with an invention that would meet with no small success. It consisted in taking advantage of a provision signed between Spain and Portugal in 1581 that stated that if a Spanish or Portuguese ship were in danger, it should be allowed to enter the nearest port and sell all her cargo. Thus "forceful arrivals" were born.

The Zárate nephews worked on both sides of the counter. They confiscated the cargo, sold it, and bought it; and did it all, of course, by using dexterous front men.

In this way, hundreds of Portuguese ships carrying black slaves and a wide variety of merchandise arrived "forcefully" in Buenos Aires. These products were sold at a significantly lower price than the legal merchandise coming from Lima. The current money generated in these operations benefited the greater part of the Porteños, who turned a blind eye on smuggling, on the knowledge that their prosperity rested on it.

The inhabitants of Buenos Aires never ceased to lobby in favor of a revision of the preposterous closing down of their port. Despite its poverty, the city managed to keep an attorney at court, and through his intercession the Porteños alternatively begged and threatened to depopulate the place and hand it over to the foreigners, and so reminded the King of their labors "in hope of the trade that was to take place between this port and the coast of Brazil," and claimed that if the trade ended, "the city would not be able to survive, because her inhabitants' only hope of sustenance comes from the little flour, tallow, and dried meat they might sell to the coast of Brazil" and were this to be closed "the city would not be able to survive and thus a very important port in service of His Majesty would be lost."[13]

Hernandarias

The government of the River Plate had lacked stability. One governor had come after the other, and none of them

---

[13] José Luis Romero y Luis Alberto Romero (eds.), *Buenos Aires, historia de cuatro siglos*, Buenos Aires, Altamira, 2000.

had the time to get acquainted with the troubles facing the country because they had either left before their term was over, totally drained, as Juan Torres de Vera y Aragón or Fernando de Zárate, or because they had died sudden deaths, as Ramírez de Velasco in 1597.

After the death of Velasco, the settlers of Asunción chose Hernando Arias de Saavedra, or Hernandarias, as their governor, who was confirmed in his post by the viceroy of Perú in 1597. On the 12th of January 1602, a sealed letter from Philip III with the official appointment of Hernandarias as governor finally arrived.

Before presenting his six-year plan of government, he set out to visit the *gobernación*, leaving his nephew, the Córdoba-born Pedro Luis Cabrera, in charge, as lieutenant-to-the-governor in Buenos Aires. Cabrera earnestly devoted himself, to the exclusion of any other duty, to smuggling black slaves.

On his return, one of the first problems Hernandarias had to face was the closing down of the port of Buenos Aires at the request of Lima merchants. So he wrote a letter to the Council of the Indies explaining that the only way to protect Perú from any invasions via Buenos Aires was by increasing its population and thus its chances for defense as, were this invasion to take place, he could not vouch for the safety of Potosí. Hernandarias had cleverly uttered the one key word the Spanish crown could not ignore: Potosí. Nothing was more important to the Crown than this city, which they couldn't afford to jeopardize in any way. As his arguments were clear and persuasive, the royal letters patent of August 20, 1602 consented to the port being partially opened.

In this document, where the influence of the Lima-Sevilla axis can be clearly appreciated, the prohibition of sea-borne commerce was retained, while making a few provisional concessions to the inhabitants of Buenos Aires: "It is not convenient," the document explains, "that in the said provinces of the River Plate a port be opened with these our lands, nor with any other; the prohibition (...) should be observed invariably, and no one, regardless of rank, should be allowed to enter or leave without my permission (...), no merchandise should be introduced (...), and neither gold nor silver nor anything else should be shipped off from the said port. But to favor the neighbors and dwellers of the said city of Trinidad and the port of Buenos Aires (...) I see it meet to grant them leave and permission (...) for a period of six years (...) of the produce of their harvest and in ships, to dispatch every year (...) up to 3500 thousand bushels of flour and five hundred quintals of dried meat and another 12,500 pounds of tallow, and take them to Brazil and Guinea and other neighbouring islands inhabited by servants of mine, so that in return they might bring what they need to their homes, such as clothes, linen, shoes, and other such things, and iron, and steel, and everything that might be consumed and is consumed in the said provinces of the River Plate."

Once in power, Hernandarias was ordered by Philip III to expel all the Jews, the enforcement of which was carried out by Manuel de Frías. But the lands of the River Plate did not take kindly to this kind of harassment: although many were expelled and still many others had to escape, the majority of those affected by the disposition remained. Some of them managed to stay by marrying "local women;" others by converting and some, being good artisans, were protected by neighbours in need of their skills. The rich, as usual, found someone to shelter them. And they were protected despite the threat of Hernandarias' enforcement of the law: in the royal letter of November 20, 1603 he issued a proclamation prohibiting the concealment of "the said Portuguese."

Another important trait of his administration was the support he gave to the marriages between Spaniards and native women, and his defense of the mission Indians, as may be surmised from this document he signed: "But the *encomenderos* began to oppress the Indians and their wives and children with heavy duties, preventing them from buying goods and driving them to misery (...). Some Jesuits set out to put a stop to so much evil (...) for which reason father Torres turned our residence in Asunción into a school (...) He received much support from governor don Hernando Arias, who had just received a letter from the Catholic sovereign urging him to convert the provinces still enveloped in the darkness of paganism with no resort to arms, but only to missionaries."[14]

Hernandarias was intent on destroying the smugglers' organization. To do so, he issued several decrees setting new conditions for the imports and exports. The inhabitants of Buenos Aires were astonished by such an unexpected display of administrative honesty. Some, known as "the Worthies" – descendants of the first settlers – decided to aid the governor, while others, known as "the Confederate" – recently arrived in the city, closely associated with illegal trade, and fearful that Hernandarias' attitude would entail greater privations for the city – took sides with the smugglers.

---

14 Nicolás del Techo, *Historia de la provincia del Paraguay y de la Compañía de Jesús*, tomo II, Madrid, Regium, 1879.

Pirates in a Frock Coat

In 1609, when his period came to a close, Hernandarias left, confident that he had performed his duties skilfully and that contraband belonged to the past. Marín Negrón, who succeeded him, tried to pursue his policies against smuggling.

One of the first serial smugglers of Buenos Aires was a Portuguese known as Bernardo the Sinful or Brother Sinner. Following his death, leadership of the Portuguese smugglers went to Diego de la Vega who, together with his wife, Blanca Vasconcelos, had entered Buenos Aires clandestinely.

Diego de la Vega, was a "son of burnt ones," as his identification papers state, because his parents, who were of Jewish extraction, had been executed by the "Holy" Inquisition. Very soon, Don Diego had become a wealthy merchant. Ships carrying slaves and merchandise would be moored directly at his city-block, bound by the present-day Alsina, Moreno, Balcarce and Defensa streets, or at his farm in Barracas. All traffic with Brazil and Portugal was under his control, and he had agents in Lisbon, London, Rio de Janeiro, Flanders, Lima, Angola and in the River Plate hinterland.

Don Diego, together with his next of kin Diego de León, Juan de Vergara, Captain Mateo Leal de Ayala and the *Hacienda Real* Treasurer, Simón de Valdez, started an organization known as The Quadrilateral, later to become the biggest smuggling band in all of Spanish America – which was no mean thing.

The goal of this society was to perfect and expand the profitable clandestine traffic. In slightly more than three years they introduced nearly 4000 "pieces," making a profit of more than 2 million ducats. Their operations observed a regulation stipulating that all confiscated products should be sold immediately. Fulfilling this requirement, as soon as a smuggled shipment arrived, the members of the gang swiftly reported it, so that the Negroes were immediately sold in auction. No one was allowed to make an offer surpassing the minimum price set by the law, about 100 silver pesos, and if anyone who was not a member of the band made a higher bid, he would lose his money and maybe even his life. The unfortunate Negroes were then sold in Potosi at a price many times greater than the one paid for them by these crooks. But the Confederate did not neglect other important legal aspects and sent the brilliant lawyer Antonio de León Pinelo to Spain, to make certain that they were acting "within the law." From Madrid, Pinelo confirmed that it was all "legal."

The person in charge of organizing these auctions, which Vergara and his partner began to refer to as "exemplary contraband," was the royal treasurer Simón de Valdez.

Simón de Valdez had been born in Tenerife of noble parents. One of his uncles had been bishop of León. Valdez sailed for the Antilles as a petty officer, and in Havana he learned that there was an English pirate looting the ports of the region and that a substantial reward was being offered for his capture. Using money obtained through illegal gambling, he put up a small fleet, chased and captured the pirate, took him to the governor, and collected the sizeable reward, which became his venture capital – an example of primitive accumulation as good as any.

Valdez would later reappear in Havana, once again fighting the pirates, and would be promoted to the rank of admiral. After meeting with much success, he traveled to Spain and the King rewarded him for his "merits" with the position of *Hacienda Real* Treasurer in the provinces of the River Plate on the 28th of June 1605.

The treasurer arrived in the port of Buenos Aires in February 1606, took up his position on the 13th of March and was accepted by the *Cabildo* on the 3rd of April. The following day, he made his social debut: at the house of the royal officers, opposite the Fort, he engaged in a knife fight with the *Hacienda Real* accountant, Hernando de Vargas.

Vargas was also a man to be feared. He had arrived in Buenos Aires in 1595 and had begun his administration by reporting the illegal dealings of Governor Zárate and bringing the case before the Audiencia of Charcas. On his return, he came across Judge Sancho de Figueroa. Don Sancho carried royal letters patent prohibiting all kinds of commerce with the port of Buenos Aires, but as soon as he became aware of the business opportunities involved, he decided not to divulge the contents of the documents he carried. Vargas found out about the royal letters in Madrid and accused Sancho, who disappeared "mysteriously."

Simón de Valdez did not arrive on his own. He was accompanied by Lucía González de Guzmán, who, according to his identification papers, "is not his legitimate wife." Mrs. Guzmán would later take an active role in his illegal organization, and thus became the forerunner of many like her yet to come. She enjoyed flaunting her wealth, and had soon acquired such a refined taste, that she would only attend Mass if borne by her slaves on a richly decorated sedan chair.

In 1610 Don Diego de la Vega was granted the status of neighbor by the city *Cabildo*,[15] since "for nine years he

---

15 The *Cabildo* or Town Council, was composed of two *alcaldes* or magistrates, and six aldermen, appointed by the Crown or the governor. It was not, as many of the supporters of the colonial days claimed it to be, a democratic or deliberative body elected by the

has kept house and significant property in town." During those years, his partner Juan de Vergara had begun performing duties in the local administration and had gradually become one of the biggest land-owners of the region, as well as cattle exporter and farmer, exploiting a large number of slaves, and Indians hired and in *encomienda*. As Jorge Gelman[16] has pointed out, the ruling classes of Buenos Aires fashioned themselves in the likeness of the Vergaras, combining the use of forced labor with participation in commerce, rural activities and the administration.

But beside the merchants whom smuggling had made rich, there lived in Buenos Aires a population who suffered severe hardships. One of the first bishops of the city wrote: "And so it goes that 20 ducats are worth in Spain more than 200 ducats here, on account of the price of things. To get a pair of shoes one must first buy the leather, then find a shoemaker, beg him for months on end, pay him an exorbitant price, be content with whatever shoes he gets, and thank the workman profusely. There are no doctors, no druggists, no medicines, no barbershops, but they all act as doctors and druggists, and as you can imagine, each

---

people, but the redoubt of high-class neighbors (i.e., property holders) who each January would "choose" the next *Cabildo* officials for the year, thus keeping a firm hold on it. Elections were supposed to be endorsed by the governor, who often vetoed them or filled in the vacancies himself. The practice of selling public positions which developed in the early years of the 17th century limited the significance of these elections even more. In Buenos Aires, land-owning council members were the majority, and their rights were hereditary.

16 Jorge Gelman, "El mundo rural en transición", en Noemí Goldman, *Nueva historia argentina*, Buenos Aires, Sudamericana, 1998.

prepares the medicines as he sees fit (...) There is neither silver nor gold, no royal or copper currency, or of any kind for that matter. Because of the lack of the former, all transactions are conducted through bartering, wine for wheat, wheat for sugar, sugar for meat, meat for maté, and so forth."[17]

That same year, 1610, the society of the Quadrilateral decided to diversify their business and opened the largest casino in the River Plate area, offering games, cards, craps, chess, *truques* (a kind of billiard) and "women in love;" it was also possible to drink alcohol. The premises were located on the corner of present-day Alsina and Bolívar streets, and they belonged to Simón de Valdez and his partner Juan de Vergara. The house was built by Florentine architect Baccio da Filicaia (1565-1635), whose works included the construction of the forts of Bahia in Brazil and the first *Cabildo* and hospital of Buenos Aires, built in 1611.

The growth of the operations carried out by the Confederates, and their impunity, finally alarmed Negrón, who came up with a procedure to expel the Portuguese, not on account of their being "illegal Portuguese" – as Hernandarias had suggested – but for "Judaizing." But the leader of the band, Juan de Vergara, was a notary of the Inquisition in Buenos Aires, and so the project was held up in the Council of the Indies.

Smuggling increased with the partial opening of the port, and the Lima people succeeding in sending a·judge from the *Audiencia* of Charcas, don Francisco de Alfaro, to assess the situation. He began his inspection tour – which can be

---

17 Juan M. Vigo, "Hernandarias entre contrabandistas y judíos", en *Todo es Historia* N° 51, Buenos Aires, 1971.

compared to present-day federal interventions – at the end of 1610, entering via Tucumán and then heading for Buenos Aires in 1611. On June 26 of that year he issued a number of regulations to combat illegal trade:

- It was forbidden to sell export permits.
- To obtain permission, three years of residence had to be proved.
- Those in charge of the vessels had to keep a record of the shipments.
- Fines were established for passengers without a license.
- Imported merchandise had to be consumed within the limits of the *gobernación*.

With this backing, Governor Negrón issued a disposition that would cost him his life: he ordered that the auctions of illegal products from "forced arrivals" should be held after the value of the merchandise was appraised by the governor and then offered at a "fair price." On July 26, 1613, Negrón died suddenly.

Obeyed but Not Followed

Back then in Buenos Aires, government positions were sold in public auction, in a solemn ceremony presided over by the highest authorities of the colony, who gathered at the main plaza, by the *Cabildo* doors. The ceremony ended with the following words: "Let this be to your true gain and advantage."

Already in 1590, a royal letters patent addressed to the governor of Buenos Aires by Philip II gives an account of the illegal manner in which posts were purchased: "Many times you have interfered by appointing judges, royal officers with a voice and a vote at the *Cabildo*, for death or absence of the true holder; and officers of our treasury, invoking their greater seniority, have acquired the post of *Cabildo* officers, through death or absence of the true holder, which has caused great inconvenience (...) And We decree that, not having a royal letters patent or any particular power granted by our person, do not interfere by appointing or granting the said titles."[18]

The Catholic sovereigns had prohibited the sale of positions, but as Bobadilla explains, "the said law should be removed, and should not take up space in the *libro de Recopilación*, because it is not observed, and the said posts are sold because of the times, and of the great needs and obligations of His Majesty."

A post was exactly like any other property, a lien could be placed upon it, it could be executed for payment of debt, sold or inherited: "And these the son and the wife can inherit, the daughter may receive as dowry if so they be promised, and they can be burdened and mortgaged like a house or a vineyard."[19]

In 1614, the purchase of positions allowed the Confederate to control the *Cabildo*. But a few days after the elections, Enrique de Jerez, a *visitador* (inspector) from the *Audiencia* of Charcas, arrived. He discovered that Negrón had been poisoned by the recently-appointed *Cabildo* magistrate and treasurer of the Holy Crusade, Juan de Vergara. Vergara, being a lover of justice, had him immediately arrested, and accused him of trying to arrest *him* on account of an "imaginary offense."

In this context, the viceroy of Lima, the marquee of Montesclaros, named a governor to put an end to the

---

18 Acuerdos del Cabildo.
19 *Ibid.*

provisional administration of Leal de Ayala, and named Don Francés de Beaumont, who had already been in Buenos Aires, dabbling in the slave trade. The new governor arrived with the ordinances of Montesclaros under his arm, a set of rules devised by the viceroy to control sea-borne commerce. Vergara, who had added to his many positions that of village representative at the Cabildo, claimed that the viceroy had exceeded his duties and suggested to the new governor that the ordinances should be "obeyed but not followed." Beaumont returned them to the viceroy for re-examination.

Hernandarias Returns

Everything seemed to be going for the Confederate when, in April 1615, dreadful news arrived: the King Philip III had appointed the *criollo* Hernandarias as governor once again. He took over on May 23.

One of his first government measures was to replace the authorities of the Confederate-controlled *Cabildo* with members of the "Worthies" minority party, loyal to the governor and to the laws of the Crown.

A few days later, he had De la Vega, Valdez, Leal de Ayala and Vergara imprisoned. The proceedings, however, were riddled with irregularities, since just a few dared testify against the band and those who did, such as bailiff Domingo de Guadarrama, were murdered.

Valdez was sent to Spain to be prosecuted, but he bribed the captain of the ship and managed to escape. Vergara bribed a guard in the prison of Perú where he had been confined and escaped as well.

The records of the case against the band of the Quadrilateral had 16,000 pages! – enlarged by the absurd chicanery of the supporters of the smugglers. For the trial to proceed, vast amounts of paper had to be brought in from other cities in the viceroyalty.

As the trial was being held up by lack of witnesses, Hernandarias asked the *Audiencia* of Charcas to grant him the faculty of "extraordinary question," that is, of applying torture. After duly torturing the witnesses, Hernandarias managed to prove, down to the very last detail, the poisoning of Negrón, the complicity of Leal de Ayala and the royal officers with the smugglers, the plan to take over the *Cabildo* and several other of the Confederate's tricks. After declaring, the witnesses were led by the free members of the band beyond the limits of the province – they turned up in Santiago del Estero – where they took back everything they had said, as it had been exacted under torture. Because the Confederate still had a great influence on the inhabitants of Buenos Aires, Hernandarias had to be on the defensive, as he felt that the people despised him and did not thank him enough for "pursuing the common good."

The arrest of the band made clear that Buenos Aires was living off illegal traffic, and scarcity spread, which increased the unpopularity of the governor.

Without evidence, and unable to continue the trial, Hernandarias ended his administration not being able to convict any of the main organizers of clandestine trade.

Fraud, 1616 Model

The Confederate needed to take over the *Cabildo*, especially the two posts of magistrate, which involved the exercise of communal justice and were essential to turn the necessary blind eye to the band's illegal business.

Like every year, on the 1st of January 1616 the outgoing members of the *Cabildo* chose the incoming members. The *Cabildo* of Buenos Aires was composed of two magistrates, Francisco de Salas and Francisco Manzanares, and six voting aldermen – on this occasion there were five, because the sixth one was in jail due to a "criminal case"[20] – Domingo Gribeo, Felipe Naharro, Gonzalo de Carabajal, Miguel de Corro, and Bartolomé Frutos, in addition to the trustee and royal standard-bearer Bernardo de León. Also, due to an accepted practice among the locals, the three royal officers voted as well. They were none other than Simón de Valdez, Tomás Ferrufino, and Bernardo de León; the first two, members of the criminal organization. In brief, the Confederate had but two votes in eight.

The crooks tried to bribe the majority electors, as it was reported on the day of the election by the first-vote magistrate and three of the aldermen; but this only contributed two more voters: the second-vote magistrate, Manzanares, who complied with the wishes of the band on the promise that he would become attorney general, and the alderman Felipe Naharro, who was offered the position of brotherhood magistrate. But they were still four to six and it was not enough.

On the day of the election, when entering the chapter house, the Worthies found out about the scheme perpetrated by the powerful Confederate of Juan de Vergara: the night before, the notary of the Cabildo, Cristóbal Remón and one of the aldermen, Domingo Gribeo, had been arrested. Instead, Juan Quinteros, who had been arrested in connection

20 José María Rosa, *Historia argentina*, tomo I, Buenos Aires, Oriente, 1971.

to the criminal case, was there. Francisco de Salas complained about Gribeo's and Remón's "ill-intentioned arrest," objected to the presence of the crook Quinteros, and after claiming that he was aware of the negotiations to get rid of another magistrate, proceeded to disallow the elections that were about to take place.

Ayala, who was presiding over the election, explained that he had arrested Gribeo in connection to a lawsuit, and refused to have him appear in court under custody.

The president began the election trying to keep the peace. They had to choose the magistrates: the five Worthies voted for Gonzalo de Carabajal, and the five Confederate for Juan de Vergara and Sebastian de Orduña. The notary nullified the vote Carabajal had conferred upon himself and said that, because the election had resulted in a draw between Gribeo, Vergara and Orduña, the governor had to break the tie with his vote. Ayala, perhaps considering personal safety a higher virtue than duty, conferred his vote on Vergara and Orduña and thus legalized the result. The whole procedure for this election was so shocking that one of the aldermen who had been elected unanimously, Captain Francisco Muñoz, refused to take office, preferring the fine and imprisonment that his denial entailed.

The Contraband of His Excellency the Governor

In 1617, Philip III finally decided to divide the vast territory of the *gobernación* of the River Plate into two jurisdictions: an intendancy with its capital in Asunción and another one based in Buenos Aires. Hernandarias was to leave Buenos Aires to take control of the new Paraguayan seat.

The man elected to fill the post of first governor of Buenos Aires, Diego de Góngora, had a prestigious background: he belonged to the Order of Santiago, and for over seven years had been fighting in Flanders, from which place he returned to Spain carrying a warm recommendation from the Duke of Lerma, which resulted in his being rewarded with a governorship in these lands, one of the most coveted posts by Spanish nobles, more interested in wealth than in glory.

The new governor, perhaps not to waste time, sailed from Spain on the 15th of April 1618 with three vessels transporting smuggled cargo worth 300,000 ducats. In the first days of June, Góngora's fleet reached port in Todos los Santos Bay, with the purpose of wintering there before continuing the journey to their destination. A few days later, a ship from Oporto entered the same port, carrying confidential information for Góngora; it notified him that four days after his departure an indictment against him had been initiated in Lisbon, and that all those who had taken part in the negotiations had testified, therefore disclosing his illegal dealings.

Góngora pretended to be shocked by the news and claimed that the whole of the cargo was "for personal use." When he realized that his arguments were not very convincing, he ordered all the cargo in question to be discharged in Bahia, and, of course, the local correspondents of the smuggler's organization took good care of it.

Finally, on the 16th of November 1618 the "illustrious" governor arrived in Buenos Aires, and took office the following day.

Góngora tried to change his subjects' "bad habits": "There is both among the men and women of this *gobernación* an abominable and filthy vice that is drinking the *yerba* with a large quantity of hot herbs to induce vomiting, causing great damage to the spiritual and temporal well-being, because it reduces the frequency of the Holy Sacrament and makes the men lazy, which is the ruin of the land, and since it is so widely spread I am afraid it will be impossible to remove unless God does it Himself."[21]

Soon after, Góngora got wind of his first business opportunity. Claiming to have been warned that the Dutch were trying to seize the port, he sent dozens of reports to the authorities saying that the place was totally unprotected and requesting that a hired force, a large supply of weapons and ammunition and "extraordinary" funding were sent to him. The attack never took place, but what did take place was a shady deal.

Some historians, like Zacarías Moutoukias, question the pertinence of speaking of "corruption" in connection to a regime whose very reason for being was illegal trade: "In the 17th century, corruption in the River Plate region consisted in the regular infraction of a fixed set of rules that limited the integration of the representatives of the Crown into the local oligarchy; that is to say, that hampered their participation in economic activities. Would it be appropriate to speak of corruption when the conditions on which the Crown organized its administrative and military structure explain the infractions, and when those same conditions were characteristic of the economic practices of the ruling elite – which also encompassed the officers – and the Crown adapted to this situation because it allowed it to finance its local administrative and military apparatus?"[22]

21 "Carta a S. M. del Gobernador de Buenos Aires", 25 de Abril de 1617, en Ricardo Rodríguez Molas, *Historia Social del gaucho*, Buenos Aires, CEAL, 1982.

22 Zacarías Moutoukias, "Burocracia, contrabando y autotransformación, de las elites. Buenos Aires en el siglo XVII", *Anuario IEHS*, III, Tandil, 1988.

The resumption of commerce and contraband brought Buenos Aires back to life, but its development would no go unchecked. The merchants of Lima reacted to the competition and the *Casa de Contratación* of Seville interceded by hastily ordering the definitive cessation of all commercial relations between the market of Upper Perú and Buenos Aires. In 1622 a royal letters patent was issued establishing a custom-house in Córdoba, whose role was to stop the traffic from Buenos Aires to Potosí. To alleviate the effects, it was established that once a year two vessels would sail from Seville to Buenos Aires, thus guaranteeing the provision of the city.

The Porteños' reflexes were quick: the *Cabildo* declared that the royal letters patent was against the interests of the city, since two annual vessels were not enough to satisfy the basic needs of the dwellers. Before the effective establishment of the Córdoba custom-house, those who had vested interests in contraband proceeded to increase the rate of traffic to Perú, flooding the market with their merchandise and causing a significant drop in prices, which exasperated the conservative *Pelucones* from Lima even more, driving them to exert their influence and voice their complaints.

But none of these dispositions managed to disrupt the penetration of Buenos Aires' goods into the markets closed to it. Its status of natural outlet for those territories into the Atlantic prevailed over the checks and prohibitions, which only served to encourage smuggling.[23]

However, during Góngora's administration the "forced arrivals" continued and even grew. This led the Crown to suspect that Góngora might be associated with the Confederate

23 Diego Luis Molinari, *Buenos Aires, cuatro siglos,* Buenos Aires, TEA, 1984.

through Simón Valdez. So a new inquirer arrived, Judge Matías Delgado Flores, who shortly after beginning his inquires described the governor, not exactly in praise perhaps, as the "lord and owner of the whole land."

Góngora did everything in his power to thwart the investigation, and had the notary of the Holy Office, who was none other than the returned Juan de Vergara, convict Flores for saying: "Smugglers are everywhere in the city. I should kill them one by one." Delgado Flores ended up being deported on a slave ship on the 21st of July 1619. He was never heard of again.

When the *Audiencia* found out about the incident, it appointed its judge, Alonso Pérez de Salazar, to investigate charges against Governor Góngora.

Suspicions were well grounded. Thanks to Góngora, Vergara's band was in control again. They had taken over the *Cabildo*, bribed the *Audiencia* of Charcas and sent their own emissaries to the Council of Indies with enough false allegations and twisted facts.

Góngora asked Hernandarias to hand over the records of the case against the Confederate, which by then added up to 19,000 pages. Hernandarias refused, claiming that the position of inquirer of the *Audiencia* of Charcas was independent from the position of governor of Buenos Aires. In November 1618, Góngora ordered the confiscation of the proceedings and the arrest of the *caudillo*, in addition to the seizure and sale of his properties.

Now that he was in control of the trial, Góngora freed the neighbors who had been imprisoned, sent the men loyal to Hernandarias to jail and banished the officers who were faithful to him, like the notary of the *Cabildo* who had acted as secretary during the trial, who was deported to Africa and died on the trip as a result of torture.

Juan de Vergara had resettled in Buenos Aires, ready to resume his activities and become the richest and most powerful man in town until his death. In Lima he had "acquired" all the posts of the *Cabildo* to perpetuity, which he distributed among his friends, one of his brothers-in-law and his father-in-law, none other than Diego de Trigueros, well-known among us because in his estancia the miracle of the Virgin of Luján took place.

In addition, during Góngora's government, Treasurer Juan de Valdez returned, whom Hernandarias had sent to Spain "so that Justice could be made." There was nothing to worry about now, and as is usually the case in these situations, impunity leads to perverse ostentation. Present-day society magazine *Caras* had not been created yet, but Juan de Vergara boasted of having seventy-five slaves for domestic service and a fifteen-room house.

According to the information supplied by Sergeant-major Diego Páez de Clavijo, Góngora died on May 21st 1623, "a few days after being affected by a fever or affliction brought about by the usual slanders of these places."

In the *juicio de residencia* carried out in his absence, Góngora was found guilty of allowing the "forced arrival" of vessels which introduced more than 5000 black slaves, and of having permitted the shipping of leather without having a license to do so. The Royal Council of the Indies examined the proceedings and the charges brought against Góngora and in a verdict dated February 18, 1631, ordered him to pay 23,050 ducats, "to be enforced on to the properties left by the deceased." On the same day, Governor Diego Páez de Clavijo – who in record time had accumulated twelve charges against him – was ordered to pay 6700 ducats in cash.

Góngora was succeeded by Francisco de Céspedes, who in an attempt to please both sides stated that the charges against the Confederate had been exaggerated, and that the fight put up by the Worthies was worthy of praise.

In 1627, Céspedes, on the advice of Hernandarias, risked his life when he imprisoned the untouchable Juan de Vergara with the intention of "giving him the *garrote* in jail." The incident caused such an uproar that the bishop, fray Pedro de Carranza, went up to the prison doors, forced them open and freed his cousin Vergara. Céspedes demanded the bishop to turn him up but Carranza, dressed as if for a Te Deum and crosier in hand, anathematized the governor, who decided to give up.

Céspedes went to Hernandarias for help. The *caudillo* traveled from Santa Fe to Buenos Aires with the authorization of the *Audiencia* of Charcas, made Bishop Carranza lift the excommunication and prosecuted Vergara far from his relative's diocese. But the leader of the smugglers immediately got the *Audiencia* of Charcas to absolve him.

In 1624, Hernandarias had been officially vindicated by judge Pérez de Salazar through an official letter issued on June 24 that said: "(…) because he deserves the favor and gratitude with which His Majesty honors and rewards those who in such posts serve him faithfully."[24]

Ten years later, at the age of 70, the first *criollo* governor of these lands died in Santa Fe, in abject poverty.

24 Jose Francisco Figuerola, *¿Por qué Hernandarias?*, Buenos Aires, Plus Ultra, 1981.

Civilization and Barbarism:
Túpac Amaru's Rebellion

If the Indians were to beat us
They'd make us sweat
As now they sweat for us,
And humiliated would we be
As much as they are now.
Not one of us could hope
For house, splendor or wealth,
No one honors will get
We'd be plebeians all:
We their Indians would be
And they would be our lords.

Anonymous Spanish Couplet, 1780

It is only fair to say that the discourse of power has been and continues to be quite shrewd, in its way. Generations of Argentines have been raised in the knowledge of how Túpac Amaru died, but they do not recall, and sometimes do not even know, what the reason for his final torment was. Thus, the last Inca has not persisted in the people's imagination as a symbol of American freedom but as the crudest illustration of quartering.

All serious historians agree that the revolt led by Túpac Amaru was the most important social movement in the colonial history of the continent. And even the most ardent defenders of the Spanish colonization admit that the Spanish Empire was at risk of disappearing. But because Túpac Amaru's ideas are so contemporary and his demands so just, it is only logical that people should be made to remember what happens to the rebellious when they take their rebellion too seriously, and at the same time made to forget their motives, the flagrant injustice that led to the creation of the fairest army that ever set foot on this continent. The revolt had repercussions in our country, and our authorities of the time had a key role in the savage repression that ensued.

On the one side, there was the millenary Inca Civilization and its heirs, who fought in defense of what belonged to them: their land, their culture and their right to live in dignity. On the other side, the barbarism of the invaders, whose only god was silver and gold, which they took in greed and unheeding of the dead they left in their wake. The punishment inflicted on Túpac Amaru's family illustrates very clearly on what side of the "civilization-barbarism" dichotomy each party stood.

Nothing like Little Colorful Mirrors

Despite the biased story that would have us believe that the original inhabitants of these lands welcomed the invaders as gods and surrendered to them like lambs in a slaughter-house, the ancient Inca Empire – like most of this continent – resisted despoilment and genocide with great heroism.

The first attempt at resistance sparked with the arrival of Pizarro in 1536 and was led by Atahualpa's brother, Manco Inca, who the Spaniards had expected would aid them in the looting of those rich lands.

In April 1536, Manco left Cuzco with the excuse of fetching some life-size statues for Hernando Pizarro, who willingly consented. Manco also said that he was going hunting – the great "chaco" or ceremonial hunting of vicuñas – though what he really intended was to perform the rituals that preceded a military campaign.

A few days later the invaders found that several contingents of Indians had gathered in Yucay. They sent armed soldiers in their pursuit, but the plan was thwarted by the natives. At that time, Manco's troops numbered 10,000 men – not counting the women who, according to the Indian tradition, accompanied the warriors.

After strenuous preparations, Manco laid siege to the city of Cuzco. Many years later, the people would still remember the fear felt by the besieged Spaniards, who found themselves surrounded by a large number of men perpetually yelling and, every night, lighting bonfires to pinpoint the contours of the siege.

To prevent Francisco Pizarro from sending reinforcements to break the blockade from the outside, Manco had also coordinated an attack on Lima. Francisco Pizarro had decided to send an expedition to Cuzco under the command of Gonzalo de Tapia through the Pisco route. On the climb to Vilcashuamán, they ran into the Inca's troops near the Pampas River. In the bloody battle that ensued, the Spaniards were routed. The native troops marched on and arrived in Parcos (Huancavelica) where they had to confront a new contingent of Spaniards trying to reach Cuzco.

A third expedition sent from Lima through Jauja was taken by surprise in Angoyacu, where its leader, Juan Morgovejo de Quiñones, was killed. The Mantaro route was cleared for the natives in two other combats: Jauja and Pariacaca.

On the 5th of September 1536, the Inca army, under the command of Quizo Yupanqui, arrived at the doors of Lima and clashed with the Spaniards in Mama, Cañete, Mala, Chancay and Ate. A contingent under the orders of Pedro de Lerma tried to stop them in the surroundings of Puruchuco, but the attackers managed to settle on the hills that surrounded the city of the kings and began to close in on the city itself. But Quizo Yupanqui had been defeated in Pachacamac by Alonso de Alvarado and, thanks to the strategic support they received from Indian troops in various locations, the Spaniards obtained their final victory in Lima. Quizo Yupanqui and Cusi Rimac, the main leaders of the Indian offensive, died in the struggle.

In Cuzco, the siege of the city ended after nine months, when Almagro's troops returned from Chile.

Manco decided to establish himself and his people in the Vilcabamba area, where he set up the Neo-Inca state – with the sacred city of Machu Picchu as its capital – which lasted until 1572. There, the old ceremonial of the Inca religion was reinstated, rejecting all the elements pertaining to the Christian cult.

Manco was succeeded by his son, Sayri Túpac, and his step-brother, Titu Cusi, who by 1560 ruled over a vast territory. Both went on fighting the Spaniards until the death of Titu Cusi in 1571. He had chosen the legitimate son of Manco Inca, Túpac Amaru, as his successor. This first Túpac Amaru would later be captured and beheaded by the Spaniards.

Thus ended the Neo-Inca state, which, for almost thirty-six years, had held the sword over the invaders' heads and had attracted thousands of fugitive Indians from mines and mills. At about the same time, the Taki Ongoy movement emerged, which in the Quechua language means "song or dance of illness." It was a quintessentially millennarian movement, "ardently anti-Catholic and anti-Hispanic."

The leaders of this movement, Juan Chocne and the Indian women Santa María and Santa María Magdalena, rejected the use of Spanish clothes, or any other Hispanic element, including names. They blamed the Church and the viceroyalty for the conditions of submission of the Indians. They also believed in a coming Deluge which would drown all Spaniards. According to their tradition, the empire had been preceded by four eras or suns, each one a thousand years long, and the very year the movement broke out, 1565, was also that of the last moon, bringing about the birth of a new humanity.

Here Comes José Gabriel

José Gabriel Condorcanqui Noguera, who would enter history under the name of Túpac Amaru,[1] was born on the 19th of March 1740, in the town of Surimana, province of Tinta (present-day Perú). He was the second son of Don Miguel Condorcanqui and Doña Rosa Noguera, and fifth-generation descendant of the last Inca, Túpac Amaru,[2] who had led a heroic rebellion against Viceroy Francisco de Toledo.

At age ten, Jose Gabriel entered the School for Chieftains of San Francisco de Borja, in Cuzco. Years later, when he was in Lima dealing with legal matters, it seems that his

1 In Quechua, the name Túpac Amaru means "blazing serpent": *túpac* blazing, and *amaru*, serpent. Ancient Incas believed that big and powerful men resembled serpents because, like them, their presence filled one with fear and respect. One of the neighborhoods of Cuzco, where the Incas kept and venerated some serpents, was called *Amaru-cancha*, "serpents' pen".

2 Don Martín García Loyola, nephew to St. Ignatius and governor of Chile in 1593, married Clara Beatriz, the only daughter and heiress of Inca Túpac. They had a daughter who went to Spain, married esquire Don Juan Henríquez de Borga, and was awarded the title of Marchioness of Oropesa. Túpac Amaru came from this same branch of the family.

permanent desire to increase his knowledge led him to attend art lessons at the University of San Marcos. He inherited the chieftancies of Pampamarca, Tungasuca, and Surimana, and a large number of mules, all of which made him a prosperous chieftain, whose main business was the transport of merchandise. On May 25, 1760, having just turned 20, he married the love of his life, Micaela Bastidas Puyucawa, who had been born in the town of Pampamarca. As a result of their union three sons were born: Hipólito in 1761, Mariano in 1762, and Fernando in 1768. All the sons of the chief were baptized by the priest Antonio López de Sosa. Túpac's marriage to that extraordinary woman encouraged him to claim official recognition as chieftain or *cacique* and the acknowledgment of his right to be considered the legitimate descendant of Inca Túpac Amaru.

A witness of the period describes him as "a man about 5.7 ft tall, with a columbine nose and lively eyes. His figure is slim and graceful, his hair is cut above his forehead and curls down to waist-length at the back; over it he wears a beaver hat. His manners are courtly and gentlemanly; his equanimity and moderation are those of a man of superior culture and are matched by his other character traits. He speaks the Spanish language to perfection and the Quechua language with remarkable grace. He addresses his superiors with dignity and the Indians with utmost formality."

Bourbon Reforms

By the end of the 18th century, the dynasty of the Bourbons, with the purpose of reorganizing the imperial structure and power, implemented a set of administrative and economic reforms. The "Bourbon Reforms" drastically transformed the relationship between Spain and the colonies.

One of the most important measures was the creation, in 1776, of the Viceroyalty of the River Plate, which included the mines of Potosí.

From that moment on, and owing to the development of maritime activities, Buenos Aires rapidly increased its population, consolidated its urban structure and became the leading commercial center among Spanish colonies in the south of the American continent.

The measure was detrimental to the Viceroyalty of Perú, where *visitador* Jose Antonio de Areche attempted to compensate for the loss of the Potosí wealth with the over-exploitation of the Indians and a suffocating increase in taxation, including the creation of new taxes which, of course, fell on the already broken Indian backs.

The closing down of the mills, the standstill of mine production and the sugar and cotton crisis extended unemployment, and thousands of Indians lost their already paltry sources of income.

To Put an End to Bad Government

In view of the situation, Túpac filed a formal petition to free the Indians from forced labor in the mines. He wrote: "In the past, the Indians died or deserted [the mines], but the towns were then well-populated and it didn't show; but nowadays, because they have been so drastically thinned out, it is impossible to comply with the *mita*, because there are no Indians left to work in the mines, and those who already have are forced to do so all over again." He denounced that the Indians had to work in inhuman conditions in the mines, and that they sometimes had to walk "for over two hundred days' journey on their way to the mines, and as many on their way back." He also demanded the closing down of the mills, virtual concentration camps where men, women, old people and children were worked to exhaustion.

Above all he targeted the system of *repartimientos* or forced labour allotments, the forerunner of the shameful payment in kind, a time-honored practice in the history of Latin American labor. To support their lavish lifestyle and increase their dividends, *corregidores* – officials in charge of the administration of a district called a *corregimiento* – forced the Indians to buy all kinds of useless stuff on which they made some profit. Túpac Amaru complained: "They give us pins, needles from Cambray, blue powders, decks of cards, glasses, small religious pictures and other such ridiculous things. To those of us who are in a better position, they give velvet, silk stockings, embroidery, buckles, Rouen cotton and chambray, as if we Indians dressed in the Spanish fashion. And at such excessive prices, that when we want to sell them back, we do not even recover the twentieth part of what we paid."

The arrogant Lima *Audiencia*, composed mainly of *encomenderos* and abusive mine-owners, didn't even deign to listen to his complaints.

Túpac was beginning to realize that he would have to take a more radical approach, and began organizing the most extraordinary insurrection that ever took place in this continent.

The poor, the sad-eyed children, the old men whose health had been ruined by the dust and the mercury of the mines, the women tired of seeing their husbands and sons die in great pain, began to organize a liberating army.

The first task was to obtain firearms, which the Indians were not allowed to own or use. Small groups raided the deposits and houses of the mine-owners and gradually the rebel arsenal began to grow. Grandfathers and grandsons devoted themselves to the making of blades, whittling canes and preparing avenging arrows. The women knitted marvellous wraps, using the colors forbidden by the Spaniards. One of these was to be adopted as the flag of the liberating army. Bearing the colours of the rainbow, it still flies over the Peruvian Andes today.

Soon Túpac realized that his rebellion would not succeed without the support of the *criollos* (American born whites) and *mestizos* (half-breeds). But the local-born property owners were not that different from their European colleagues. They were very much a part of the social status quo, their wealth derived from the exploitation of Indian labor in the mines, haciendas and mills.

The kind of independence that Túpac proposed not only entailed political changes, it also involved the transformation of the social structure that prevailed in Spanish America.

While José Gabriel Túpac Amaru's revolt against abusive *corregidores* and the iniquitous organization of mine labor lasted, it shook Perú to its foundations, spurred significant local transformations and had a great impact on the rest of America. "Death to bad government, death to false officials (...). And deserved death to those who are not true to justice and greedily steal under the cloak of the Customs-House."

The high taxes and the new *repartimientos* created on the arrival of Viceroy Agustín de Jáuregui[3] led Condorcanqui

3 Agustin de Jáuregui was the 33rd Viceroy of Perú. He ruled from 1780 to 1784, and spent the three first years of his administration trying to put down Túpac Ameru's rebellion. Then he was summoned by the King of Spain, Charles IV, who, rather untimely, admonished him for his behavior regarding the trial and execution.

to unleash his rebellion. The opportunity arose when *criollo* bishop Moscoso excommunicated the *corregidor* of Tinta, Arriaga, whom the Indians despised. On the 4th of November 1780, Túpac Amaru, relying on his authority as *cacique* of three towns, ordered the arrest of Antonio de Arriaga and forced him to sign a letter requesting money and arms from the authorities, and summoning all the peoples from the provinces to Tungasuca, where the offender had been imprisoned. He was sent 22,000 pesos, some bars of gold, 75 muskets and mules. Arriaga was summarily judged and executed at the square of Tungasuca, on the 9th of November.

Túpac Amaru issued a proclamation claiming the sovereignty of those kingdoms for himself, saying: "The sovereigns of Castile have been usurping my crown and the rule of my people for almost three centuries, burdening my subjects with unbearable duties, taxes, customs-houses, sales taxes, property registers, tithes, viceroys, *audiencias, corregidores,* and all the other officials: all equal in tyranny, selling justice in auction with the notaries of this faith, everything going to the highest bidder, the church and secular posts as well, without fear of God; working the natives of this kingdom like beasts; taking the lives of those they couldn't steal from, all of this deserving the harshest punishment. For this reason, and for the clamor that has often reached Heaven, in the name of God Almighty, we order and demand that none of the said people pay or obey in any respect the intruding European officials."

Wherever the liberating army went, slavery, the *mita* and the exploitation of human beings ended. To this army, which came to put an end to the "race of the domineering," everyone was equal. People lifted their heads once again, were proud of who they were.

According to Julián Santisteban Ochoa, "On November 13th the rebel arrived at the mills of Pomacanchi, which he had promptly opened, and in the presence of the various chieftains of the neighboring towns that had been summoned by him, he told them that his mission did not end with the hanging of five *corregidores,* but that he would also burn down every single mill, and put people of his trust in charge. He had all the clothes taken out and distributed among the people."

On the 18th of November 1780 the first battle, known as the Battle of Sangarará, took place, and the rebels defeated the royalist army led by Tiburcio Landa. From then on, the rebellion took on a more radical character. Túpac proposed: "Let us all live like brothers congregated in a single body. Let us all take care of the protection and preservation of the Spaniards; *criollos, mestizos,* mulattos, and Indians, for they are all fellow countrymen, born in this land and sharing the same origin."

According to Boleslao Lewin, Túpac Amaru's biographer, the rebel's agenda included the following demands:

• suppression of the *mita*;
• eradication of the mills;
• nullification of the forced labor allotments (*repartimiento*) for the *corregidores*;[4]
• abolition of all taxes;
• liberation of all slaves who joined the rebellion.

---

4 The *repartimiento* or *reparto*, as the Indians called it, constituted a system of progressive indebtedness through which the employer gained permanent control over the employee's workforce. It forced the native population to purchase European and native goods on credit and at inflated prices, and the Indians had to work in the haciendas or mills, or relinquish a production surplus; seldom, if ever, being able to pay off their ever-growing debts.

"As from the 10th," reads a document of the period quoted by Pedro de Ángelis, "he began writing letters to various chieftains, ordering them to capture their *corregidores*, lieutenants and their assistants, and giving orders for the confiscation of their properties. Those letters were accompanied by the edicts these chiefs were to publish in their respective provinces, announcing that the taxes of the *repartimientos*, customs and *mita* of Potosi would end once the *corregidores* were exterminated."

On the 23rd of December 1780, Túpac Amaru addressed the *criollos* in particular, saying that "seeing the heavy yoke that oppresses us and the tyranny of those who hold these posts, who have no consideration for our misfortunes; exasperated by them and their ruthlessness, I have decided to break the unbearable yoke and to face up to the bad government that we suffer, for which reason the *corregidor* of Tinta died on the public scaffold, on whose aid came a bunch of *chapetones* [Spaniards in America] from the City of Cuzco, dragging my beloved *criollos* with them, who paid for their foolhardiness with their lives. I am only sorry for the fellow *criollos*, as my will is that no harm shall befall them, but rather that we all live like brothers congregated in a single body, and destroy the Europeans."

From Salta to Cuzco, about 100,000 Indians decided to follow the rebel. In Oruro, where *mestizo* participation ran high, a street poster from April 1781 read:

In Cuzco there's an order,
To shake, and it's no joke
The foreign king's yoke
And crown the rightful owner.

Americans, arise!
And take arms at last
With fury in your hearts
Kill, kill without fear
The tyrannical officials.

And in March 1781, the following words were written on the door of the *Audiencia* of Charcas:

Long live the Inca general
Let's swear him in as our king
Because justice and the law
Must let him come into his own.
All the American born must rally
Their right to defend
As Charles in his haughtiness
Despoils them and takes their lives
And everything he does
Is nothing but plain theft.

According to the Peruvian historian Valcárcel, "the role played by Doña Micaela Bastidas Puyucawa is crucial to the understanding of the Tinta revolt. It may be claimed that, from the very beginning, she was Túpac Amaru's main counselor, together with the renowned Council of the Five. And although the leader did his own will, her ideas and initiative gave this energetic and heroic woman all the qualities of a truly remarkable character."[5]

Some of the Spaniards in Cuzco must have been truly frightened, since, according to a contemporary source quoted

---

[5] Daniel Valcárcel, *Rebeliones coloniales sudamericanas*, México, FCE, 1982.

by De Ángelis, not only did they seek refuge in the churches, but they "begged the sacristans to unbolt the vaults and bury them alive." The powerful never forgive those who force them into public fear. Past fear, and present "disgust" at the idea of the "barbarians" making justice here on Earth, made them extremely uneasy.

Manuel Godoy, King Charles IV's and – above all – his wife's favorite, gives in his memoirs an account of how panic spread, and even reached the court in Madrid: "No one ignores that in the years 1781 and 1782, the whole of the Viceroyalty of Perú and part of the Viceroyalty of the River Plate was nearly lost, when the famous Condorcanqui, better known as Túpac Amaru, raised the banner of insurrection."

Terror even reached the shores of Buenos Aires, as Doctor Pacheco, an official in the recently created Viceroyalty of the River Plate, pointed out: "It is the opinion of this Official that the chieftain Túpac Amaru can be considered a rebel, and if he does not surrender, or is turned in by his supporters to the counterclaims or requirements allowed by the situations of each party, every subject of the King, either from the rebellious party or from the one that may defeat it, is hereby authorized to capture or kill him, on his Excellency the Viceroy's behalf, so that the troops belonging to each party may coexist in the greatest harmony. Buenos Aires, the 15th of January 1781."

In one of his pronunciations, Túpac said: "A humble young man with a stick and a sling and a unlearned shepherd freed the unhappy people of Israel from the power of Goliath and of the Pharaoh, as the tears shed by these poor captives moved to compassion, demanding justice from Heaven, so that in a few years they were delivered from their torments and martyrdom and led to the Promised

Land. And after many tears and much crying their desire was finally fulfilled. Whereas we, unfortunate Indians, having breathed more sighs and shed more tears, in all these centuries have not been able obtain any relief (…). The pharaoh who chases, abuses and harasses us is not one but many, as iniquitous and depraved at heart as are all the *corregidores*, their lieutenants, tax collectors and the rest of the catchpoles: men unquestionably diabolical and perverse (…) To tell of their hellish doings would turn (…) the Neros and Attilas, whose inequities History relates, into veritable saints (…). But these might be forgiven since, after all, they were infidels; but the *corregidores*, having been baptized, gainsay Christianity with their doings, and they are more like atheists, Calvinists, Lutherans, because they are enemies of God and of men, and worshippers of gold and silver. I cannot think of a single reason for such base behavior but that they are poor and of very humble birth."

To disparage Túpac, it was said that he had contacted the English, who at that time were at war with Spain. Halfway between criticism and admiration, a newspaper from Arequipa described in January 1781 the figure of the rebel and his comrades in the following words: "The army was very remarkable and in addition to infantry he was accompanied by more than a thousand horsemen, Spaniards and *mestizos*, carrying firearms; and Túpac Amaru was escorted by two blond men of good appearance, who looked English. Túpac Amaru was riding a white horse with embroidered harness, a pair of blunderbusses, pistols and sword; he was dressed in blue velvet, trimmed with gold braid; his cabriole was likewise ornamented, in scarlet cloth, and he wore a gold braid round his forehead. He also wore a three-cornered hat, and over his dress a vest or *unco*, like to a bishop's chasuble, sleeveless and richly embroidered, and round his neck he wore a gold chain, with a sun of the same metal pending from it, emblems of the princes, his ancestors."

After the victory of Sangarará, Túpac Amaru did not march on Cuzco; instead, he returned to his general headquarters in Tungasuca without entering the city, in an attempt to facilitate peace negotiations.

The Spanish Commander reports on the calamitous state of the royalist troops after the battle with the liberating army: "The troops under the command of Field-Marshall don José del Valle returned to Cuzco greatly reduced in number on account of the casualties and desertion, and on seeing those who did enter the city one was moved to pity, because they were infested with lice, many or the majority walking barefoot, and many in rags. They went straight to the hospitals, because the bad food had given them dysentery; they had no mattress, hospital or doctor to take care of the sick, and their tents were in tatters, so rotten and ragged were they. It is said that one cannot read the journals of Valle and Avilés without tears, and that these unfortunate gentlemen who left Lima's mild climate, the peace and quiet of their homes in order to serve the King as His faithful subjects, have not been paid yet."

The situation led the viceroys of Lima, Agustín de Jáuregui, and of Buenos Aires, Juan José de Vértiz, to join forces. The Viceroy of Lima sent the *visitador general* José Antonio Areche to Cuzco, with full powers in matters economic and military, together with the Field-Marshall José del Valle, troops inspector of the viceroyalty, and the Colonel of Dragons, don Gabriel de Avilés, leading an army of more than 17,000 men. Vértiz, the "Viceroy of the Lights" as he was called, sent Lieutenant Colonel Ignacio Flores, governor of Moxos, and appointed him general commander of all the provinces "that were upset in the jurisdiction under his command", with ample faculties to act freely.

Vértiz and his collaborator, the unspeakable Marquis de Sobremonte, wrote to the Viceroy of Perú in these terms: "Peace and order will only be established after we extirpate the seed of all the evils suffered by the peoples, cutting off the head of the ambitious rebel José; I have ordered that 10,000 silver pesos be offered to any of the faithful subjects or any other person who performs this service, and 20,000 of the same for whoever turns him in; so that justice can be made on his person as a lesson and example to the rest of the rebels, his accessories. And if any of the latter, ashamed of his mistakes and wretchedness, execute the same service, in addition to the pecuniary reward he shall be pardoned for his offense. May what I dispose be known and published in a suitable manner."

With *Visitador* Areche's and Inspector Jose del Valle's arrival in Cuzco, the scales were tipped against the rebels.

Fearful that they might end up decorating the scaffold that the rebels had promised to set up, the Council of War of Cuzco decided to add some clever political measures – some of them meeting Túpac Amaru's demands – to military presence:

• definitive abolishment of the *repartimientos* for the *corregidores*;

• general pardon to everyone who had taken part in the revolt, except for the leaders;

• debts contracted by the Indians with their *corregidores* would be condoned.

These measures, together with a terrorist campaign consisting in the sacking of the towns and the slaughter of the Indians, succeeded in making many of them desert from the rebellious to the royalist army, thus paving the way for the defeat of the rebels.

Túpac attempted a master stroke and attacked first, but the royalist army had been warned by an escaped prisoner and the surprise attack failed. On the night of the 5th to the 6th of April, the unequal battle between the two armies was waged.

According to a military dispatch from the royalist army, "more than a thousand were put to the sword and the rest were routed entirely."

Túpac Amaru tried to flee. "Realizing all was lost," continues the military dispatch of April 8, "he ordered his wife and children to escape as well as they could, and jumped into a wide river, which he managed to cross. But on the opposite bank, the colonel of Langui, who had been appointed by Túpac himself, hoping to obtain our pardon, took him prisoner and turned him in to us (…) as well as his wife, his children and the rest of the his confederates. (…) At six in the morning that same day, Francisco Túpac Amaru, uncle to José Gabriel, and another chief called Torres, both well-known captains under the orders of the rebel, were taken prisoner. The former was wearing royal garments, the kind the Incas used to wear, with the arms of Túpac Amaru embroidered in silver and gold on the angles."

The traitor was Francisco Santa Cruz, a deputy and comrade of Túpac's, who had been advised to proceed in this manner by the priest of Langui, Antonio Martínez, who proudly wrote to *Visitador* Areche: "Your Highness can well see how cleverly I disposed of all."

Túpac was taken prisoner and conveyed to Cuzco. *Visitador* Areche bolted into his cell and demanded, in exchange for a series of promises, the names of his accomplices. Túpac Amaru answered with contempt: "You and I are the only conspirators; Your Honor for having burdened the country with intolerable taxes, and myself for having tried to free the people from such tyranny. Here I am to be punished alone, so that the other people's lives are spared and I am alone in my punishment."

For several days, Túpac Amaru was subjected to the most horrifying torture. In one of the interrogation sessions, he retorted to the sadist judge Mata Linares in this way: "Being a descendant of the Incas, and as such, seeing that his fellowmen were in distress, abused and persecuted, he thought he was in the obligation of defending them, to rid them of such oppression."

The rebel chief had his hands and feet tied together. A hundred-pound iron bar was attached to the rope that fastened these bonds, then his body was raised more than six feet off the ground, causing the dislocation of one his arms.

Túpac Amaru did not betray anyone, he kept the names and location of his comrades to himself and to posterity. Even the sinister *Visitador* Areche had to acknowledge the courage and resistance of that extraordinary man. In a report addressed to the viceroy, he stated that, despite the continued days of torture, "the Inca Túpac Amaru has a very strong spirit and nature, and an imponderable serenity."

At the torture chamber, his courage led him to mock his torturers; when he was asked who the letter he had written in his cell, with his own blood, was addressed to, he replied: "That draft is for a Higinio de Marcapata, Spaniard, mine-owner, blond hair and blue eyes, who rode with the defendant on a white mule. Find him if you can."

Túpac was "judged" according to the principles of the so-called Spanish justice – an heir of the Inquisition – and sentenced to death. The same sentence was imposed on his family. The greatest atrocities were about to be perpetrated on the rebel leaders and on the family of the Inca, unprecedented in these lands before that day.

The sentence, read on the 17th of May 1781, speaks volumes about the Spaniards' hatred and fear of the insurrection. The document began by listing the "crimes" of the rebels: "In the case pending before me, that of the Royal Justice against José Gabriel Túpac Amaru, chieftain of the town of Tungasuca, in the province of Tinta, for the horrendous crime of revolt or general uprising of the Indians, *mestizos* and other castes, conceived of more than five years ago and carried out in almost all the territories of this Viceroyalty, and that of Buenos Aires, with the purpose (which he carries with much conviction) of being crowned as their Lord, and liberator of what he has called the oppression of the kinds of inhabitants that he managed to entice, the undertaking of which he prompted by hanging his *corregidor* don Antonio de Arriaga."

An then it sentenced: "I condemn José Gabriel Túpac Amaru to be taken out to the main public square of this city, dragged out to the place of execution, where he shall witness the execution of the sentences imposed on his wife, Micaela Bastidas; his two sons, Hipólito and Fernando Túpac Amaru; his uncle, Francisco Túpac Amaru; and his brother-in-law, Antonio Bastidas, as well as some of the principal captains and aides in his iniquitous and perverse intent or project, all of whom must die the same day; and once these sentences have been carried out, the executioner will cut out his tongue, and he will then be tied or bound by strong cords on each one of his arms and feet in such a way that each rope can be easily tied or fastened to others hanging from the saddle straps of four horses so that, in this position, each one of these horses, facing opposite corners of the square, will pull toward their own direction; and let the horses be urged or jolted into motion at the same time so that his body be divided into as many parts and then, once it is done, the parts should be carried to the hill or high ground known as "Picchu," which is where he came to intimidate, lay siege to, and demand the surrender of this city; and let there be lit a fire which shall be prepared in advance and then let the ashes be thrown into the air and a stone tablet placed there detailing his main crimes and the manner of his death as the only record and statement of his loathsome action. His head will be sent to the town of Tinta where, after having been three days on the gallows, it shall be placed on a stake at the most public entrance to the town; one of his arms will go to the town of Tungasuca, where he was chief, where it will be treated in like manner, and the other in the capital of the province of Carabaya; one of the legs shall likewise be sent for the same kind of demonstration to the town of Livitaca in the province of Chumbivilcas, while the remaining one shall go to Santa Rosa in the province of Lampa along with an affidavit and order to the respective *corregidores*, or territorial judges, that this sentence be proclaimed publicly with the greatest solemnity as soon as it arrives in their hands, and on the same day every year thereafter; and they will give notice in writing of this to their superiors in government who are familiar with the said territories. His houses will be pulled down, and salted before all the neighbors of the town or towns where he had them, or existed. All his possessions will be confiscated, for the purpose of which, the corresponding commission is given to provincial judges. May all the individuals who compose his family, who have not come or shall not come under the power of our weapons and the justice that desires to punish them with equal severity, be declared infamous and incapable of acquiring, possessing or obtaining by any mean or means any inheritance or legacy, if there came a time when they so wanted or claimed their right to. May the proceedings regarding his offspring be collected in the said Royal *Audiencia* and burnt publicly by the executioner in the public square of Lima, so that no traces of such documents may be left."

Finally, it was suggested that all his offspring should be exterminated to the fourth degree of consanguinity.

The sentence written by *Visitador* Areche was very much like an ideological manifesto, and went as far as banning all the vestiges of the Inca culture: "In like manner shall be prohibited and confiscated the trumpets or bugles that the Indians use for their ceremonies, being seashells with a strange and mournful sound that celebrate the mourning and pitiful memorial they make for their antiquity; and there shall also be prohibited the custom of using or wearing black clothing as a sign of mourning, a custom that drags on in some provinces in memory of their deceased monarchs and also of the day or time of the conquest which they consider disastrous and we consider fortunate since it brought them into the company of the Catholic Church and the very loving and gentle domination of our kings. And so that these Indians renounce the hatred that they have conceived against the Spaniards, and that they adhere to the dress which the laws indicate, adopting our Spanish customs and speaking Castilian."

Barbarism

On the 18th of May 1781, Túpac Amaru and his people were at the mercy of the beasts who wanted revenge for the moments of humiliation and abject fear they had suffered on his account.

The following is a verbatim transcription of the report of the death of Túpac Amaru's family as told by his murderers:

"On Friday, May 18, 1781, the militia of the city of Cuzco surrounded the public square and the following persons were brought forth: José Verdejo, Andrés Castelo, a sambo, Antonio Oblitas (the executioner of *Corregidor* Arriaga), Antonio Bastidas, Francisco Túpac Amaru, Tomasa Condemaita, *cacica* of Arcos; Hipólito Túpac Amaru, son of the traitor; his wife Micaela Bastidas, and the rebel leader himself. They were all brought out together, one after the other. They came out handcuffed and shackled, in the kind of baskets used to bring maté leaves from Paraguay, and dragged along behind a harnessed horse. Accompanied by guards and by priests who offered them spiritual consolation, they were brought to the foot of the scaffold, and there the executioners meted out the following deaths to them:

"Verdejo, Castelo, the sambo, and Bastidas were simply hanged. Francisco Túpac Amaru, the rebel's uncle, and his son Hipólito, had their tongues cut out before they were thrown down the steps of the gallows. The Indian woman Condemaita was garrotted on a little scaffold provided with an iron screw made for this purpose (...) The Indian and his wife witnessed all these punishments, even that of their son Hipólito, who was the last to go to the gallows. Then Micaela went up to the scaffold, where, in the presence of her husband, her tongue was cut out and she was garrotted, suffering infinite agony all the while, because since her neck was very slender the screw could not strangle her, and the executioners had to dispatch her by tying ropes around her neck, each pulling in a different direction, and kicking her in the stomach and breast. Last to die was the rebel leader, José Gabriel. He was brought into the middle of the square, and there the executioner cut out his tongue. Then they took off his chains and laid him on the ground. They tied four ropes to his hands and feet and attached the ropes to the girths of four horses, which four *mestizos* drove in four different directions. Cuzco had never before seen a spectacle of this kind. Either because the horses were not very strong or because the Indian was really made of iron, they simply could not tear him apart, although they tugged at him for a long time, while he dangled in the air like a spider. Finally *Visitador* Areche, moved by compassion, decided to end his suffering and sent an order from the Jesuit College that the executioner should cut off his head, and so it was done. Then they laid his body under the gallows and cut off his arms and legs. They did the same to the women, and the heads of the others were cut off and sent to be displayed in various towns. The bodies of the Indian and his wife were borne to Picchu, where a great bonfire was made, into which they were thrown and reduced to ashes, which were thrown into the air and into the little river that runs through there. Such was the end of José Gabriel Túpac Amaru and Micaela Bastidas, whose pride and arrogance reached such a pitch that they called themselves Kings of Perú, Chile, Quito, Tucumán, and other parts…

"A considerable number of people gathered on this day, but no one gave a cry or even spoke; many, and I among them, noted that there were no Indians in that multitude, at least not in their customary dress; if there were any, they must have been disguised in cloaks or ponchos (…) Although the weather had been very fine and dry, that day dawned with the sky heavily overcast, and at twelve o'clock, when the horses were tugging at the Indian, there arose a gust of wind followed by a downpour that forced all the people and even the guards to run for shelter. This has caused the Indians to say that the heavens and the elements were mourning the death of their Inca, whom the inhuman and impious Spaniards were putting to death with such cruelty."

According to Valcárcel, the young Fernando Túpac Amaru,[6] of ten years of age, attempted to turn his head round and cover his eyes, but he was forced to witness the sacrifice of his parents and brothers and so "let out a scream so full of external fear and inner suffering that for a long time it would remain in the ears of those present."

A Spanish document titled *Distribution of the Body or Its Parts, of the Nine Principal Leaders of the Revolt, Executed at the Square of Cuzco, on the 18th of May, 1781,* makes any further comment unnecessary:

José Gabriel Túpac Amaru.
Micaela Bastidas, his wife.
Hipólito Túpac Amaru, his son.
Francisco Túpac Amaru, uncle of the first.
Antonio Bastidas, his brother-in-law.
The *cacica* of Arcos.
Diego Verdejo, commander.
Andrés Castelo, colonel.
Antonio Oblitas, executioner.

Tinta
The head of Túpac Amaru.
An arm to Tungasuca.
One arm of Micalea Bastidas, idem.
Another one of Antonio Bastidas, to Pampamarca.
The head of Hipólito, to Tungasuca.
An arm of Castelo, to Surimaná.
Another one to Pampamarca.
One of Verdejo's arms, to Coparaque.

6 Fernando Túpac Amaru, son of José Gabriel, was walked below the gallows and banished for life in one of the prisons of Africa.

Another one to Yauri.
The rest of his body to Tinta.
An arm to Tungasuca.
The head of Francisco Túpac Amaru, to Pilpinto.

Quispicanchi
An arm of Antonio Bastidas, to Urcos.
A leg of Hipólito Túpac Amaru, to Quiquijano.
A leg of Antonio Bastidas, to Sangarará.
The head of the cacica of Arcos, idem.
Castelo's head, to Acamayo.

Cuzco
The body of José Gabriel Túpac Amaru, to Picchu.
Idem his wife's, along with her head.
An arm of Antonio Oblitas, on the road to San Sebastián.

Carabaya
An arm of José Gabriel Túpac Amaru.
A leg of his wife.
An arm of Francisco Túpac Amaru.

Azangaro
A leg of Hipolito Túpac Amaru.

Lampa
A leg of Jose Túpac Amaru, to Santa Rosa.
An arm of his son, to Iyabirí.

Arequipa
An arm of Micaela Bastidas.

Chumbivilcas
An arm of Jose Túpac Amaru, in Livitaca.
An arm of his son, to Santo Tomás.

Paucartambo
The body of Castelo, in its capital.
The head of Antonio Bastidas.

Chilques and Masques
An arm of Francisco Túpac Amaru, to Paruro.

Condesuyos of Arequipa
The head of Antonio Verdejo, to Chuquibamba.

Puno
A leg of Francisco Túpac Amaru in its capital.

On hearing of the slaughter, the noteworthy bishop of Buenos Aires, friar Sebastián, issued the following "pious" sermon: "Yesterday, the 23rd of the present month, we received by mail from Chile factual and accurate news, that on the 8th of April, the traitor José Gabriel Túpac Amaru was defeated and taken prisoner, together with his wife, children, brothers and other aides that accompanied him and refused to obey God and Our Catholic Monarch. And which faithful and loyal servant will not rejoice in the capture of the rebel? Which true Spaniard does not feel an overwhelming joy in his heart on hearing such plausible news? Which Christian will not offer the most generous gifts to God, for having granted us such great benefit? Yes, beloved sons, this incident is worthy of all our vows and most fervid prayers. The love we owe to our King and to the Religion that we profess requires that we bring our hearts to our mouths in songs and in praise. Finally, we urge all our servants to remain in the obedience to Our Catholic Monarch, and in the respect that we owe to his viceroys and governors and ministers, observing the principle of the Apostle, who reminds us that every soul is subject to the highest authorities. Given to us in our Episcopal Palace, signed by our own hand and substantiated by our secretary, on the 24th day of June, 1781."

An Echo From the Andes: The Revolt Continues

The heroic deaths of José Gabriel Condorcanqui, his comrades and his family, despite their brutality, did not put an end to the revolt. His next-of-kin Diego Andrés Túpac Amaru and Miguel Bastidas, and the leaders of the neighboring regions, such as Julián Apaza, also known as Túpac Catari, kept up the fight. The Túpac Amarus concentrated in the Cuzco area, while Túpac Catari fought in the Upper Perú area.

The capture of Tomás, one of Catari's brothers who were related to Túpac Amaru, was one of the many incidents that extended the revolt. As beloved as the Inca, Tomás Catari was one of the leaders who most fervently addressed the Spaniards, including Viceroy Vértiz himself, on behalf of his people.

From 1781 to 1784, the Catari brothers held the sword over the Spaniards' heads, but after a few military victories and many betrayals they were finally captured. Túpac Catari was defeated in 1781, when one of his aides led him to a Spanish ambush. He and his wife, Bartolina Sisa, shared José Gabriel and Micaela's fate.

Diego Cristóbal's fortune was as tragic as his brother Túpac Amaru's and Túpac Catari's: despite the amnesty of 1782, the standard-bearers of Western Civilisation captured him in 1783, burnt him with red-hot tongs and hanged him.

The list of rebel cities and leaders is too long to include in these pages. But it would be unfair to leave out Vilca-Aspasa, who did not believe in the amnesty and continued fighting until his death in 1784. It would also be unfair to disregard some of the women leading the revolt, such as the chiefs Marcela Castro and Tomasa Tito Condemaito – who abandoned everything to go to war, including her husband, and always fought in the vanguard. Both were tortured to death.

Between February and March 1781, there began the revolt of the Tobas from the mission of St. Ignatius in the Chaco and Puna regions of Jujuy.

José Quiroga, the mission's interpreter, took advantage of his relationship with the Tobas and other groups to organize a movement in support of Túpac Amaru in the north of Argentina. The military governor of Jujuy, Gregorio Zegada, reported what follows: "The Toba Indians have spread the news, through their interpreter and leader José Quiroga, a Christian who has taken sides with them, saying that the poor want to protect themselves from Spanish tyranny, and that once these are all dead, including breast-sucking babies, the Indians will govern themselves, under their Inca king, whose bloody name has made theses Indians lose their mind."

In the puna, the *criollo* sergeant Luis Lasso de la Vega proclaimed himself governor of the region in the name of Túpac Amaru. The movement extended to Rinconada, Casabindo, Santa Catalina and Cochinoca.

But some chiefs and *criollos* betrayed the revolt and doomed it to failure. According to a note sent to the viceroy by the *Cabildo* of Jujuy, the traitor Pedro Serrano denounced that Quiroga had told him that "their aim was to defend the lowly people, for they were all being killed in this town, so that the said Inca king would have less vassals." Serrano feigned to participate in the uprisings as captain, with the purpose of learning about Quiroga's plan and denouncing him.

The outcome was the combat waged in Zapla, where Governor Zegada took prisoners and forced the Indians to hide in the forests. The Indians then besieged and took San Salvador de Jujuy. Zegada asked the governor of Tucumán for help, but he had his hands full trying to put down other rebel attacks in Salta.

Quiroga and his second-in-command, Domingo Morales, were captured and tortured before they were killed. The prisoners were tried; the leaders sentenced to death and the rest were branded with an "R", which stood for "rebel", and sentenced to several years of forced labor.

What was keeping Salta governor Mestre busy was a fresh uprising, that of the Wichi Indians.

He and Zegada were in charge of administering correction, as is stated in a letter sent to Viceroy Vértiz: "I had been informed that Commander Cristóbal López and Governor Don Gregorio Zegada had managed to defeat the said Mataco Indians, and to capture 65 fully-armed, 12 children, 12 women, and the old woman they carried as fortune-teller and was guiding them to the city. But considering the disgust of the neighborhood, and the impossibility of securing them and carrying them to the hinterlands without great expenditure to the royal treasury (...) And to conclude, that their intention was to help the Tobas carry out their plans, demonstrating the usual ingratitude, disregarding the compassion with which they had always been treated, who were kept despite their not being part of any *reducción*, and considering how bothersome it would be to provide for their subsistence, I decided to have them put to the sword and hang them from the trees, as a lesson to the rest."

Despite the dispersal of their forces, and the fact they had lost their leaders, both the Tobas and the Wichis (Matacos) continued fighting until 1785. The brutal retaliation of the Spaniards finally put down the revolt, although there continued to be sporadic outbreaks until the end of the 18th century.

Those who never surrendered were the Chiriguanos, who took up the torch and towards 1796 began a new offensive in the north of Argentina and in Upper Perú against cities and Indians living in *reducciones*. The Spanish repression, carried out by the governor of Cochabamba, Francisco de Viedma and by the governor of Potosi, Francisco de Paula Sanz, was never entirely successful: although they burnt their lands and food, poisoned their rivers and killed whoever crossed their path, the Chiriguanos conducted a guerrilla warfare of sorts, and would attack and disappear into the forest. When in danger of being captured by the Spaniards they would jump off a cliff.

The campaign initiated by Sanz in 1805 ended in the Spanish retreat, after a number of clashes with Chiriguano groups allied with the Chanés.

Tucumán, La Rioja, Córdoba, Mendoza, Santiago del Estero, not a single region escaped the rebel fever.

Many years later, the struggle in Charcas and the repression across Perú was not yet over.

Fear of a new revolt left its traces, and soon after the massacre, the Spanish authorities decided to suppress the system of *corregidores* and *repartimientos*. In its place, a system of intendancies was established. Some years later the creation of the *Audiencia* of Cuzco, one of the demands of the rebellion, became a fact.

To be on the safe side, as late as 1782, the Spanish authorities prohibited any book that portrayed the days of the Inca Empire as a Golden age to yearn for. The circulation of *The Royal Commentaries of Perú*, by the Inca Garcilaso de la Vega, was considered politically dangerous for the population.

The revolutionaries of 1810 would later be referred to as "tupamaros" in the Spanish documents of the period, and this name would be proudly adopted by the rebels, as it can be seen in an anonymous couplet that circulated in those days:

Don Fernando, our good friend
Far away we'll fling,
Because We Tupamaros
Don't want to have a king.

The English Invasions or Water and Oil

It is curious, to say the least, that the episode known to the Argentine as "the English Invasions" is almost exclusively reminiscent of a gastronomic incident: the pouring of hundreds of gallons of – boiling – oil from the rooftops above the narrow streets of colonial Buenos Aires.

When recalling this episode there are some who wax nostalgic and regret the fact that "the English were kicked out," suggesting that we should compare present-day Argentina to the United States, Australia and Canada. Without much evidence to support their claim, these people believe that thanks to the drive of the "Anglo-Saxon race" Argentina would have become a world power and not a former English colony with the majority of its population wallowing in utmost misery, like India, Bangladesh, Pakistán or Tanzania.

According to Robert Clive, an English official who led the conquest and occupation of Bengal (present-day Bangladesh), around 1757, the textile centre of Dacca (capital of Bengal) was as "vast, populated and wealthy as London." Before the arrival of the English, the city had 150,000 inhabitants, hundreds of textile mills, a thriving textile industry, and fertile and prosperous lands. In *An Inquiry into the Nature and Causes of the Wealth of Nations*, one of the fathers of economic liberalism, Adam Smith, deplores the havoc wreaked by the English in the region. He writes: "Thousands die each year due to the conditions imposed by the conquerors, who turn dearth into famine, ploughing up a rich field of rice or other grain in order to make room for a plantation of poppies when it is foreseen that extraordinary profit is likely to be made by opium." By 1840, after almost a century of British rule, the population of Dacca had fallen from 150,000 to 30,000. As Sir Charles Travelyan testified before the Select Committee of the House of Lords, "Dacca, which used to be the Manchester of India, has fallen off from a flourishing town to a very poor and small one."[1]

The key to the development of the U.S., Canada and Australia does not lie in English colonisation – which in all three countries was brutal, cruel and bent on genocide – but in the development in each of these countries of a bourgeoisie, selfish and abusive as they are wont to be, but which nonetheless had the sense to link the fate of their fortunes to the economic growth of their respective countries, something that never happened in Argentina. As early as 1806, during the struggle for the reconquest, Liniers exclaimed: "Would I not work the year round after throwing the English out of Buenos Aires to turn a population of merchants and rich landowners into warriors! Here, the mildness of the climate, the fertility and richness of the soil, weaken the soul and diminish its energy (...) Servants are more able than their masters."

1 Noam Chomsky, *Política y cultura a finales del siglo XX*, Buenos Aires, Ariel, 1995.

The English Invasions were much more than "water and oil." They entailed the incorporation of the River Plate region into the world conflict between England and France, the two leading capitalist powers of the time, and the end of the decadent Spanish Empire. As far as local politics were concerned, the Invasions evinced the fragility of the local authorities, apparent in the creation of popular militias and in the unprecedented destitution of a viceroy and the appointment of a new one by the will of a people whose *criollo* voice already sounded stronger than that of the Spaniards.

Europe at War

In the second half of the 18th century, the English dominion of the seas seemed incontestable. As in a bad joke, the Spanish "Invincible Armada" had long been vanquished, and gone as well were the days when Dutch Admiral Michel de Ruyter would be portrayed holding a broom in the guise of a sceptre, as a symbol of the Dutch's power to sweep all its enemies off the sea.

For the French, Dutch and Spanish ships, sailing the seas had become dangerous business. Between 1702 and 1808, Spain and England went to war no less than six times. This led American colonies to acquire the necessary supplies through the smuggling of different goods, particularly British, provided by the sons of "His Most Gracious Majesty." Isolation seriously affected the military defense of Hispanic possessions. By 1806, the defendants of Buenos Aires would remind each other that the last infantry regiment coming from Spain had arrived in the capital in 1784.

America for the English

From the onset of the conquest of America, the various English governments looked greedily on the wealth of the New World. Foreign policy in the British Empire evolved from the support of the great pirates – so dear to Hollywood and to the future political leaders of the U.S., who took them as an example – to the great smugglers of the 17th and 18th centuries, who were all hired and rewarded by Great Britain. The Treaty of Utrecht, signed in the territory of present-day Netherlands, on the 11th of April 1713 by Great Britain, Portugal, The United Provinces, Savoy, Prussia and Spain, concluded the War of the Spanish Succession and granted England the sole right to the slave trade with Spanish America. In this way, the English were granted a peculiar "monopoly of contraband." Ships carrying slaves not only transported what they declared, but their holds were crammed with manufactures – and of course they never returned empty-handed. They took in the raw materials (in our case, leather, jerked beef and tallow) needed in their developing factories, which were about to take the great leap of the Industrial Revolution.

During the far-from-boring 18th century there were constant discussions, in the English political and commercial circles, about the advantages of supporting the independence of South America and taking over its wealthy markets. For instance, in 1741, a plan proposed the liberation of the Spanish colonies, since, as the document went: "It is convenient for a free people such as the English to place other countries under the same condition, for English trade would benefit from the existence of free nations in South America, and thus England would gain positive friends and allies." Other plans to free South America were presented to British authorities throughout that century, in 1742, 1760, 1766, 1780, and 1785.

The Industrial Revolution, which began in the last quarter of the 18th century, gave English capitalism a strong impulse and forced the highly competitive British manufactures, which had already saturated local markets, into the search for new ones.

Like every hegemonic power in history, from that moment on the English state would set a double standard, manifested in the duplicity of its commercial policy: at the national level, the State would implement tight protectionist polices in order to protect industrial development, but at the foreign level, it would promote and impose free trade for its products to compete freely and to purchase raw materials in peripheral countries at a menial price. "Do as I say, not as I do."

Meanwhile, The Spaniards, who thanks to their network of spies were aware of these projects, would often warn the viceroys about new threats. Thus on the 1st of December 1783 the royal official José Gálvez wrote to the Viceroy of Buenos Aires: "The King has been notified that a foreign power is endeavoring to send to our Indies emissaries in disguise with the wicked purpose of stirring up a revolt among its naturals and inhabitants." The viceroy was ordered to find these agents and punish them "as befits the enormity of their offense."

In such a context, London ears were ripe for the ideas of the Venezuelan revolutionary Francisco de Miranda. Miranda was a romantic character who was lover to Princess Catharine II of Russia, a soldier in Washington's army and a general in the French Revolution.

In March 1790, Miranda had presented the English Prime Minister William Pitt "The Younger"[2] with a plan to conquer

---

2 He was called this way because when he took up office as Prime Minister for the first time in 1783 he was only 24 years old, and also to distinguish him from his father, who preceded him in the post, and who since then was referred to in English history as "The Elder."

American colonies, transform them into a constitutional monarchy, and crown a descendant of the House of the Incas as Emperor of America. In his report, Miranda enthusiastically wrote: "South America has a very large market which could be preferentially offered to England, and has enough funds to honor its obligations for services rendered (...) Considering this to be of mutual interest to both parties, South America hopes that by forming an association with England through a Solemn Pact, establishing a free, similar government and implementing a reciprocally beneficial trade policy, both Nations will establish the most respectable and influential Political Union in the world."

Miranda believed that incidents such as Túpac Amaru's rebellion and the Comuneros' uprising in Paraguay and New Granada were clear signs of the hatred developing against the metropolis and the king, when in truth they were isolated streams that had not yet been able to find a common channel.

In 1796, while Spain, in alliance with France, declared war on England, Pitt was presented by a member of his government with a new plan to organize expeditions to South America, more ambitious than the one proposed in 1790. A few ships were sent to the River Plate on a reconnaissance mission, but in 1797 the idea was dropped as the European situation had become critical. That same year, the indefatigable Miranda proposed yet another plan of British aid in the liberation of his home continent, but, once again, the project did not take off.

On one occasion, however, luck was on the side of the Venezuelan revolutionary. On the 5th of October 1804, being 25 leagues away from Cádiz, four Spanish frigates commanded by the governor of Montevideo José de Bustamante, carrying silver and gold from Upper Perú, were attacked by four English vessels that worked their way into the midst of the Spanish fleet and opened fire.

The English attacked because they suspected that this treasure, valued in 2 million pounds, was headed for France and destined to finance Napoleon's[3] campaigns as part of the subsidy that the Spanish King Charles IV regularly paid the French Emperor with the purpose of, he hoped, placating his uncomfortable ally.

To round off a successful attack, the English captured three vessels and blew up the fourth. During the attack on the latter perished the mother of Carlos María de Alvear – future dictator of Argentina – and eight of his nine brothers. Carlos and his father Diego de Alvear survived but were taken captive with the rest of the fleet. They spent some time in England, where Carlos María finished his studies and established lifelong contacts with major English leaders.

In the midst of the commotion caused by this episode, and after Spain declared war on the 12th of October 1804, Pitt and his cabinet members discussed Miranda's plan with Sir Home Popham, and it was agreed that it should be concluded and presented immediately.

Canadian historian H.S. Ferns says that Popham "was one of the most able, imaginative and successful officers in

3 Napoleon Bonaparte was born in Corsica in 1769 and in his early youth enrolled in the French Military Academy. After the coup on the 18th Brumaire (November 9, 1799), he ruled France with ample powers. In 1804 he was crowned Emperor. He conquered many territories until 1812, when he was defeated in Russia. After a brief period of recovery, he was finally defeated in Waterloo on the 16th of June 1815. He was banished to the Island of St. Helena where he died on the 5th of May 1821.

the Army. His sailing exploits, his contribution to the improvement of signals, and his mastery of joint operations justified both his promotion and his incorporation to the Royal Society. He had been convicted of corruption charges by a military court and had succeeded in having the sentence revoked."[4]

It seemed that Miranda was getting away with it, and he often got carried away while writing about the objectives of his plan: "The emancipation of South America from its Tyrannical Government, its Oppressive Administration, Arbitrary Extortions and its exorbitant advances over all European Articles." Undoubtedly, Miranda knew that with the English government he had to speak the tongue of trade rather than that of freedom, if he was to obtain any support for the emancipation and protection of South America.

"As far as the South American question is concerned," wrote Popham accompanying Miranda's report, "I believe it is unnecessary to draw the attention of the His Majesty's ministers to its positive wealth and commercial potential, as these have certainly been meditated upon; and a kind of universal anxiety is bent on guiding this infallible source of wealth into any channels but those that now drain it."

In his letter, Popham supported his claim with over-whelming commercial evidence. He claimed that the English were perfectly aware of the fact that two-thirds of the riches Spain extracted from South America were shipped straight to France, and that this would continue until Napoleon decided to invade America and exploit the colonies' raw materials himself.

4 H. S. Ferns, *La Argentina*, Buenos Aires, Sudamericana, 1973. *The Argentine Republic: 1516-1971*, New York, Harper & Row Publishers, Inc., 1973.

For the English Cabinet, which had just suffered the loss of its colonies in North America, this was something to be avoided at all costs. Popham concluded by quoting the former minister of the United States in London, who believed that the independence of Spanish America was the only way of preventing the defeat of Great Britain at Napoleon's hands.

Pitt's government had reasons to fear that the French would soon try to take over the River Plate region, so he took intelligence measures to be warned on time.

At first, Pitt was supportive of the Popham-Miranda plan. But when in December 1804 the expedition had to be postponed, Popham, who could not stay put for any lengthy period of time, decided, in the summer of 1805, to embark on an expedition to take the Cape of Good Hope, in South Africa, from the hands of the Dutch, who were Napoleon's allies. Before Commodore Popham set off, Pitt informed him that the plan to attack South America had to be temporarily postponed, as the government was trying to separate Spain from France on peaceful terms.

Napoleon's chief enemy in the Old World, and the main obstacle to French expansion, was England. Napoleon began to dream about conquering both margins of the English Channel, and since the distance separating his dreams from reality was as scant as his height, it was not long before the clash between the combined fleet of France and Spain on one side, and the English on the other, finally took place on the 21st of October 1805 in Trafalgar, near Cádiz. There, the expertise of Admiral Horatio Nelson gave the British their victory. The French-Spanish fleet, commanded by French Admiral Pierre Charles de Villeneuve, was almost entirely destroyed and 2400 men perished. It was a rough ride for the English as well: they lost 1587 men, among them Nelson himself – but after it control of the major commercial routes of the world was theirs.

Subsequently, one of the most important squares and commercial centres in London would be named Trafalgar Square, and the use of a black tie became mandatory for all members of the Royal Navy, in memory of Admiral Nelson.

Victory soothed the English. Napoleon would not invade London and control of sea routes gave way to the quest for new markets that could alleviate the Liverpool, Manchester and London factories, which were on the verge of bankruptcy, and the Bank of England, which for the first time in history had had to abandon the gold standard, that is to say, had had to operate with an inconvertible paper currency.

Forty days after Trafalgar, Napoleon took revenge on the Austro-Prussian army by defeating them in Austerlitz, to the north of Vienna, and had the famous Arch of Triumph built in the centre of Paris.[5] Following these two crucial battles, European power was split in two: the sea belonged to the English and the continent to the French. It is said that on hearing about the victory of the French Emperor, William Pitt, the English Prime Minister, folded up a map of Europe and said: "We will not be needing it for the next ten years."

At the same time he found out about the French-Spanish disaster, Popham received from the Admiralty the order to

5 The monument, about 492 feet high, is located on the Boulevard des Champs Élysées. The construction began in 1806 but the monument was inaugurated in 1846. On its surface Napoleon had the names of 386 of his generals and 96 of his victories engraved. Following the First World War, the monument to the unknown soldier was built underneath.

send a frigate to a point somewhere between Rio de Janeiro and the River Plate to gather intelligence on the enemy's activities and preventing a likely French attack. A few days later he received news from his old friend and former partner in the slave trade business, the American resident in Buenos Aires Pío White, who warned him about the total vulnerability of the ports of Buenos Aires and Montevideo and about the existence in the capital of the Viceroyalty of a fabulous treasure worth more than a thousand silver pesos from Potosí, which was about to be shipped to the Peninsula.

Popham owed White a large sum of money, and it would not be entirely unreasonable to suppose that this might have encouraged the Commodore to attack Buenos Aires, with the purpose of paying his debt off with the *porteño* bounty.

In any case, Popham went before Commander Baird and expressed his intention of taking over the River Plate, with or without the support of his army. Baird accepted the offer and provided him with the 71st Infantry Regiment, the necessary artillery, and 1000 men to carry out his plan.

The commander was not entirely confident on the success of the enterprise. Therefore, in order to retain some measure of control, he decided to promote Colonel William Carr, Viscount of Beresford,[6] to General with the order of appointing him vice-governor and thus prevent the eventuality of Buenos Aires' independence. Popham imagined that the arrival of British forces would immediately kindle enthusiastic and spontaneous support from the followers of free trade. Reality would prove him wrong.

6 Beresford had enrolled in the British Army in 1785 and had served in the campaigns of Egypt and South Africa. In one of these he had an eye accidentally shot out.

The reasons Baird had for authorizing the expedition can be found in a letter addressed to Robert Stewart, Viscount of Castlereagh, Secretary of State for War and the Colonies on the 14th of April 1806. Under the influence of his subordinate Popham's ideas, and fully aware of the Crown's interests, Baird appealed to the commercial potential of the nation: "I believe the possession of a colony on the South American coast to be full of advantages, both for our Nation and for the colony in question, and I consider it unnecessary to point out to Your Honour the benefits that might be derived from the opportunity of opening a new and profitable outlet for the exports of our national industry, which the French government is so intent on obstructing and diminishing."

Before Castlereagh's reply arrived, the expedition had already sailed from Cape City on April the 14th. On the Island of St. Helena, Popham persuaded the governor to lend him, without a return warranty, about 250 men and two cannons from the Garrison of the East India Company. Thus the task force was to be composed of 1500 men, 36 of which were officers. Out of the five vessels, the Narcissus carried the commanders, who halfway through the trip discarded Beresford's plan to set foot on Montevideo and decided to attack Buenos Aires straight away. Thus, on June 8th the expedition were within sight of Montevideo and on the morning of the 25th the English vessels reached Buenos Aires.

Their landing had something ominous to it. The invaders were welcomed by a furious downpour of rain and hail.

The Task Force Arrives

On the night of the 24th of June 1806, Viceroy Sobremonte, pioneer in the art of employing public funds for personal use, was celebrating the birthday of his assistant and son-in-law to be, Juan Martín de Marín, with a lavish dinner-party at the fort. When the feast ended, the group headed for the House of Comedies, where the play *When a Girl Says Yes* by Fernández de Moratín was being performed. There, the viceroy received a message from the Commander of Ensenada de Barragán, Navy Captain Santiago de Liniers,[7] reporting that an English war fleet was approaching, and had opened fire on his position.

At 11 o'clock in the morning of the 25th, nearly 1600 soldiers from the 71st Highland Light Infantry Regiment, among them 36 Chinese artillerymen and a number of Germans, landed in Quilmes, and in a few hours, marching from the south along present-day Montes de Oca Street and another narrow one later to be called Defensa (defense) Street, occupied Buenos Aires, which in those days numbered some 45,000 inhabitants.

Mariquita Sánchez, future performer of the National Anthem and an eye witness of the invasion, wrote down her impression of the episode and recorded the earliest apparition of the mini-skirt in this region: "The 71st Scots came into the Square commanded by Colonel Pack; the loveliest troops I have ever seen, wearing the most poetic uniform: scarlet cross lace-boots leaving part of the leg

7 Santiago de Liniers and Bremond was born in La Vendée, France, in 1753. He studied in Malta, where he was made a Knight of the Order. In 1775, during the war against the Algerians, he joined the Spanish fleet and after that campaign arrived in the River Plate with Pedro de Cevallos. He returned to Europe for a short period where he rejoined the Spanish army, at war with the English. In 1788 he was posted to the River Plate again, where he married the daughter of the wealthy merchant Martín de Sarratea.

uncovered, a brief skirt, a black-feathered bonnet, a tartan ribbon and a tartan shawl over a scarlet short coat."

The 71st Regiment, also known as the Royal Scots, under the command of Colonel Pack, was, of the British Army corps, one of the most glorious and, on reaching Buenos Aires, still unvanquished. It had excelled in campaigns both in India and Europe. In 1799, in the famous battle of St. John of Acre (present-day Israel) it had set up an impenetrable line of defense against Napoleon's famous army in Egypt, and before arriving in Buenos Aires it had just carried out a successful campaign in Sicily.

Viceroy Sobremonte, less concerned about the CV of his attackers than about clinging onto his privileges, fled to Córdoba in an attempt to hide the royal funds. Before taking off, he left his unforgettable last instructions: "Retreat to the fort to obtain an honorable capitulation." Of course, the roads were then in a worse state than today, and it took three days for the Viceroy to get to his house in Luján, long enough for the English to find out about the escape of the representative of the King of Spain, and above all, to discover the location of the coveted treasure. The Viceroy arrived safely home, but the treasure was handed over to an English escort in Luján on June 30. On July 2, the terms of surrender were signed in Buenos Aires, including the relinquishing of the treasure by the Spanish authorities.

Inside the famous chest taken from the Viceroy there were 1,291,323 silver pesos. Part of the bounty was distributed among the troops. The leaders of the expedition, William Carr Beresford and Home Riggs Popham, received 24,000 and 7000 pound respectively. The rest, more than 1 million pounds, was shipped to London.

Once in London, the bounty was paraded on eight coaches pulled by six horses adorned with blue lace, while a band performed "God Save the King" and "Rule Britannia." The procession stopped off in front of the Admiralty, went through Pall Mall and St. James Square and finally reached the building of the Bank of England, where the Buenos Aires bounty was deposited. This goes to show that sometimes the English lose their usual composure and restraint and indulge in the same kind of carnival they often criticize South America for.

Those who pressed and finally made Sobremonte hand over the treasure were the *Porteño* capitularies, that is to say, the wealthiest property-owners of the City of Buenos Aires, honourably called "the healthiest people in the neighbourhood." Owning up to Beresford's threat to collect from them what he could not obtain from the viceroy, they decided to set a shameful and successful precedent for the years to come and prompted the State to take responsibility for private expenditure, and "suggested" the Viceroy to hand over the public funds.

On hearing about the incident, Manuel Belgrano bitterly observed: "Merchants don't know of any homeland, king or religion other than their own interest."

In the *Book of the Luján Cabildo,* years 1806-1814, folio 6, there is an account of the behavior of the English escort, bearer of a "superior culture" as we have often been told, during the period they resided in the chapter house. In addition to mishandling documents, using school desks as fuel and stealing 16 pesos out of the 28 in the cashbox, on going to fetch the ball they were playing with broke – perhaps in anticipated retaliation for Maradona's "hand of God" – all the tiles of the prison roof, as "they walked on the tiles as if they were walking on solid ground."[8]

---

8 E. Udaondo, *Las invasiones inglesas y la villa de Luján,* Buenos Aires, Raigal, 1928, p. 108.

In December 1805, Sobremonte was geared up to resist the English attack he believed was about to take place in the River Plate region. But the fleet that raised the alarm, having collected supplies in Bahia, Brazil, never made it to Buenos Aires. That fleet was none other than Baird's and Popham's and was headed for the Cape of Good Hope, with the purpose of sailing to Buenos Aires from that port.

Sobremonte's disgraceful flight inspired the *Porteños* to write verses such as these:

> *On hearing the first shot of the brave*
> *Sobremonte chose to visit his relatives.*
> *This man, the falsest rogue*
> *Buenos Aires can provide*
> *Is a precarious marquis;*
> *Over the hill he flees**
> *And downhill goes our fate.*[9]

For those readers who would like to try this at home and prepare their own Sobremonte, this is the recipe. The ingredients, unfortunately, can be easily found today, well into the Twenty-First Century, in some offices, coteries, foundations and comradeship dinners:

> *Ingredients to prepare a fifth-generation Marquis of Sobremonte*
>
> *A quintal of hypocrisy,*
> *Three pounds of braggadocio,*

* Translator's note: "Sobre-monte" means, in Spanish, "over the hill," thus the precarious pun.

9 Anonymous popular couplet, in Arturo Capdevila, *Las invasiones inglesas*, Buenos Aires, 1938.

And fifty of thief,
Fifteen of fancy
And three thousand of cowardice;
Mix all the ingredients well,
In an English cauldron,
Throw in capons and hens,
And out will come the coat of arms
Of the despicable marquis.
Not even while surrendering
Did they have their wits about them,
As the terms were agreed upon
By two hens and a capon.
Quintana's coat of arms[10]
We must learn to forget
And from Your Excellency learn,
He who out of fear shits his pants
Where should he be interred?[11]

Sobremonte's behaviour left much to be desired. The sentence reached by the Council of War held in Cádiz in 1813, however, declared the absolution of the former viceroy, of the charges brought against him for his military behaviour in Buenos Aires, during the events of 1806 and 1807. The attorney requested that, in exchange for his services, Sobremonte be given a similar post to the one he held in America, be paid whatever salaries were owed to him, and promoted to field-marshal, in addition to being appointed to the India House. Quite a precedent!

10 The verse refers to Hilarión de la Quintana, military chief of the city who, as the tango song would later put it, "surrendered without a fight."

11 John Street, *Gran Bretaña y la independencia del Río de la Plata*, Buenos Aires, Paidós, 1967.

On the 28th of June 1806, Beresford began to organize his military government. He summoned the existing Spanish authorities and told them they would be allowed to continue as before the conquest, in compliance with government law.

The prior of the Dominicans, Fray Gregorio Torres, thanked the invaders for their kindness and said that, "the loss of a government under which a people has grown is usually a great misfortune, although in many other cases this has been the beginning of its glory." And he went on, "I do not dare foretell the fate of our glory, but I am certain that the suavity of English rule and the sublime qualities of Commander Beresford will comfort the People of their recent loss." The prior finished his speech by saying that, "religion teaches us to respect secular authorities, whatever their creed, and if some kind of fanatical or ignorant wretch dare oppose such useful truths, let the penalty reserved for the traitors to the Fatherland and the Gospel be his."

Popular sense of humor did not even spare the ecclesiastical hierarchy:

If the prior took it to his head
That this English general
Would make him provincial
For his sycophantic fawning,
He should think again.
As this dear sir
Dislikes flattery of any kind,
And prefers sermons pronounced
by the cannon's mouth.[12]

12 In Ignacio Núñez, *Noticias históricas,* Buenos Aires, Jackson, 1957.

Encouraged by so many varied blessings, Beresford wrote a report to the War Office saying: "I am pleased to say that of the People who most fervently wish to be freed from Spanish rule, none show greater goodwill than the Church; they have not only been tyrannized but literally robbed, and have expressed their Feelings more openly than what mere Politics, under the present circumstances, should advise; which can been gathered from the speech read publicly to me by the Principal Prior of the Preachers in the presence of the rest of the other Buenos Ayres prelates, which he then handed to me, whishing to have it published."

Many were the obsequious officers, wealthy landowners, and merchants who presented themselves at the fort to pledge allegiance to "His Most Gracious Majesty George III" and pay Beresford a visit. These adulators, on learning that the British commander had a sweet tooth, brought him large trays containing local desserts, such as milk jam and pumpkin jam. It is said that Beresford, probably ignoring the customs of the country, believed the silver trays to be part of the gift, and had them sent to England conveniently crated.

On his part, Mariano Moreno wrote: "From the swiftness with which the British army took over such a large city, it can be gathered that either the government was neglectful, or the city dwellers indifferent; this sole doubt should prompt every citizen to voice his genuine opinion on the matter."

In his first declaration, Beresford said that the population of Buenos Aires was "protected by the honor, the generosity and kindness of the British character." He hastily established free trade and appointed José Martínez de Hoz as administrator of the Customs House. This official reciprocated by promptly reducing the tax on British imports.

The commander sought to give himself peace of mind by saying that: "At present, it pleases this Commander to communicate to the People that the system of monopoly, restriction and oppression they have been suffering under has come to an end, and that from now on the People may enjoy the products of other countries at a reduced price, that the manufactures and produces of the land are free from the check and oppression that smothered them and prevented the country from being what it is destined to be, the most flourishing in the world, and that the object of Great Britain is the happiness and prosperity of these Countries."

At first, and before the copious bounty reached London, news of the occupation of Buenos Aires did not go down well with the Admiralty, and the lords expressed, in the polished language of British diplomacy, their "disapproval at the fact that such an important step had been taken without His Majesty's sanction" but voiced their "total approval of the judicious, able and spirited behavior shown" by Popham and those under his orders at the time of the attack. In other words, the English government was ready to praise the operation if it had a successful outcome or condemn it energetically if it failed.

The most forward-thinking *criollos* which supported the idea of drastic change became absorbed by profound discussions. Manuel Belgrano chose to retire to his country house in the Banda Oriental (present-day Uruguay). Before departure, he uttered his famous phrase: "We want our old masters or none at all."

From the capital of the Viceroyalty, admiral Popham wrote to Francisco Miranda a phrase which was meant to last: "My dear General, here we are in possession of Buenos Aires, *the best country in the world.*"[13]

---

13 Letter from the English Admiral Home Popham to the Venezuelan revolutionary Francisco de Miranda, in Gustavo Gabriel Levene, *Breve historia de la independencia argentina*, Buenos Aires, Eudeba, 1966.

News travelled slowly in those days, and exactly one month after the reconquest of Buenos Aires the London *Times* would say, believing that Buenos Aires was still a British colony: "At present Buenos Aires belongs to the British Empire, and when we consider the consequences resulting from this situation and its commercial potential, as well as its political influence, we do not know how to express ourselves in a manner that can properly reflect our idea of the advantages that this conquest will present to our nation."[14]

A few days later, the *Times* would be so kind as to inform us that, thanks to the fertility of our soil, Argentina was destined to become "the granary of the world."

In Spain, on finding out about the loss of Buenos Aires to the English, the director of the *Caja de Consolidación* worriedly observed: "The loss of Buenos Aires may lead to a catastrophe in the rest of America and result in the bankruptcy of the State if this evil be not immediately remedied by seeking a reconciliation with the English."[15]

Due to a complaint filed by the wealthy *criollo* of French descent Juan Martín de Pueyrredón, where he stated that the Negroes "had become unruly as they believed the English had come to free them," Beresford had to put down an early emancipation movement of black slaves. Through a band, he reminded them of their allegiance to their rightful owners and established severe punishments for those who tried to escape.

It seems that the English General was not a good reader of Adam Smith, who claimed: "The experience of all ages and nations, I believe, demonstrates that the work done by slaves,

14 *The Times,* September 13, 1806.
15 Julio Irazusta, *Breve historia argentina*, Buenos Aires, Independencia, 1982.

though it appears to cost only their maintenance, is in the end the dearest of any. A person who can acquire no property can have no other interest but to eat as much and to labor as little as possible."[16]

The best vehicle for the circulation of British ideas was the periodical *Southern Star*, edited both in English and Spanish, which during the occupation had been set up in Montevideo.

In its editorial pieces, *Southern Star* contrasted the characteristics of the British and Spanish government, and the baseness of Napoleon and his followers, to the generosity and heroism of the British.

The English officers mingled with the leading *Porteño* families, stayed at their homes, and attended the increasing number of parties held in their honor. It was common to see the very conservative ladies Sarratea, Marcó del Pont and Escalada strolling arm in arm with the "heretics."

But it would be a mistake to believe that this condescending attitude spelled a resolute political support from the *Porteños*, who did not make up their minds whether to cooperate with the invaders or not, recalling perhaps incidents such as that of Martinique, returned by the English to the Spanish three times after as many invasions, or that of Guadalupe, which held the record of five successive invasions and devolutions.

Belgrano phrased this very clearly in his *Autobiography*: "England would abandon us if this improved its situation in Europe, and we would then fall under the Spanish sword."[17]

---

16 Adam Smith, *An Inquiry into the Nature and Causes of the Wealth of Nations.*

17 Manuel Belgrano, *Autobiografía*, Buenos Aires, Carlos Pérez, 1968.

Beresford admits to this in a letter dated July 11, 1806: "I have been informed that the People of this City are not only glad about the Change of Masters, but would rather remain under the protection of His Majesty, and only the fear of falling again under the Rule of their previous masters prevents them from expressing this openly, and the scantiness of our force cannot give them sufficient Confidence not to fear the Consequences of such occurrence, and as I am ignorant of what the intentions of the Government of your Majesty might be, I am necessarily careful not to advance something that might compromise His Majesty or the people of this City, and until I am given instructions on this point, I will be satisfied to leave everything as it is. However, if at least we retained this place during the War, and if Instructions allow, we might act here in hope of undoing the affections of the People for the Spanish yoke, which, in the case of being restored, would find it extremely difficult to rule them."

Beresford's instructions, however, arrived several days after the surrender, and they represent a curious document on the limits of British "liberality" and their support of American revolutionary movements.

As for the guarantees he was allowed to give to the people, in the event that a peace treaty were in the future signed with Spain, Beresford was told to stick to the tactics of not making declarations that would oblige the British government to follow a particular course of action. "You shall abstain from interfering in any local disorder, in case there were one, and refuse to take sides with any kind of person involved in it, unless, and this only to a certain extent, if it were to protect those persons who might be related to you on a commercial deal or to prevent a major and immediate act of violence and cruelty in any particular case where your interference may be employed without risks and in an effective manner."

England was not interested in plans *à la Miranda*. They were too dangerous a weapon in the context of the European war. It was, however, willing to encourage the creation of a commercial outpost on the South American coast, provided the costs were not too high in any sense.

Applying the policy of the carrot and the stick, on the second dispatch Beresford was informed about the king's "entire approval" of his and his troops' behavior. The general was told: "In fact, every lie adopted prudentially and with the purpose of illustrating the inhabitants of Buenos Aires and adjoining Provinces on the difference between the oppressive government that has ruled them so far and the benign and protective rule of His Majesty, must be deemed of great importance in securing, in the most effective and satisfactory manner, the brilliant projects a vista of which the army of His Majesty has opened before our eyes."

At last, King George III issued two orders – on the 17th of September and on the 1st of October 1806 – regulating the trade of Buenos Aires, ratifying Beresford's provisional changes and placing the River Plate region in the same commercial category as the British colonies in the West Indies and South America. As we have already pointed out, when these orders were issued, Buenos Aires was once again under Spanish rule and was therefore in no position to enjoy the "benefits" of British administration.

Subversion

Except for the usual flatterers and sycophants, the majority of the population, which was both hostile to the invaders and outraged at the incompetence of the Spanish authorities, began preparing the resistance.

The Ranqueles – as the Tehuelche Indians were called in those days – were the first to react against the invasion: they sent a delegation to Córdoba to have an appointment with Sobremonte and offer him their best lancers. The Pampa Indians also offered their brave horsemen to the *Cabildo* of Buenos Aires. Ten chiefs went into the chapter room where an interpreter translated the following message: "We wished to meet you through our own eyes and, pleased to have done so, we once again offer you the number of twenty thousand of our subjects, each of them a warrior and each possessing five horses, for we want them to be the first to attack those reddies who seem to incommode you."[18] But the local landowners were a bit shocked by the looks of the Indian throng, however collaborative they purported themselves to be, and refused their aid. Anyhow, the unilateral truce proclaimed by the Aborigines was very valuable, since it permitted frontier corps such as the Blandengues to join the resistance.

Also in those years there emerged the first attempt at an urban guerrilla in our history, composed by a group of *criollos* and Catalans who met clandestinely in circles of five at the bookshop of don Tomás Valencia. Led by Felipe Sentenach, an engineer and mathematician by profession, and Gerardo Esteve y Llach, they took upon themselves to blow up the fort and all the English positions. They made explosives that were supposed to go off under the Fort of

[18] Actas del Cabildo, December 22, 1806. Acuerdos del Extinto Cabildo de Buenos Aires. Serie IV, t. II, lbs., LIX, LX, LXI, and LVII, 1805-1807.

Buenos Aires, where Beresford and the English officers were residing, and below *La Ranchería* Theatre, which had become the general headquarters of the standard-bearers of Western culture. To achieve their goal, they rented a house next to *La Ranchería* to begin their excavations from.

Another Catalan in the group, José Fornaguera, suggested organizing a secret band of knifemen to cut the English throats. When they decided it was time to take action, they distributed a manifesto signed by Sentenach: "If we have the good fortune of achieving the reconquest, we will organize round-table discussions where everyone will be equal and no one will be superior to the rest, and where all the members of the council shall rule with equal character or authority."[19]

The group set the revolutionaries of North America, who only ten years earlier had declared their independence, as an example to emulate. Sentenach said that the time had come to "be men and finally declare our free Republic from the King Our Lord and from Spain." When the seditious finally had everything ready to turn Beresford and his assistants into the first astronauts of the River Plate, Liniers and his troop appeared, and for security reasons, it was agreed that the attack should be called off.

Martín Rodríguez, on his part, had planned to kidnap the commander of the invaders. This he recalls in his memories, dictated to his loyal scrivener Rivera Indarte thirty years after the incident: "I devised a plan to abduct Beresford and his retinue, for which purpose I made arrangements with ten young men, suitably armed and horsed, and we agreed that on the day he came out we would pounce upon him and

---

19 Enrique de Gandia, *Nueva historia de América*, Buenos Aires, Claridad, 1961.

his followers. One of my friends, Don Antonio Romero, came to see me and begged me dearly to cancel a plan that, if carried it out, would drive the English to take revenge on the population."[20]

Martín de Álzaga, black slave trader and prosperous practitioner of commercial monopoly, whose business extended from Potosí to Lima and from Chile to Buenos Aires, and who would have been badly affected if the English declared free trade, claimed that he was ready to finance any kind of action against the invaders. He rented a house in Perdriel, later to be used by Juan Martín de Pueyrredón as training grounds for the military resistance. On learning of this, Beresford led a force of 550 men which surprised and defeated Pueyrredón and his people on the 1st of August 1806.

In that same country house in Perdriel, today a beautiful museum in San Martín district, José Hernández, descendant of Pueyrredón and author of *Martín Fierro,* would be born on the 10th of November 1834.

Álzaga was far from being a humanitarian. According to one of his contemporaries, a few days before the invasions, "Álzaga loaded 300 Negroes in the Port of Mozambique and crammed them below deck, where they died of thirst or the plague and had to be tossed into the waves. When he reached Santa Catarina (Brazil) he hardly had thirty Negroes left. Once in Montevideo, Governor Ruiz Huidobro did not let him enter the port as a hygiene measure. The captain of the ship, a deft dodger of shipping regulations, obeyed and sailed away, but immediately returned claiming that he had run aground in a storm. Álzaga alleged there

20 Martín Rodríguez, *Memorias*, Biblioteca de Mayo, Senado de la Nación, 1962.

was no danger in his landing, since the Negroes had not died from the plague but of thirst. The governor of Montevideo ordered the removal of the ship. The case reached Viceroy Sobremonte, who approved the measure. Álzaga continued to complain and wrote to the Viceroy: 'I assume that it is not beyond the discernment of His Excellency that surgeon Molina exaggerates the perils that slave trade presents to public health, describing the former as inhuman and execrable. These odious adjectives by which the said surgeon characterizes slave trade are not compatible with the object of so many royal letters patent and orders in which His Majesty recommends this profitable industry.'"[21] Thus spoke Don Martín de Álzaga, who was one of the fathers of the revolution, according to the opinion of some pro-Hispanic historians. He certainly knew how to hide it well.

To monopolists such as Álzaga, writes Ignacio Núñez, contemporary to the events, free trade with England was enormously detrimental "for once British manufactures were admitted, the profit obtained through their smuggling would be greatly reduced. The common class of smugglers knew how to slow progress and expected to sell for 200 what they had bought for 50."[22]

The commander of the Fort of Ensenada de Barragán, French Navy officer Santiago de Liniers, left for Montevideo and started organizing the troops to recover Buenos Aires.

An odd document testifies to the existence of a plan devised by Liniers and Pío White to liberate, with British

21 José Luis Lanuza, *Morenada, una historia de la raza africana en el Río de la Plata.*
22 Ignacio Núñez, *op. cit.*

aid and approval, the River Plate from Spanish rule. It also adds that Beresford tried to entrust his forces to Santiago de Liniers, whom he had met in Montevideo. But Liniers, continues the document, "seeing the low number of the troops and that they could be easily defeated by the Viceroy, with any number of people he managed to gather, refused the offer of the General, escaped to Montevideo and placed himself at the head of the reconquest."[23]

Liniers embarked with a thousand men, among them various French privateers commanded by Hipólito Bouchard, and sailed from Tigre. As he was approaching the city, neighbors joined his troops. When he reached the Corrales de Miserere – present-day Miserere Square or *Once* Square – he ordered the English commander to surrender.

It was there the episode of Manuela Pedraza, "La Tucumana," occurred. This woman, wife to a corporal, went up to the Square with her husband, killed the first Englishman that came within her reach with her own hands and, taking possession of the dead man's rifle, continued the fight among the "shooters." Liniers recommended her to the King, and Charles IV appointed her sub-lieutenant of infantry with a right to the uniform and a salary.

In the thick of the fray Don Simón, a dexterous lassoer from the slaughter-house, managed to lasso two English soldiers. Since he was crippled in combat, the government gave him leave to beg in the streets. Don Simón became a very popular beggar of the Buenos Aires of yore.

The *Porteño* children also took an active role in the reconquest, as some *Cabildo* papers explain: "Children eight

---

23 Susana Rato de Sambucetti, *La Rrevolución de Mayo*, Buenos Aires, Siglo XX, 1983.

and ten years old were seen running to the rescue of our artillery and, clinging to the cannons, they helped fire them and put themselves in the line of fire; they would rip off the very clothes on their backs to feed the cannon's fire; would run boldly around within reach of the enemy, defying undaunted their fire in spite of their tender years and the loss of their mates, whose fortune it was to be the tender victims of a heroic Childhood."[24]

In the last days of June 1806, the exceptionally low tide in the River Plate left the English ship Justine stranded on its bed, and the leader of the defense, Santiago de Liniers, ordered a group of horsemen to attack it. In a few minutes they succeeded in dexterously defeating the powdered sailors. The leader of this operation was called Martín Miguel de Güemes.

Another future protagonist of our history also risked his life in action. As described by Pascual Ruiz Huidobro, governor of Montevideo, in a letter dated August 15, "The Blandengue corps aide-de-camp Don José Artigas, has returned from Buenos Aires where he was on a mission assigned by me in the service of the King, for the accomplishment of which he almost died in the river as the boat that was taking him capsized, on which occasion he lost his suitcase containing clothes for everyday use, saddle, poncho and the rest of his stuff; and to make up for the said loss and for the expenses that the mission itself has cost him, I consider that in all fairness the Royal Treasury in charge of His Excellency should compensate him with the sum of three hundred current pesos, as soon as possible. May God grant you many years of good life."

24 Oficio del Cabildo de Buenos Aires, 12 de agosto de 1806.

Beresford made a last attempt to prevent the failure of his adventure, and negotiated what might have been an offer of English support for the emancipation. One of the English commanders commissioned Pío White to meet Pueyrredón before the attack. On the 11th of August White wrote saying that he had "something very interesting" to inform him of, and requested an appointment. But the revolt broke out before it was expected, and White and Pueyrredón couldn't have their meeting.

According to some sources, Liniers tried to reach an agreement with the British government with the purpose of declaring the independence of the Viceroyalty of the River Plate.

In any case, after having lost about 300 men, counting both the dead and injured, and being confined to the Fort, Beresford finally capitulated on the 12th of August 1806.

The *Times*, used to extolling the glories of the Empire, was struck with bewilderment: "The attack on Buenos Aires has failed and for a long time there have not been any British soldiers on the Spanish territories of South America. This is perhaps the greatest disaster this country has suffered since the beginning of the revolutionary war."[25]

The capitulation, signed on August 20th, established that English prisoners would be exchanged for the "Spanish" ones. But on finding out about the terms of the surrender, and fearing that the English might counter-attack on returning to their ships, the *Cabildo* and the people of the city commanded Liniers to send the prisoners to the hinterlands as a precaution, and rejected the validity of the capitulation.

25 *The Times*, London, September 11, 1806.

On the 5th of February 1807, while Beresford was imprisoned in Luján, Saturnino Rodríguez Peña, Álzaga's secretary, tried to talk him into supporting American emancipation, as the use of arms would only gain Great Britain more enemies, and offered to liberate him if he favored his ideas. The British general enthusiastically supported and offered to communicate them to General Achmuty, the conqueror of Montevideo, and to the English government. On this cue, and with the complicity of several friends and the consent of Álzaga and Liniers, Rodríguez Peña arranged Beresford's and Lieutenant Colonel Pack's escape on the 17th of February 1807.

Beresford remained in Montevideo until March 26th, when he left for England. In May 1811, aided by the troops of the Spanish general Francisco Javier Castaños, he defeated the French marshal Nicolas Jean de Dieu Soult in La Albuera, Badajoz, and together with Arthur Colley Wellesley participated in most of the major military actions of the conflict. The latter had wanted his portrait painted by Goya, but when he realized that the Spanish artist had done a half-hearted job of it, he expressed his dissatisfaction, in response to which the great Spanish painter, who might not be able to hear but understood perfectly well, took one of his pistols and almost put an end to the life of the man who was to defeat Napoleon in Waterloo.[26]

When Miranda found out about the Buenos Aires disaster, he addressed a letter to Popham in these terms: "How do you expect eighteen million people, settled in the vastest and most impregnable continent on Earth, located four to

26 Ramón de Mesonero Romanos, *Memorias de un setentón*, 2 vols., Madrid, Oficinas de la Ilustración Española y Americana, 1881.

six thousand miles away from Europe (...) to be conquered and subjugated with a handful of men who believe they can boss them about as their masters? It is not possible, my dear friend, the affair is neither natural nor feasible nor possible." Thus the Venezuelan general reminded the Englishman that it wasn't conquest that would win them the Latin Americans' favor.

Complying with Liniers' dispositions, a contingent of prisoners, soldiers and officers, was taken to the province of Catamarca. But the local prison did not meet the necessary safety requirements, and so they were lodged in family homes, but because the neighbors refused to receive these compulsory guests and dangerous heretics, the government had to rent a few houses to lodge them until their return to Buenos Aires.

An Englishman who took part in the invasion recalls: "While we were in jail many local families expressed their wish to have English soldiers as servants, not so much to benefit from their services, but rather because they wanted to spare them their captivity. It was apparent that the English women preferred the English officers. The only obstacle in the way of more intimate relationships was the difference of creed."[27]

Love Interlude

In those days, Anita Perichón, known as "La Perichona" glowed in all the *Porteño* social gatherings. She had arrived in Buenos Aires with her parents in 1797. Vicente Fidel López claims that she was not only Liniers' but also Beresford's mistress, and that it was due to her "good offices"

---

27 Alejandro Gillespie, *Buenos Aires y el interior*, Buenos Aires, A. Zeta, 1994.

that Beresford agreed to such a benevolent capitulation. She was described as pretty, elegant, witty, attractive, cosmopolitan, sharp and possessing a great sense of humor. She was married to Tomás O'Gorman – brother to Miguel O'Gorman, proto-physician in Cevallos' expedition and founder of the Medical School of Buenos Aires – but it wasn't long before the Irishman abandoned her.

Madame Perichón is also remembered as the grandmother of Camila O'Gorman, the young girl who was executed by Rosas in 1848 for eloping with Tucumán priest Uladislao Gutiérrez.

Subordination and Valor

Given the possibility of a new invasion, and the ineffectiveness of the Spanish regular troop, the neighbors organized themselves in militias. Every citizen of the capital of the Viceroyalty became a member of a militia. Things were different in those days, and Liniers did not think twice about letting each man take his weapons home, although he trusted the ammunition of every combat unit to the chief alone.

Those who were born in Buenos Aires formed the Patricio corps, composed mostly of poor workers and artisans; men from the Hinterlands formed the Arribeño ("upperers") corps, which received its name from the fact that its members were mainly rural workers and day laborers from the "upper" provinces. Slaves and Indians formed the corps of Pardos and Morenos. On their part, the Spanish created the Galician, Catalan, Cantabrian, Montañeses and Andalusian corps. Leaders and officers were democratically elected by the members of each of the militias.

Among the chosen leaders stood some of the young *criollos* who for the first time took up a position of power and popularity: Cornelio Saavedra, Manuel Belgrano, Martín Rodríguez, Hipólito Vieytes, Domingo French, Juan Martín de Pueyrredón and Antonio Luis Beruti.

The city became militarized but also politicized. The militias were a natural ground for the discussion of political ideas, and thus a conspiratorial spirit began to take shape, slowly but steadily.

Spanish authorities were not exactly keen on these popular militia formed by *criollos* because, as Saavedra tells us, "the former were used to looking down on the sons of the country as if they were their servants, and to treating them with the demeanour of conquerors; they did not like to see them with arms in their hands, even less so since with them they became respected for their good services and for their decision of preserving the order of society."[28]

One of the officials of the viceroyalty described the attitude of the members of the ruling classes who had joined the militia in these terms: "These individuals are more intent on defending their properties than the Supreme Dominion of the Royal Crown; rather than observing the principle of subordination that is expected from soldiers, they went into combat because they wanted to keep their personal wealth and rights."[29]

In London, the Cabinet was fuming. The 165 dead bodies strewn on the streets of Buenos Aires had a *je ne sais quoi* that led an outraged Lord Melville to declare: "Neither in

---

28 Cornelio Saavedra, *Memoria autógrafa*, Buenos Aires, Biblioteca de Mayo, tomo II, 1966.
29 Testimony of Miguel Lastarría in John Street, *op. cit.*

the history of our country nor in that of any other will we come upon the example of an expedition conducted with less judgement and ability."

In for a Penny, in for a Pound

Whether in a mood of revengeful sportsmanship, or in the perverse desire to repeat their own mistakes, the English decided to have another go at it and, as was to be expected, on the 16th of January 1807, a new English expedition, this time consisting of 12,000 men and 100 merchant ships carrying British products, under the command of Lieutenant General John Whitelock, landed in Montevideo.

The situation was getting difficult and both the *Cabildo* and the *Audiencia* had to own up to the rather "slippery" behavior of the viceroy, the Marquis of Sobremonte, whom future president Mitre, a man who usually minced his words, in a fit of rage accused of "doing everything in his ineptitude's power to hamper the defense." Paul Groussac, a friend of Mitre's, in every bit as good as him, describes the Viceroy as a "collection of incapacities."

Anonymous pamphlets written along the following lines began to circulate: "The People request that, having received no answer regarding their petition, namely, to remove the *Audiencia* and hang all traitors and allow no one, be he rich or poor, to leave the city, Sobremonte be deprived of all his power and have no say in our affairs, and that Don Santiago de Liniers be given full powers to lead us and rule us; and if our demand be not met before Sunday we will put each and every member of the *Audiencia* to the knife for refusing. So the People demand."

On the 6th of February 1807 the people clamoured at the top of their lungs "death to the traitors, death to Sobremonte" calling for the destitution and imprisonment of the Viceroy, and there even appeared some graffiti saying, "Death to the Viceroy and to the aldermen, away with the *Audiencia*, long live freedom and let us hoist the Republican flag!" On the 10th the Viceroy was relieved of his duties. This episode set a precedent of popular self-determination which would not be overlooked by the reactionary Spanish authorities. Sobremonte, a man of absolutist ideas, did all in his power to disavow the resolution, and the members of the *Audiencia*, no less absolutist than him, tried to justify their procedure by inserting it within in a pre-existing legal framework. The aldermen devised a plan to conceal the fact that the Viceroy was being removed from office on account of his ineptitude and cowardice and through the will of the people of Buenos Aires, claiming that "the Marquis of Sobremonte was too sick to govern, so that we considered it fit that his person be treated as circumstances require, reserving to His Majesty the knowledge of the operations of the said person in the matters in question."

Thus popular intervention was toned down, and a colonial legal continuity of sorts was guaranteed.

Attorney Villota, another recalcitrant conservative who would flaunt his intolerance in the May Week of 1810, observed that "the Council of War did not have the faculty to judge the actions of the Viceroy, that there was no authority in these dominions who could do so" and that before removing him from office a legal solution should be sought out, that is to say that the Viceroy himself should renounce on his own will. Like the aldermen, Villota feared that "the same thing might occur with the rest of the army on the other side of the river under His Majesty's orders, resulting in new turmoil and fostering doubts with regard to true authority." He concluded by saying that what had happened in Buenos Aires was "a noxious example" and that "the people should not be allowed to impose their will."

According to Francisco Saguí in *The Last Four Years of Spanish Rule in the Old Viceroyalty of the River Plate* "some of the aldermen had their own ideas and were working in favor of the viceroy, so that the people began to suspect that they were trying to reinstate him."

The interested party, Sobremonte, described in this way the *Cabildo* of the 14th of August 1807 which put an end to his administration: "Two or three despicable youngsters were the ones who raised their voices in that so-called Congress, and with a contemptible fury attempted to prove that the people had the authority to choose their leaders when the defense of the city was at stake. Should we permit the order of civil, military, and political affairs to be thus upset, the Viceroy to be deprived of an essential portion of his employment and privileges, a military and political governor to be daringly created? Should he by such horrid means be prevented from entering his Capital, and this seat set such a pernicious example to the subjects in the remaining viceroyalties?"[30]

It was a complex issue. It was one thing to give arms to the people to throw the English out, and another to let the people express their opinions and go as far as to impose their will.

The removal of the Marquis of Sobremonte which began in Buenos Aires on the 12th of August 1806 and was enforced on the 10th of February 1807 was, undoubtedly, the first victory of the people over the authority of the king. Not because Liniers – who was, after all, another conservative

---

30 Enrique de Gandía, *op. cit.*

– was designated, but because it advanced the idea among them that those officers who were cowardly, corrupt and inefficient could be removed by the people if they organized themselves.

A report sent by the Spanish brigadier Curado describes this state of popular effervescence: "Those who in appearance are invested with public power are the ghosts of their past glory and are often insulted and always subjected to the people, whose anarchy is so excessive and complete, that they even dare object the commands and dispositions of their rulers when these do not comply with their objectives."

Towards the end of June 1807, the invaders tried to take Buenos Aires. With relative ease they overrun the Square and after laying siege to the city they took it by storm.

The plan of English general John Whitelocke consisted in attacking the city with heavy artillery, "house by house and street by street, until there be no place left for the guerrillas and snipers to hide." Once the houses were demolished, they would direct their fire on the fort, where the English flag would be hoisted once again.

If he succeeded, Whitelocke was to be appointed "General Governor of South America" by the British Crown, with an annual salary of 12,000 pounds.

But by that time the capital of the viceroyalty was no longer unprotected. Santiago de Liniers and Martín de Álzaga, its mayor, had managed to draft 8600 men and organize the neighbors. Until recently, the improvised officers had been civilians, such as landowner Cornelio Saavedra.

"When the 110 sails of the great British armada were made out on the horizon," would recall the British agent and friend of President Rivadavia's Manuel José García in his *Memoirs*, "this spectacle, capable of intimidating even the most daring of men, did not as much as stir the settlers."

And when the English thought they would once again march in triumph along the narrow streets of Buenos Aires, they collected shots, stones, and torrents of boiling water coming from balconies and rooftops.

The future *vocal* (council member) of the First Junta, Domingo Matheu, wrote in his *Memoirs*: "The English entered the city causing havoc, killing and plundering and forcing the women, and in this way advanced deep into the city. But as soon as they reached the area where people were waiting for them on the rooftops the party was over, as the soldiers came under a fire so deadly that in less than two hours more than 1500 were killed and those injured and taken prisoner added to more than 4000."[31]

Years later, the invading general would write: "The kind of fire our troops were exposed to was extremely violent. Shrapnel at the corners of all streets, fire from rifles, hand grenades, bricks and stones from the rooftops, each homeowner defending his abode together with his slaves, and each home became a fortress, and perhaps it would not be and exaggeration to say that the whole of the male population of Buenos Aires was engaged in its defense."[32]

Both scalded and surprised, the English decided to surrender, although among the articles of capitulation they unsuccessfully attempted to include a clause granting them authorization to freely sell the plentiful cargo they had brought on their ships.

Whitelocke commissioned his deputy, Gower, to begin conversations with the enemy and to coordinate the

31 Domingo Matheu, *Memorias*, Biblioteca de Mayo, tomo II, Buenos Aires, 1966.
32 Whitelocke's oficial report, June 10, 1807.

surrender of his army. Like *de facto* President Galtieri 175 years after him, Whitelocke refused to use the term "surrender." Just like the alcoholic general, the Englishman resorted to all kinds of euphemisms to inform his country about the unconditional surrender: "In the afternoon the fire had ceased and on the following day, July 7, 1807, a national agreement was signed." Just in case – one never knows what might happen in the future – on the 11th Liniers hosted a banquet for the defeated chiefs, where both the Kings of Spain and England were toasted and a band of bagpipers played "God Save the King."[33]

In the context of the victory celebrations, a ballot was cast over 686 slaves distinguished for their bravery in combat and 70 obtained their freedom.

Napoleon sent congratulations for the recovery of Buenos Aires to Charles IV who, as usual, didn't have the slightest idea of what was going on. Emperor Bonaparte, who was apt to have his say without much caring whom he was speaking to, put special emphasis on the fact that the "victor" was a Frenchman.

On the 2nd of August 1807, Father Grela delivered a sermon from the pulpit of the Church of Santo Domingo, attacking Sobremonte's behavior and commending Liniers with enthusiasm. The usual adulators went up to former Viceroy Sobremonte, staying in San Isidro at the time, and told him the effects that the sermon had caused. Outraged, Sobremonte took up the pen and on the 5th of August 1807 addressed the following note to Liniers: "Don Santiago de Liniers: I have been informed than on the second day of the present month at the service in Santo Domingo when the

---

33 Domingo Matheu, *op. cit.*

preacher proceeded to commend the victory against the enemies of the said capital, a comparative judgement was uttered containing expressions the purpose of which could only have been to disparage my administration, something that in an act both so serious and so public and especially because the sovereign was not present to judge them should not be allowed, and given that the laws of the kingdom contain a strict and special prohibition against the said verbal excesses being proffered from the pulpit, I cannot but express to Your Excellency my just feelings so that with your authority you may take the necessary measures to stop them before they reach the press, as it may happen; as such speeches are unnecessarily offensive and opinionated when praise could have been formulated in a just and dignified manner without making such hateful comparisons. May God protect you. San Isidro, August 5, 1807. The Marquis of Sobremonte."

On the 30th of December 1807, the *Cabildo* of Buenos Aires addressed to the Spanish king a petition penned by Mariano Moreno: "The City of Buenos Aires, which has gloriously recovered the City of Montevideo and the Banda Oriental of this river, who has defeated in a single campaign the superior forces on which the enemy's hope of triumph rested; which has disturbed the meditated speculations through which Great Britain was preparing the conquest and enslavement of this region; which with the blood of its faithful and courageous inhabitants has freed the provinces from the heavy yoke that threatened to fall upon them, which they might not have been able to resist by themselves; beseeches His Majesty humbly deign to confer upon this *Cabildo* the title of "Preserver of South America and Protector of the remaining *Cabildos* of the Viceroyalty."

The truth be told, despite the surrender of Whitelocke's troops, there remained in Buenos Aires and Montevideo some 2000 British merchants arrived in either one of the two invasions. This is how Matheu tells the story: "What they did not achieve through occupation, they gained in failure, since during those two months they sold merchandise for more than 8,000,000 pesos worth for less than one third of their market value, so as not to carry it back to England. Buyers were mainly wealthy Spaniards and some natives of similar condition. All the deserters of the defense took money on an interest rate of over 15% in order to smuggle it into this market. Useless were the complaints to the Consulate and to Viceroy Liniers, who remained in this as deaf as his predecessor."[34]

The soldiers returned to London, but the merchants and their goods remained in the River Plate. They British had not been able to conquer the cities, but they had conquered the markets since, as a British historian has pointed out, "what the English government and people were after was not really the territory, but trade and cash."[35]

Military justice

On the 28th of January 1808 the trial against Whitelocke began in London. At times the English general tried to defend himself by saying things like, "I was expecting to find a large number of citizens willing to support or goals. But the country turned out to be completely hostile towards our purposes."[36]

34 Domingo Matheu, *op. cit.*

35 C. K. Webster, *Gran Bretaña y la independencia de América Latina*, Buenos Aires, Paidós, 1971. *Britain and the Independence of Latin America: 1812-1830*, London, New York, Oxford University Press, 1938.

36 Gillespie, *op. cit.*

Whitelocke concluded his defense with strong words, "I daresay there is not in history a single example that is comparable to what has occurred in Buenos Aires, where all the inhabitants, free residents and slaves, fought with a sense of determination and belonging such as could have not been expected from even religious or patriotic enthusiasm or the most inveterate hatred."

The words of the prosecutor manifested the imperial indignation: "With this unfortunate episode, any hopes sensibly and reasonably entertained of discovering new markets for our manufactures, of opening new horizons for the inclination and activity of our merchants, of finding new sources for the Exchequer and new fields to satisfy the needs of countries that have only recently left the state of barbarism, or to supply the demands of luxury and refinement of those faraway lands of the globe, have vanished."

The verdict of the court expressed the annoyance of a conceited monarchy, not used to suffering defeats so humiliating as to wipe the ever-lasting smile off "His Most Gracious Majesty's" face. It instructed that "the said Lieutenant-general Whitelocke be dismissed and declared unfit and unworthy to serve His Majesty in any military rank." And it added, "may this be set as an example of the fatal consequences officials invested with power are exposed to when, in the performance of the very important tasks assigned to them, they lack the sense, care and personal effort which their Sovereign and country are entitled to expect of them."[37]

While this was happening in London, in the Buenos Aires liberated from the English but still subjugated by the Spaniards, a new era was about to begin. Things would never be the same again.

37 *Ibid.*

The May Revolution

Do they think that the sons of this country
can be put back in chains? Do the enemies
not know that, even if they exterminate us,
our sons will avenge the death of their parents?

MARIANO MORENO

Were one to ask if the May Revolution was an economic, a political or a military incident, the answer would be: none of these. It was a school play. This is what the birth of our nation has come to mean in the end: little more than a bittersweet memory of small cake, burnt cork makeup and street vendors.

Historical anaesthesia is administered by the powers-that-be to a people too crushed by the struggle for survival – and in the case of half of the country's population, by poverty and hunger – to spare the time to think about our historical roots, and it is the cause of many a present evil.

At the most, the system encourages the discussion of issues as significant as the presence or absence of umbrellas in the days of 1810, or the discrepancy between the state of the weather in the patriotic song "The sun of the 25th is on the rise" and that of the illustrations of *Billiken* magazine, the *Simulcop*[1] and school textbooks, where the sky is quite

---

1 The *Simulcop* consisted of a notebook containing all the illustrations required for the school year – for example, 6th grade *Simulcop*. These would then be transferred to the class notebook by applying pressure with a pencil. Publishing was discontinued in the late 1960s.

unquestionably overcast. Consciously or not, this is what the process that would determine the future of our nation has been reduced to. Little wonder then that throughout our history the high and mighty, and their spokesmen, start squirming in their seats when it comes to discussing a series of historical events that involve all of Argentina's basic unresolved issues: justice, equity, the economic model, dependence and corruption.

All of these issues are encompassed by the May Revolution, its context and circumstances. It is the starting point for a "they" and a "we" that has not ended and will not end, neither by recourse to absurd vindication or slandering defamation, even when many believe that it is in the latter that novelty lies.

Changes in Europe and America

The May events cannot be understood without reference to the European context, because they are the result of a complex series of causes among which the European conflict plays an essential role.

In Europe, the two leading world powers, France and England, were at war. The Industrial Revolution initiated in England had unleashed the conflict to gain control of the European market. It is in this, and not in the personal ambitions or in the alleged madness of Napoleon, that lie the causes of the war.

Bonaparte was the best representative the French bourgeoisie could have hoped for, and his conquests cleared the path for new business opportunities for the class that had triumphed in the French Revolution, a class that by fire and sword managed to turn a revolutionary process into an Empire. The preeminence of economic determinations becomes apparent in the "continental blockade," declared by Napoleon after the victory at Austerlitz, against British products and in favor of French manufactures.

In January 1808, the Napoleonic troops that had invaded Portugal – England's traditional ally – in order to guarantee the implementation of the blockade, decided to remain in Spain and take possession of the entire Iberian Peninsula, then under the rule of Charles IV, whose only virtue, if it may be deemed such, was a rather peculiar notion of tolerance, which led him to surrender the Kingdom of Spain, including his wife the Queen, to her favorite Manuel Godoy, the self-called "Prince of Peace." Napoleon succeeded in making Charles VI abdicate in favor of his son Ferdinand, who in turn renounced his rights to Joseph Bonaparte, brother to Napoleon, nicknamed "Joe Bottles", on account of his taste for wine.

Ferdinand VII, whom Spanish writer Benito Pérez Galdós describes as "the most despicable being,"[2] congratulated Napoleon on the appointment of his brother Joseph and urged his subjects to submit to and befriend the Emperor's brother. But while the politicians and the Spanish grandees accepted the suggestion of the Bourbons and got ready to do business with the French, the Spanish people rejected this irregular situation and with the purpose of resisting the invaders organized themselves, in all the major cities, into juntas or councils, coordinated by the Central Council of Seville.

Former King Charles IV, the former Queen and her official – but in no way former – lover Manuel Godoy, were taken to the Palace of Fontainebleau, France. The fleeting King Ferdinand VII – he actually got to rule for a few days

2 Benito Pérez Galdós, "La corte de Carlos IV", en *Episodios nacionales*, Madrid, Alianza, 1971.

before his deportation – known as the "the Desired One," together with his wife and some members of his court, were transported by Napoleon to France and lodged in the Castle of Valençay, in the valley of the Loire, attended by servants and enjoying every comfort. In addition, Napoleon politely invited him to his wedding with the Archduchess Marie Louise of Habsburg. According to some witnesses, Don Ferdinand grew hoarse yelling "Long live the Emperor!" congratulating him at the same time on the victories that his troops were achieving in Spain – that is to say, on the massacres perpetrated against his own people.

Ferdinand's supporters, who erroneously took him for some kind of patriot, made plans to arrange the escape of the "captive" king and return him to Madrid, but Ferdinand himself turned them in to Napoleon, and all their loyalty got them was a good standing-place before the firing squad.

When Napoleon invaded Portugal, King John II, his family and court fled to Brazil. The Portuguese princess Carlota Joaquina, sister to Ferdinand VII, argued that she represented the Spanish Bourbons and claimed her rights over the territories of the River Plate until don Ferdinand returned to the Spanish throne. The Central Council of Seville sent her a note "thanking" her for her concerns but asserted that Ferdinand's rights were duly secured by them. With the transfer of the Portuguese court to Brazil, the influence of the British over the region increased.

Changes in Buenos Aires

In Buenos Aires, the acting viceroy, Santiago de Liniers, turned from popular leader and "hero of the reconquest" into one of the most corrupt and unscrupulous viceroys of these sub-kingdoms.

The governor of Montevideo, Javier de Elío, tried to take advantage of Liniers' status as a French subject and, therefore, as a potential ally of Napoleon's, to request his removal. Liniers asked him to offer evidence for the charges levelled against him but Elío refused to acknowledge his authority and created a government council independent of Buenos Aires.

Liniers' opponents, led by Liniers' old rival Martín de Álzaga, tried to take advantage of the election at the *Cabildo* on the 1st of January 1809 to remove him from office. But Liniers was defended by the *criollo* militias, which succeeded in curbing the protest. The Spanish militias were disarmed and dissolved. The leaders of the "*asonada*" or mutiny – as it was then called and as it has come down in history – among them Álzaga himself, were arrested and sent to the territory now occupied by Carmen de Patagones. Soon after they were rescued by Elío and taken to Montevideo.

What was Buenos Aires like in 1810?

"At siesta time, only dogs and doctors can be seen in the streets of Buenos Aires." This is how a French traveler described the *Gran Aldea* (Big Village). It seems that siesta was the favorite *Porteño* pastime – not that there was much else to do. The main activities were farming and commerce, which could be run with little labor and the odd visit to the places of production and service.

"Going shopping," did not take up much time either. One only had to cross Victory Square and walk along the *Recova* (arcade), where could be found the stands of the "*bandoleros*" (brigands) – as the drapers were called in those days – facing a double row of clothes and novelty shops. This left ample time for a lively nightlife, which found its most elegant expression in the social gatherings. Wealthy families would entertain travelers, neighbors and friends so as to enjoy themselves and make business deals. These social gatherings lasted until well past midnight, and were enlivened with *empanadas*, music or poetry recitals, and discussions on politics and fashion. One of the most famous gatherings was hosted by the O'Gormans. Don Tomas O'Gorman and his wife Anita Perichón entertained the *crème* of society, including Viceroy Cisneros. A regular guest at these meetings, the Englishman John Parish Robertson, delighted in the good conversation of the *Porteño* ladies and in the precocity of the girls, who at age seven could dance the minuet to perfection. These gatherings were, in addition, the proper – and only – occasion for teenage girls to find a fiancé.

Once a week, the "healthiest portion of the neighborhood" as the *Cabildo* described its own members, that is to say, the *Porteño* landowners, would go to the theater for the opera nights or the plays of Lavardén. Since its inauguration by Viceroy Vértiz in 1783, the House of Comedies, also known as the *Teatro de la Ranchería,* became, until destroyed by fire in 1792, the center of all lyrical and dramatic activity in Buenos Aires. In 1810 the Provisional Coliseum of Comedies was reopened, giving new impulse to dramatic art.

Both rich and poor thronged to the bullfights. In 1791 Viceroy Arredondo inaugurated the small bullring of Montserrat – located at the present-day intersection of 9 de Julio and Belgrano Avenues – with a capacity for 2000. When the population of the city grew, it was demolished and a new bullring for 10,000 was built at the Retiro area. Don Juan Lavalle was once among its matadors.

During their brief stay, the English had introduced cricket, a game very similar to the "chueca," the favorite sport of the Pampa Indians, who were baffled to see the *huincas* (white men) practicing it. In addition, the city dwellers would often visit the suburbs for pato (played on horseback, somewhat like polo), cockfighting, tug-of-war and horse racing. Roulette and games of chance had their venue at the house of Martín Echarte, a colonial casino of sorts where chess was played and politics were discussed.

The cafés were the natural meeting point and the place where heated arguments took place in May 1810. The most famous ones were the Café de Marco, the Café de la Victoria, and the Catalans' and Martín's Café. They all had billiard tables and large patios.

There were not many options to eat out. At the French Cafeteria one could order a drink, but the Fonda of the Three Kings was the only restaurant of Buenos Aires. Its sole competitor was *monsieur* Ramón, an authentic French chef who prepared take-away meals. Many ladies would send their slaves to learn cooking with *monsieur* Ramón.

Eventually, the revolution would change many of these traditions, and slowly but steadily the Spanish influence would start to weaken, as the change in the habits and the manners of speech and dress of the *Porteños* would soon evince. The women would continue wearing the mantilla, the back comb and the fan, but progressively adopted the dress of French ladies. The men, on the other hand, would dress in the British style, top hat and all.

Muffled Noises

In 1809, appointed by the Central Council of Seville as regular viceroy in replacement of acting viceroy Liniers, there arrived in Buenos Aires Don Baltasar Hidalgo de Cisneros, called "the deaf" on account of his impaired hearing – a cannon shot had exploded too close to his ear during the Battle of Trafalgar.

In the Banda Oriental, Elío dissolved the Council of Montevideo and accepted the authority of the new viceroy, who reassembled the Spanish militias and granted a pardon to those who had conspired against Liniers.

Cisneros' greatest obstacle was the lack of economic resources. Commerce with Spain was almost entirely paralyzed, smuggling was on the rise and so was the pressure of leather exporters to trade directly with England. A young lawyer, Mariano Moreno, presented the Viceroy with a text called *The Representation of the Landowners,* where he explained the economic problems facing the region and suggested that Cisneros authorize free trade.

The viceroy, in view of the treaty signed by Britain's Secretary of State for Foreign Affairs George Canning, and the representative of the Central Council of Seville, Juan Ruiz de Apodaca, on January 14, 1809, opening the Spanish and colonial markets to British products, signed a free trade agreement on November 6 that same year, which for the most part benefited British ships and merchants.

The Insubordinates of Chuquisaca and La Paz

The problems of the Viceroy did not end with the signing of this treaty. Despite his hearing impediment, Lieutenant-General Cisneros[3] had to listen to the complaints coming

3 Don Baltasar Hidalgo de Cisneros y la Torre Ceijas y Jofré, Knight of the Order of Charles III, was a distinguished navy officer born in Cartagena in 1755. His performance as Vice-Admiral of the Spanish Armada in the Battle of Trafalgar gained him the recognition of the English and his promotion to Lieutenant-General of the Royal Spanish Armada.

from two cities in Upper Perú (present-day Bolivia.) On the 23rd of September 1808 there arrived in Chuquisaca the news about the imprisonment of the Spanish sovereigns and the creation of the Central and Supreme Council of Seville. The fire of controversy raged in intellectual and university circles, partly kindled by our fellow-countryman Bernardo de Monteagudo, who posited a question that would trigger the rebellion: "Should we follow Spain's fate or should we resist in America? The Indies are a personal dominion of the King of Spain; the King cannot rule, therefore, the Indies must rule themselves." This argument, known as the "syllogism of Chuquisaca" would be adopted by the revolutionaries who rushed out to the streets of this university city on the 25th of May 1809, and of La Paz on June 16. The people rebelled against the abuses of the local authorities and created councils as in Spain. The Council of La Paz was exclusively composed of Americans. This greatly worried the Spanish authorities, who did not want their example to be followed in the rest of the Americas.

One of the claims of the rebels, among which Monteagudo was to stand out, went as follows: "We have kept a silence akin to stupidity. It is high time we raised the banner of freedom in these unfortunate colonies, which have been acquired without any title whatsoever and maintained with the utmost injustice and tyranny."

Cisneros ordered a violent repression, resulting in hundreds of deaths and included cruel episodes of torture and quartering, regardless of sex or age.

At about the same time, the brilliant Monteagudo had written his *Dialogue between Atahualpa and Ferdinand VII* which, unsigned, circulated clandestinely throughout Upper Perú. In a passage of the *Dialogue*, Ferdinand would say to the Inca Atahualpa, "The most infamous among living men, that is to say, the ambitious Napoleon, deceitfully ripped me away from the sweet bosom of my land and kingdom, and accusing me of false and fictitious offenses, took me prisoner and transported me to the center of France." Atahualpa retorted, "I sympathize with your misfortunes, especially since I have suffered in the flesh the great pain of being unjustly deprived of scepter and crown."

The sentence passed against the captured rebels read: "For subversion against public order I hereby condemn you to the gallows, to which place you will be dragged tied to the tail of a packsaddle[4] beast and hanged by the executioner until you lose you life." Six hours after the execution the heads of Murillo and Sáenz will be cut off and placed on a tenterhook.[5] The first will be borne to the entrance of Upper Potosí, and the second one to the town of Croico, in order to satisfy offended majesty, vindicate the kingdom and be a lesson to all.[6]

As the news of the massacre perpetrated by the Spaniards Nieto, José Manuel de Goyeneche, Córdoba and Francisco de Paula Sanz in Chuquisaca spread, indignation grew among all the *criollos* of the viceroyalty, who couldn't help but notice the behavior of the new viceroy, who rewarded the insurgents if they were Spaniards like Álzaga and those involved in the "asonada" against Liniers, but massacred them if they were American rebels, such as the La Paz and Chuquisaca martyrs.

---

4 A saddle specifically designed for supporting the load on a pack animal.

5 A sharp hooked nail used especially for fastening cloth on a tenter.

6 In Bartolomé Mitre, *Historia de San Martín*, Buenos Aires, Eudeba, 1971.

To avoid the eventuality of similar episodes occurring, and "since the news has reached us that in these dominions a certain class of wicked and poisonous men is spreading, prone to subversive ideas that upset and disturb public order and established government," the viceroy decided to create a Tribunal of Political Surveillance, designed to prosecute "those who promote or hold the loathsome maxims of the French party or any other system opposed to the preservation of these dominions in union and dependence of the metropolis."[7]

The economic groups of Buenos Aires were at this point dividing into two factions: the monopolist merchants and the exporting farmers. On the one hand, Spanish merchants held on to the privilege of being the only ones allowed to introduce and sell foreign products shipped from Spain. These products were very costly because Spain first had to buy them from other countries such as England or France and then resell them in America. On the other hand, American farmers wanted to trade directly and freely with England and other countries which were the leading clients and purveyors of products in these regions. Spain had turned into an expensive, inefficient and therefore, unnecessary intermediary.

Only Rumors

It was clear that the fortune of these colonies was tied to the vicissitudes of the European war and French and British politics. The *Porteños* would anxiously wait for fresh news regarding the Spanish situation, which would arrive

7 Ricardo Levene, *Historia argentina*, Buenos Aires, Lojouane, 1937.

by ship, usually two or three months late. Consequently, on many occasions popular imagination filled in the lack of information with rumors and fantasies, thus enlivening the unexciting atmosphere of the viceroyalty. "Ferdinand has been murdered," "Napoleon has surrendered," "Ferdinand is back," "The Council of Seville has been removed," anything could be claimed – until the ships confirming or gainsaying these rumors arrived.

A Ship Fraught with News

On the 13th of May 1810 the English freight John Paris arrived at the port of Montevideo carrying shocking news: on January 13 Seville had fallen into Napoleon's hands. The Central Council, the last bastion of Spanish power still recognized by the Americans, had been dissolved and a phantasmagorical Council of Regency had been created to replace it, integrated by the bishop of Orense, don Pedro de Quevedo; State counselor don Francisco de Saavedra; General Francisco Javier Castaños; the Commander-In-Chief of the Navy, don Antonio Escaño; and the representative of the Viceroyalty of New Spain (Mexico), Miguel de Lardizábal y Uribe.

At first the viceroy tried to keep the news to himself, confiscating all the newspapers in the ship. But, according to Mario Belgrano,[8] one of them reached the hands of Belgrano and Castelli, who took it upon themselves to spread the news. From then onwards, Cisneros could not but share the information, which seriously questioned his legitimacy, in a proclamation issued on May 18 to calm things down.

---

8 Mario Belgrano, *Belgrano*, Buenos Aires, Instituto Nacional Belgraniano, 1999.

The proclamation, a true expression of wishful thinking, read: "The throne of the Catholic sovereigns will subsist in Spanish America, even if it succumbed in the Peninsula (...) The authorities shall take it upon themselves not to take any decision without the previous consent of all the representations of the capital, together with that of the provinces under it, until, in accordance with the rest of the viceroyalties, a representation of the sovereignty of Ferdinand VII be established."[9]

The last viceroy would never cease to regret not giving what little hearing was yet his to the advice of José María Romero, informer and functionary of the Royal Treasury, who had clearly understood that the days of the viceroyalty were numbered: "On the morning of the 12th of May 1810 I pointed out to Cisneros the need to deport immediately Saavedra, Chiclana, the Pasos, Castelli, the Vieytes, the Balcarces, the Castellis, the Larreas, Guido, Viamonte, Rodríguez Peña, Dr Moreno, presbyter Sáenz, canon Belgrano, Mercedarian friar Manuel Aparicio and Bethlemite friar Juan Salcedo."[10]

England All the Time

On the 21st of February 1810 the administrator of the Customs House informed the viceroy that since the opening of the ports four months earlier, 400,000 pesos had been collected by the said organization, "a figure never before collected by this Customs House in such a short period of time." This placed the Viceroy at a crossroads. On the one

---

9 Proclamation by Cisneros, of May 18, 1810.
10 Biblioteca de Mayo, vol. 5.

hand, thanks to the opening, the finances of the viceroyalty were recovering from the calamitous state Liniers had left them in, and the negative effect caused on them by the European situation and the subsequent disappearance of France, one of the Viceroyalty's leading clients. But, on the other hand, it was clear that free trade had a detrimental effect on the interests of the most influential Spaniards living in the city, such as Martín de Álzaga and José Martínez de Hoz, whose wealth depended on the restrictions imposed by monopolist commerce, which allowed them to carry out their most profitable activity: smuggling. Cisneros decided that his priority was to maintain the political support of the most conservative members of society and, probably "encouraged" by monopolist smugglers, he nullified the decree authorizing free commerce.

In response, the English formed a committee led by the influential merchant MacKinnon and asked Captain Doyle, chief of the British squadron at the River Plate, to negotiate with the viceroy appealing to England's position as Spain's ally in the struggle against Napoleon. At last, Cisneros gave in and granted the English four months to conclude their businesses. The term was due on the 19th of May 1810.

Strange Faces Will Come

Despite what we were taught in out tender years, the famous May Week was far from being the quiet round of street vendors – the self- and under-employed of their day – and posh ladies with hoop skirts. There were varied interests at stake, both foreign and national, and the passions, sometimes legitimately and in other cases motivated by financial interests, ran riot.

Contrary to the viceroy's illusion that everything would develop according to his will, on the same night of May 18 supporters of change gathered at the house of Rodríguez Peña, where they decided to demand Cisneros to call a *Cabildo Abierto* – an open city council – on May 18, with the purpose of considering the situation of the viceroyalty after the episodes in Spain. The group commissioned Juan José Castelli and Martín Rodríguez to arrange an appointment with Cisneros and demand the calling of the "open" *Cabildo*. They met on May 20. The viceroy attempted some speechifying and spoke of insolence and impertinence, but Rodríguez reminded him that it was not the right time to demonstrate his histrionic abilities and told him he had five minutes to make up his mind. Cisneros answered: "Since the people do not love me and the army has abandoned me, do as you please," which in simple terms meant that they had obtained the open *Cabildo* for May 22.

On the same night of the 20th the majority of the insurgents went to the theater to see Voltaire's *Rome Sauvé*, a tragedy about tyranny. Domínguez, the alderman of the police, forced actor Morante to call in sick and replaced the original playbill with the play *Misanthropy and Repentance* by the German poet Kotzebue. The theater was filled to capacity and rumors of censorship spread swiftly. Getting on their feet, the audience required the presence of Morante who, in view of the clamor, appeared on stage and performed the role of Cicero in the programmed play.

Morante, as if he had chosen the passage on purpose, began by saying: "Between ruling the world and being slaves, choose to be victors of the Earth." The *criollos* gave a round of applause and booed the *Audiencia* attorney Cape, who by not taking his hat off showed his disapproval of Morante's words, which ended, "Glory of Rome, wounded majesty, from your sepulcher the fatherland awakens." The ovation forced the few remaining Spaniards to leave the theater.

As usual, at nine o'clock in the morning of the 21st the *Cabildo*[11] assembled to discuss the affairs of the city. But a few minutes later, the members had to interrupt their activities. Victory Square had been taken by nearly 600 men, armed with pistols and knives. These groups of revolutionaries, led by Domingo French and Antonio Luis Beruti and known by the name of "Infernal Legion," were suspicious of the viceroy's pledge and demanded with shouts that the open *Cabildo* be declared. The *Cabildo* members conceded to the demands of the crowd. Syndic Leiva came out to the balcony and formally announced an open *Cabildo* for the following day. But the "infernal lads" would not calm down and demanded that the viceroy be suspended. The situation got tense and the Chief of the Regiment of the Patricians, Cornelio Saavedra, had to intercede, calming them down by guaranteeing that the military supported their demands.

The Great Debate

The members of the open *Cabildo* began to arrive since early morning. Out of the 450 guests, only 251 managed to get in: to this end, the lads of the Infernal Legion resorted,

11 The present-day building of the *Cabildo* is the result of a reconstruction carried out in 1940 by the architect Mario Buschiazzo, who respected the original plans but reduced the scale, eliminating six of its original arches. From the original *Cabildo* only the chapter room remains. It was in that room where the heated discussions of the open *Cabildo* of May 22 took place and where the First Junta or Council of Government was elected.

rather than to lace blue and white or of any other color historical tales have told us about, to the persuasive knives, blunderbusses and rifles they carried.

A witness refers how the lads of the Infernal Legion, strategically positioned at the corners of the *Cabildo*, and under the close supervision of their leaders French and Beruti, exercised the "right of admission": "As soon as the session began, a compact and organized group of six hundred people, mainly young men who had been gathering since early morning on the part of the Square adjoining the *Cabildo*, and who were led and guided by French and Beruti, began to offer insult to the viceroy and to demand the immediate calling of an open *Cabildo*. They all carry firearms and knives, because they are determined and intrepid men. They go by the name of Infernal Legion, which has reached every ear by now; and no one dares mess with them."

As well as applying direct pressure, the *chisperos* (a Spanish term for low-brow dandies and braggarts) used other methods to neutralize the influence of the royalists. The press of The Home for Foundlings, where the cards authorizing the *Cabildo* members had been printed, was run by Agustín Donado, one of French and Beruti's boys. It appears that Donado printed a few extra cards and distributed them among his comrades, who could then take up the place of several royalists and thus prevent them from getting in.

Those invited to the *Cabildo* can be grouped as follows:
- 94 merchants, neighbors and landowners;
- 93 civil servants and officers;
- 60 chiefs and officers of land and sea;
- 27 of the liberal professions;
- 25 priests and clergymen.

In a letter, the attorneys of the *Audiencia* complained about the scheme perpetrated by the *criollos*: "In the Council held on November 22 the absence of many distinguished European residents and paterfamilias was conspicuous, while the number of Patricians was much greater than usual, among them a large number of officers from that corps and the sons of families who still did not have the status of neighbors. Many conferences and subversive versions preceded the election."[12]

The situation reached boiling point with the start of the speeches about whether the viceroy should remain in office or not. Silence was broken by the most reactionary of the Spaniards, Bishop Lué y Riega. Héctor Ramos Mejía tells us that the bishop was "dressed with exceptional ecclesiastical luxury. He was wearing all the chains and crosses of his rank, rich gold scapulars, and four familiars standing behind him held the miter, a magnificent missal, the laws of the Indies and several other volumes destined to crush his adversaries." Buttressed by such impressive props, the head of the local church began by saying that as long as there was a Spaniard left in America, Americans should pledge allegiance to him.

"Not only should we let the viceroy be; even if in Spain there remained not one region unvanquished, the Spanish residents in America would take up the rule, which could only be exercised by the sons of the country were there not a single Spaniard left in the place. Were there a single alderman remaining in the Council of Seville, and were he to reach our shores, we should receive him as our sovereign."

12 Carlos Alberto Pueyrredón, *1810, La revolución de Mayo*, Buenos Aires, Peuser, 1953.

Francisco Saguí describes Bishop Lué in the following manner: "More than anyone else, the prelate drew attention to himself and his ultramontane views: he seems to believe he is still living in the days of Gregory VII or Boniface VIII, and has temporal jurisdiction, so oblivious is he of his holy ministry of peace; getting involved in all kinds of political events (...) Just envisage what the character of the said bishop of Buenos Aires Don Benito Lué y Riega was like, that he thought we did not even know how to write. When he saw the circulars he had commissioned the notary to print, in order to be sent to the priests of the diocese, the bishop made the following commentary to the notary, Don Gervasio Antonio de Posadas, 'The handwriting is good, and they are well-written. Has it been learnt here or have the circulars been written by a Spaniard?' Posadas looked at him while pointing in our direction and responded, 'Yes, sir, they have been written by a son of the country, and it is something we also teach.'"[13]

But the main course had not yet been served: the voice of the revolution had not spoken yet. There stood Juan José Castelli, the orator who could pierce stones with his critical, vibrating words. A report from the *Audiencia* describes him as "destined to mesmerize the attendants."[14]

Castelli, who like his friend Mariano Moreno had studied at the University of Chuquisaca, was steeped in the theory of popular sovereignty, a recurrent topic among the Spanish

13 Francisco Saguí, *Los últimos cuatro años de la dominación española en el antiguo Virreynato del Río de la Plata , desde 26 de Junio de 1806 hasta 25 de mayo de 1810. Memoria histórica familiar*, Buenos Aires, Imprenta Americana, 1874, Senado de la Nación, Biblioteca de Mayo, Buenos Aires, 1960, pp. 35 y 176.
14 Pueyrredón, *op. cit.*

jurists of the 16th and 17th centuries. These ideas were developed by authors such as Domingo de Soto, Juan de Mariana, Francisco Suárez, and Francisco de Vitoria, who proved that the right of the people to elect their own government was not conditioned by any other right, not even the divine right. American revolutionaries like Castelli expanded these concepts by combining them with the notions of "pact" and "social contract" developed by the theoreticians of the French and English revolutions, Thomas Hobbes, John Locke, and Jean-Jacques Rousseau. The ideas of the latter, interpreted by the voice and the pen of Mariano Moreno, would be crucial in the early moments of the revolution.

Castelli said on that memorable 22nd of May 1810: "It is my duty to give the bishop an answer, and if I am not allowed to, I will appeal to the people for my rights to be respected."

Castelli was interrupted by the bishop: "It amazes me that men born in a colony believe they have the right to meddle in the affairs that only those who were born in Spain are entitled to discuss, on account of the Conquest and the Bulls through which the Popes have declared the Indies to be the exclusive property of the Spaniards."

Getting slightly nervous, Castelli retorted: "No one has ever been able to accuse all the members of a nation, nor the individuals who have expressed their political opinions, of delinquency." And with wonderful irony he added: "If the right of conquest originates in the conquering country, it would only be fair that Spain prove the Bishop right by giving up resistance against the French and yielding, as under the same principles Americans are expected to submit to the towns of Pontevedra. Rule and reason must be applied equally to all. There are neither conquerors nor conquered here, just Spaniards. The Spaniards from Spain have lost their territory. The Spaniards from America are trying to keep theirs. Let the Spaniards from Spain deal with their own affairs as best they can; we Americans know what we want and where we are going. I therefore suggest that we take a vote: may the viceroy be replaced by a new authority, which will respond to the metropolis if the latter is saved from the French, or which will be independent if Spain is overpowered."

Visibly upset, the representative of the most conservative Spaniards, Attorney Manuel Genaro Villota, said that "the people of Buenos Aires do not have the right to decide on the legitimacy of the Government of the Regency by themselves, but together with the rest of the national representatives; and even less so to chose, by themselves, a sovereign government, as this would be tantamount to breaking up the unity of the Nation and establishing within it as many sovereignties as peoples there are."

Juan José Paso cut him short, arguing as follows: "Attorney Villota is right when he says that the general will of the remaining peoples of the viceroyalty has to be consulted; but the perils which this capital is currently exposed to must also be taken into consideration. Buenos Aires must take urgent measures to protect itself from the dangers resulting from the power of France and the sad state the Peninsula is in. To further this end, one of the first steps should be the creation of a provisional Council to govern in Ferdinand's name, and it in turn should proceed to invite the remaining peoples of the viceroyalty to participate in the creation of a permanent government by sending their representatives."

The debate that took place on the 22nd was very heated and kindled passions on both sides. Colonel Francisco Orduña, supporter of the viceroy, would recall in shock that while he spoke he was treated like a madman for not sharing revolutionary ideas, and at the same time, "those who did not vote against the boss (Cisneros) were spat at, mocked, insulted and booed."

In the meantime, Manuel Belgrano, positioned on one of the windows of the *Cabildo*, had agreed with the *chisperos* on a system of signals. If things got rough, he was to wave a white handkerchief to the lads, who would promptly break into the chapter room. In the end it wasn't necessary, as almost all the participants voted for the deposition of the viceroy, although they did not reach an agreement as to who should replace him, and how. Castelli suggested that the people elected a government council through vote. The leader of the Patricians, Cornelio Saavedra, proposed that the *Cabildo* itself should elect the new government, and in the end his argument won the day: the viceroy would be deposed but the conservative redoubt that had formed at the *Cabildo* would designate a Council of Government.

On the morning of the 23rd, the *Cabildo* reassembled in order to count the previous day's votes and then issued the following document: "After careful counting of the votes it is decided that His Excellency the Viceroy must hand over command which will fall provisionally on the most excellent *Cabildo* until a Council is created by the most excellent *Cabildo*, in the manner it sees fittest."

As was to be expected, official receiver Leiva and the conservative members of the *Cabildo*, who supported the Viceroy, came up with a stratagem: they designated a Council presided by Cisneros, thus making mockery of the will of the people. This caused the immediate reaction of the militias.

Colonel Martín Rodríguez pointed out that the scheme perpetrated by the *Cabildo* was "treason against the people, who were being treated as imbeciles." Rodríguez warned them that he neither could nor would keep his troops at bay. Leiva tried to calm him down by claiming that Saavedra would play an important role in the new government. But Rodríguez insisted: "Were we to support this combination that keeps Cisneros in office, in a few hours we would have to open fire against our own people and our own soldiers would abandon us; everyone, without exception, calls for the removal of Cisneros."

The revolutionaries' idea was to use armed violence and put pressure on Saavedra to make him react.

Muffled Noises

In his memoirs, Tomás Guido recalls that "in face of this situation, Don Manuel Belgrano, Major of the Regiment of the Patricians, who in full uniform was listening to these discussions from the adjoining room, slouched on a sofa, almost prostrate because of the long hours of watch, on noticing his friends' indecision, suddenly jumped to his feet and, with his face flushed by the fire of generous blood, bolted into the room and, after casting a look around, placed his right hand on the cross of his sword and said: "I swear to my country and to my comrades that, if by tomorrow afternoon at three o'clock the viceroy has not resigned, as I am a gentleman, I will knock him down by the force of my arms."[15]

What follows are Cisneros' memories of his last hours in power: "That same night, when the first session of government was held, some of the aldermen informed me

15 Tomás Guido, "Reseña histórica de los sucesos de Mayo", en *Los sucesos de Mayo contados por sus autores*, prólogo de Ricardo Levene, Buenos Aires, El Ateneo, 1928.

that a part of the people disagreed with my receiving the command of the arms and demanded my total deposition, and that the danger of commotion still loomed ahead, so much so that in the headquarters of the regiment of the Patricians some officers and civilians were hollering shamelessly, and that is what they call the people, but it is plain to everyone's eyes that the general mass of the people, including all the civil servants and tribunes of this city were rejoiced, as if they had just been spared of some great danger, when they saw me in office again, and that contentment was manifested by the display of city lights and in the compliments that were paid to my person by all the corporations, magistrates and neighbors. I did not consent that military command be handed over, as requested, to the lieutenant-colonel of Urban Militias Cornelio Saavedra, and thus taken from the hands of a general who would have always preserved them and defended them with honor, and to whom His Excellency had entrusted them as his viceroy and general captain of these provinces; and rather than submit to such demands, I agreed with the aldermen to renouncing my post and allowing the *Cabildo* to govern."[16]

On the night of the 24th, a delegation led by Castelli and Saavedra, followed by a large escort, knocked on Cisneros' door with a not-so-friendly attitude and wrenched the resignation from him. The Council was dissolved and a new *Cabildo* was called for the following morning.

On the morning of the 25th, various groups of neighbors – with and without umbrellas, since, even though they

---

16 Baltasar Hidalgo Cisneros, "Informe dando cuenta al rey de España de las ocurrencias de su gobierno, Buenos Aires, 1810", en *Memorias de los virreyes del Río de la Plata*, Buenos Aires, Bajel, 1945.

existed, they were a luxury item[17] – congregated at the plaza before the *Cabildo*, actively supported by the militias led by French and Beruti. They expressed their opposition to the maneuver and demanded the definitive overthrow of the viceroy, and the creation of a new Council.

When everyone thought that the session was taking too long, Antonio Luis Beruti, the leader of the *chisperos*, broke into the room and said menacingly: "Gentlemen of the *Cabildo*: The time for toying around is past; and we are not to be made the laughing stock of your nonsense. If so far we have proceeded with caution, it has only been to avoid bloodshed and havoc. The people, on behalf of whom we speak, are in the headquarters, armed, and a large portion of the neighborhood is only waiting for us to send word. Would you like some proof? Ring the bell, or else we will give a call to arms, and you will see the face of the people, whose presence you seem to be missing. Yes or no! Quick, gentlemen, say it now, because we are not willing to suffer delays or deceits and, if we return with our arms in our hands, we cannot answer for the consequences."[18]

The members of the *Cabildo* took the threat very seriously and announced the creation of the First Council of Government presided by Cornelio Saavedra, with lawyers Mariano Moreno and Juan José Paso acting as secretaries. Six aldermen completed the list: Doctor Manuel Belgrano and his cousin Juan José Castelli; army officer Miguel de

17 The inventory of a Buenos Aires store in 1795 can be found in the General Archive of the Nation. Among the items listed are 27 rubber umbrellas costing 4 reales each.

18 "Palabras de Antonio Beruti ante el *Cabildo* del 25 de mayo de 1810", en Neptalí Carranza, *Oratoria argentina*, Buenos Aires, Sesé y Larrañaga Editores, 1905.

Azcuénaga; clergyman Manuel Alberti and the Spanish merchants Juan Larrea and Domingo Matheu.

Ignacio Núñez, contemporary to the events, observes that Saavedra's designation was not due "to the importance of his person but to how much he weighed in the regiment where, undoubtedly, he possessed an influence superior to the rest of the officers."

In his *Memoirs*, Saavedra recalls: "Cisneros himself persuaded me to accept, in order to please and placate the people. At last I gave in and was received as president and alderman of this most excellent Council (...) For political reasons, it was necessary to place the Council under the cloak of Ferdinand VII, in whose name it was created and under whose authority it issued orders and made decisions."[19]

Ferdinand's Funny Mask

The Council hurriedly declared that it would rule in the name of Ferdinand VII. The record that was signed on that day read: "In the name of the king, the viceroy has been deposed."

The text of the oath went as follows: "Do you swear to perform your duties loyally and to defend the unity of this part of America for our Sovereign Don Ferdinand VII and his legitimate successors, and to observe faithfully the laws of the Kingdom?" Thus a political move became apparent: the Council refused to be subordinated to the Spanish councils which had bestowed upon itselves the representation of Ferdinand.

19 Cornelio Saavedra, *Memoria autógrafa*, en Biblioteca de Mayo, vol. II, pp. 1050-1051, 1966.

In his *Memoirs*, Alderman Matheu described the members of the Central Council and the Council of Regency as follows: "As we realized than in Spain the men who were supposed to save the country were plotting and scheming, we began to suspect everyone; especially when the members of the Central Council were kicked out on account of their slyness and trickery, and the few who managed to get together designated a Council of Regency without the participation of the remaining provinces and began to offer employment all over the Americas, we decided not to recognize their authority. For, being the Americas part of the Monarchy, what right had three men, unknown to the majority of the free, to rule them from a rock?"

The so-called "Mask of Ferdinand" was, contrary to what many believe, a clear act of independence. In those days, no one in his right mind could think that Napoleon would be defeated and that Ferdinand would return to the Spanish throne and would recover his American colonies. Therefore, pledging allegiance to a phantom king – rather than to an existing Council of Regency – was quite a declaration of principles, which cleared the path for the will to independence, which British pressure prevented from being made explicit.

"Unquestionably, there were reasons," points out Argentine historian Tulio Halperin Donghi, "to conceal rather than exhibit a by now mature belief in independence: in addition to the vitality of the tradition of monarchic loyalty among the popular masses, there existed the international juncture, which made it highly advisable not to lose the benevolence of the English."[20]

20 Tulio Halperin Donghi, *Historia contemporánea de América Latina*, Madrid, Alianza, 1974.

The English had set their priorities on the European conflict and the war against Napoleon, so they needed to preserve what was left of Spanish power in the Peninsula to combat the French on every front. In this sense, their alliance with Spain prevented them from openly supporting the American revolutionaries, and although they had very good political and commercial relations with the Council, they disapproved of the formal declarations of independence that were being voiced all over Spanish America.

The *criollo* bourgeoisie supported the movement in order to take over the State apparatus, and thus secure and increase their rate of return. Domingo Matheu, one of the aldermen of the First Council, admits to this: "In hindsight, it can be said that what took place was not a revolution but a popular movement, the expression of social and domestic needs with the purpose of securing the public persona and, as far as foreign affairs were concerned, to preserve commerce or commercial subsistence, otherwise any transformation or reform could be called a revolution; the mistrust and selfishness of the those who wanted to be in control but had no title nor base to refer to were the cause of the turmoil, the struggle and the movements."

They Left Never to Return

Neither the Council of Regency nor the Spaniards residents of the ex-viceroyalty believed in the story of the "loyalty to our beloved captive king" and refused to accept the new situation.

The Spanish chief of the Naval Station in Montevideo, Captain José María Salazar, who did not recognize the authority of the First Council, wrote: "The revolution of Buenos Aires had been meditated upon for the past eight years, as Doctor Castelli has publicly confessed to the viceroy, had been attempted on many occasions and thwarted an equal number of times; it has been, rather than a popular movement, a military conspiracy. The leading agitators have been a handful of petty officers. Saavedra is a cunning fox, concealing a most fierce ambition behind his hypocrisy, and so are all the members of the Council, who are of the people the poorest and least distinguished. The most excellent *Cabildo*, the Royal *Audiencia* and Reverend Bishop (Lué) remain loyal to the King."[21]

On the night of the 25th of May 1810, former Viceroy Cisneros sent José Melchor Lavín to Córdoba with correspondence for Santiago de Liniers, where he asked him to be ready for a likely and necessary military intervention against the Council.

The members of the *Audiencia* – something like the Supreme Court of the colony, composed of a variable number of members – refused to pledge allegiance to the new authorities.

According to a document of the time, the attorney of the *Audiencia*, Don Antonio Caspe y Rodríguez, attended the ceremony "picking his teeth with a toothpick, a grossness intended to manifest how much he looked down on the Council. After being admonished, he swore amidst the angry shouts of the people, who were outraged at his attitude." It appears that the judges had agreed on their demeanour because, the documents adds, "the next day Judge José Manuel de Reyes repeated Caspe's operation, but lacking a toothpick, he used his fingernails instead."[22]

21 *Mayo documental*, vol. XII, Buenos Aires, Facultad de Filosofía y Letras, 1961.

22 Julio Lafont, *Historia de la Constitución Argentina*, Buenos Aires, El Ateneo, 1935.

A few days after the dental episode, the judge was informed, while at home, that the president of the Council had sent for him urgently. When he reported, Saavedra denied having called for him. Slightly frightened and no longer in the mood for tooth picking, he left the Fort, but as he walked by a place known as the "Four Corners", he was assaulted by five masked men, who left him badly wounded. The judges blamed the episode on the "band of trouble-makers that has been created in Buenos Aires" at the house of Rodríguez Peña where Castelli resided, also integrated by Chiclana, Moreno and Belgrano, and pointed their finger at Chiclana as the instigator of the incident. Investigations did not produce any concrete evidence, but the Council issued a decree on June 11, calling on the people to avoid similar episodes in the future.

However, it appears that the members of the *Audiencia* did not trust the goodness of the Council and on June 15 secretly pledged allegiance to the Council of Regency, sending circulars to every city in the hinterlands inviting them to disobey the new government. That same day, Bishop Lué informed the Council that he meant to take a tour of his diocese. The royalist agent's attitude raised suspicions and he was forbidden to visit the Cathedral and leave his home.

As spies were all about, Moreno got wind of their scheme and decided to go right into the meat of things, summoning all the conspirators to an urgent meeting at the Fort (present-day Government House or *Casa Rosada*). When the conspirators arrived, they were received by the stern looks of Juan José Castelli and Domingo Matheu who informed them that their lives were in danger and that they should embark immediately on the British vessel Dart, which was waiting for them to sail off. The Captain of the ship, Marcos Brigut, hired and paid for by Larrea, had orders not to land in any

American port and to disembark all the members of the *Audiencia* and Viceroy Cisneros himself on the Canary Islands.

Brigut fulfilled his command. Despite the pleas and attempted bribes through which his "select" passage tried to convince him to let them get off in Brazil, the human cargo was deposited in Las Palmas of Great Canary Island on the 4th of September 1810, after 65 exhausting days at sea, during which the fights among the deported were, according to the story the captain tells, "the worst of the journey."

Following the expulsion of the Spanish authorities, the Council appointed a new *Audiencia* entirely composed by *criollos* loyal to the revolution.

These episodes seemed to be the signal that Liniers and the unemployed ex-Spanish officials were waiting for to rebel in Córdoba, but the uprising was swiftly put down by patriot troops under the command of Francisco Ortiz de Ocampo. Liniers and his followers were taken prisoner. The Council of Buenos Aires ordered their execution but Ocampo excused himself, because he had fought at Liniers' side during the English invasions. The task was performed by Castelli, who had Liniers and his accomplices shot on the 26th of August 1810.

The First Council soon understood that it was necessary to carry the goals of the revolution to other cities, in addition to securing their survival, for it was clear that the Crown was not going to sit back and watch. Thus several military expeditions were organized and a subscription created to raise funds to finance the campaigns. Moreno set the example by donating six ounces in gold. Belgrano, Matheu and Larrea renounced to their salaries as aldermen. The periodical *La Gaceta* published the lists of donors. They were mainly poor people since "those who have got nothing, give everything for the revolution," as Castelli would put it.

"The slave María Eusebia Segovia, with her master's leave, has donated one peso and offers to cook for the troops. The mulatto Santos González, of ten years of age, has donated 4 reales. Juan Reynoso puts his entire properties and his person at the Council's disposal. The boy Pedro Agüero, age 9, has donated 2 pesos and, with permission, has offered his person for whatever service his tender years be fit for. The mulatto Julián José Agüero, age 5, has donated 1 peso. Anastasio Ramírez has donated 4 reales with words worthy of praise, especially as they were uttered by an eight-year old, who already is capable of showing the love and loyalty his fatherland deserves. Juan José Gómez has contributed with 1 peso and a pair of shoes for a soldier to wear, and has given his word to give 4 monthly reales for a period of four months."

Referring to these offerings, Moreno commented in the very same *Gaceta*: "It moves one to see how the people struggle to help the exchequer with the expenses of the expedition. The poorest classes of society were the first to bestow upon their country a part of their scarce fortunes; soon the wealthy will begin to make the contributions corresponding to their wealth and care, but although the bulk of a rich merchant's donation might move one to admiration, he shall not compete with the poor on the commendable merit of promptness of offer."[23]

When the independence campaigns began, many slaves filled in the patriotic ranks. Many of the so-called "Patrician" families would rather send their house slaves than their sons to war, and so it came to pass that there were many black soldiers

---

[23] Álvaro Yunque, *Breve historia de los argentinos*, Buenos Aires, Futuro, 1957.

in the revolutionary armies. These stood out not only because of their color, but for the courage and bravery manifested in their country's defense. This is one of the reasons why the blacks of Buenos Aires would practically disappear.

A few days after May 25, the parish priest of Soriano, in the Banda Oriental – still in the hands of the Spaniards – Presbyter Tomás Javier Gomensoro, made the following entry on the parish record of deaths: "On the 25th day of May there has expired in this province of the River Plate the tyrannical jurisdiction of the viceroys, the despotic rule of the Spanish Peninsula, and the outrageous influence of all the Spaniards. Thus the unbearable yoke of the most unjust and arbitrary authority has been shaken off, and the foundations for a glorious independence have been laid, which shall situate the brilliant Provinces of South America in the rank of the free nations, and shall give them a national representation next to the great and glorious empires of the globe."[24] A few days later, priest Gamensoro was removed from the parish.

According to Mariquita Sánchez de Thompson, who was getting ready to play the National Anthem, we were breaking free from the links of "the three chains that had fastened this great country to the metropolis: terror, ignorance and the Catholic religion. Ignorance was most thoroughly honored. We had absolutely no teachers; we had no books, except insignificant devotional books; we did have a commission from the Inquisition to go through all the books that arrived, despite the fact that they were coming from Spain, where the same kind of persecution existed."[25]

24 A. J. Pérez Amuchástegui (director), *Crónica histórica argentina*, Buenos Aires, Codex, 1968.

25 Mariquita Sánchez, *Recuerdos del Buenos Aires virreinal*, Buenos Aires, 1953.

The revolution was on the march. The question was which path it would follow.

Winds Announcing Tempests

During the colonial period, the Viceroyalty of the River Plate experienced unequal economic development: the regions of the centre and northwest were densely populated and their economy was related to the mines of Potosí, in Upper Perú. The Littoral, on its part, was sparsely populated, its main economic activity being commerce and contraband.

In addition, each region specialized in a certain line of products it would then exchange with those of other regions. The Cuyo area produced wine and spirits; Paraguay produced maté; Tucumán, mules and carts. Thus a truly interregional commercial circuit developed. At the same time, in each of these areas subsistence crops such as corn, vegetables and cereals were grown.

The political economy of the revolution, based in an opening of commerce conceived of as gradual and provisional but which in fact was brutal and permanent, caused irreparable damage to the hinterlands. Now it was impossible to revive the profitable mule traffic that had existed between the Littoral and Perú, or reestablish commerce with Upper Perú, essential to the provinces of the centre and the north.

An English merchant observed at the time: "For much of the leather we bought, we paid three and a half pennies per pound. Three months later, it was sold in Buenos Aires at five and a half pennies per pound; and perhaps six months later it was sold to the tanners in Liverpool and London at nine or ten pennies per pound. Supposing the profit on a piece of leather or another to be twenty shillings, the profit was ten times the price paid to the owner for the animal in his establishment. Undoubtedly, much of the steer, calf and stud leather thus sold and transported to England, returned by the same route in the form of boots and shoes."[26]

The administration of the Customs House gave Buenos Aires resources no other area could aspire to. The Customs House was the main source of income for the entire country, and a very important political weapon. The ruling classes of the capital decided which products were allowed to enter or leave the country, and could thus prevent any province from developing its own industry, farming or agriculture, just by blocking the entrance of a piece of machinery or product they thought might jeopardize the *porteño* economy. On the other hand, all the provinces contributed to increase the wealth and power of the city-port through the custom dues they paid.

When the May Revolution took place, the Viceroyalty of the River Plate was far from being a political unit, and even less so an economic one. The process that led to independence accentuated these differences, and thus a peculiar concept of nationality emerged, people feeling they belonged to a city and its surroundings rather than to any country. A person was from Tucumán, Jujuy or Corrientes, but the idea of an "Argentine identity," did not appear, except in the River Plate area, until several decades later.

At first, in the cities, the *criollo* elite was the main beneficiary of political emancipation: it was able to remove the Spaniards from the bureaucratic and commercial positions, to create republican independent governments and, in the case of those who had been born in the Viceroyalty, to fill government and political posts.

26 William Parish Robertson, *Cartas de Sudamérica*, Buenos Aires, Hyspamérica, 1985. *Letters on South America; comprising travels on the banks of the Paraná and Río de la Plata*, London, J. Murray, 1843.

Compared to the pre-Revolutionary period, however, the position of the urban elite was weakened, for a variety of reasons: the properties and prestige of the Spaniards, who had been a significant part of this elite, had disappeared, and more importantly, foreign merchants had arrived – above all, English – whose relevance grew as the Spaniards' decreased.

The collapse of a colonial system consisting of a metropolis exercising its power through the cities which constituted its political and administrative centres, brought about, after 1810, the emergence of a new power system based in the countryside, and effected a great shift of power from urban groups to landowners and caudillos. The revolution brought about an important change, as it put an end to a system where birth regulated social difference and where the urban elites monopolized wealth. In this way, the urban elites lost part of the material base on which their power had rested, and the power they lost went to the rural groups.

Regional differences became particularly noticeable in the economic field. Buenos Aires and the Littoral competed in the exportation of products such as dried meat and leather, and for the importation of all kinds of products. Free trade was functional and essential to both. Disagreements between these two regions arose around the control of the port and the Customs House, exercised by Buenos Aires. The so-called "inner provinces," on the other hand, lacked products they could export but had a precarious industry – textiles, sugar and wine – capable of supplying the home market, which was negatively affected by the importation of these same products. They thus called for protectionist regulations but, unfortunately, would not be able to join in their demands, as one of the consequences of Spanish colonization had been the prevalence of local loyalties and the preeminence of particular interests.

In spite of these differences – which would only increase and, eventually, lead to an endless civil war – when the war against Spain broke out, the patriotic armies were able to rely on the invaluable support of the people from the interior, who would provide men and provisions for the successive liberation campaigns.

The Execution of Santiago de Liniers, "Hero" of the Reconquest

To concede too much to the people is
tantamount to condescending, in private life,
to the whims of a child who, having asked for all,
throws a tantrum when he is not given the moon he has
seen reflected in a tub of water.

SANTIAGO DE LINIERS

Among the adjectives frequently leveled at those responsible for Liniers' execution is that of "Jacobin[1] terrorists;" and this without any mention of the circumstances: namely, the threats and dangers to the revolution, so ardently worshipped by those who question the decision of the Council to put a stop to the counter-revolution that would have killed our national independence in the cradle.

Those who are so eager to call Moreno, Castelli and French terrorists seem to forget that the same epithet should be levelled against those who murdered Túpac Amaru and his entire family, against the murderers and torturers of the revolutionaries of Chuquisaca and La Paz, and against all the murderers that would later spatter the pages of Argentine history with human blood. Even nowadays, many get squeamish about employing the word "terrorist" to refer

---

1 "Jacobins" was the name given to the members of the most radical party of the French Revolution. It was founded in 1789 as a Society of Friends of the Constitution. The club derived its popular name from the monastery of the Jacobins (Parisian name of Dominicans), where the members met.

to the State apparatus of the last dictatorship, which they euphemistically call "the last military government." Undoubtedly, it all depends on the "status" of the victims and that of the killers.

Burn Those Letters

On the 19th of May 1810, Viceroy Cisneros received a letter from Santiago de Liniers, who at the time was residing in Córdoba, informing him about the move for independence in Buenos Aires. In this way, Liniers was betraying the trust placed on him by some of the conspirators, who would not believe that the former viceroy had taken sides with the Spaniards: "I have received several warnings and letters reporting the existence of an organized plan of insurrection, the implementation of which is waiting on the arrival of bad news from the Peninsula. If on an earlier critical situation I told Your Excellency that there was nothing to fear from the people, today I tell you that the ideas of independence prevail, fostered by the rebels which have gone unpunished. My beloved Cisneros, the situation is serious; I would give my little finger to have an hour of conversation with you. You are surrounded by scoundrels, and some of the people you trust the most are deceiving you. Tell me, if we received unfortunate news from the Peninsula and popular turmoil broke out, where could you expect help from? From Perú, undoubtedly, but, what officers are there able to lead an army? Because of his ailments, Nieto is incapable of suffering the toils of war. I can only think of Goyeneche, whose influence, however, might not be equal to mine in the task of rallying the defenders of the rights of our beloved Ferdinand against the party of independence and anarchy."

These words were penned by Santiago de Liniers, who on the 28th of May 1802, in a petition submitted to Viceroy Don Joaquín del Pino, claimed to be as poor as a church mouse: "Since all the expectations I had regarding the use of gunboats have long vanished, and my considerable family prevents me from returning to Spain; and particularly because of the hardships and adversity I have suffered for my compliance with the orders of the Sovereign in relation to the ill-fated establishment that my brother, the Count of Liniers, came to plan in this capital. Under these circumstances, I will be forced to retire at an age when my services might still be of some help, unless Your Excellency deigned grant me some occupation in His Province that was of his Superior liking, confident that due to my prudence, activity and the love I have for my country I would perform my tasks in a manner that may fulfill the expectations and trust His Excellency would have placed on me."[2]

Liniers' position would change in due time, especially during his short period as viceroy. In his *Memoirs*, Domingo Matheu complains about the viceroy's arbitrary behavior: "I do not know who my monarch is. Liniers has become a legislator, he institutes rights, offers employment of all kinds, gives promotion to veteran troops, artillery and navy. I realize I am Liniers' vassal. As Customs Administrator we now have a cunning Frenchman, Liniers' godson, who has Potosí pay double duties and taxes that have already been paid. Contraband is carried out so shamelessly that even a five-year old child could give evidence. Their despotical

---

2 Archivo General de la Nación Argentina, División Colonia, Sección Gobierno, Marina de Guerra y Mercante, 1794-1803, sala IX, cajón I, anaquel 4, número 1.

behavior must be seen to be believed. In broad daylight they unload their cargo and transport it with an escort. If God does not put and end to this I do not know what will become of us."[3]

Manuel Moreno, on his part, does not spare invectives to describe Liniers' administration: "His vicious nature, his corruption and prodigality will never free his memory from the execration that public affairs have gained him. Not just dissipation, gambling and baseness degrade the private character of this man. He is now indulging in all kinds of disorders, in which so far these provinces had been untaught."[4]

Patriotic Fund, 1808-1809 Model

On the 23rd of August 1808, José Manuel de Goyeneche, the emissary of the Central Council of Seville, arrived in Buenos Aires, demanding obedience and capital to finance the resistance against Napoleon. Collections were started, in order to raise funds to be sent to "our motherland," and soon donations from all over the viceroyalty began to arrive.

On the 20th of April 1809 the syndic of Buenos Aires, Don Matías de Cires, wrote to the King of Spain: "As soon as the news about the critical situation of the Peninsula arrived, there arose among the people the desire to excel and surpass others in the nature and amount of the donations."

The residents of Buenos Aires competed to see who donated more money to help expel the French from the Peninsula. The *Cabildo* opened a subscription list and very

---

3 Domingo Matheu, *Memorias*, tomo II, Buenos Aires, Biblioteca de Mayo, 1966.

4 Manuel Moreno, *Vida y memorias del Dr. Mariano Moreno*, Buenos Aires, Eudeba, 1972.

soon "a large sum was collected, far superior to what the fortunes of the contributors might have led to expect."

But while the "patriotic fund" grew in Buenos Aires, Viceroy Liniers seemed in no hurry to send it to Spain. Liniers had considerably increased the number of employees working for the administration of the Viceroyalty, designating friends and relatives in the main posts. And arguing the possibility of a third English invasion, he kept a very large number of troops and remarkably increased the officer's wages.

In those days, many there were who lived off public funds, and they, of course, became Liniers' most fervid supporters against the attacks of his old enemy, Martín de Álzaga.

A letter from the Royal Exchequer addressed to the viceroy reminds him of the debt contracted with this organization – advance payments, as they would be called today: "For this reason, and according to the report of the General Secretaries of the Royal Treasury dated the 6th of this month, the supplements made by Your Excellency from the 23rd of May 1807 to the 16th of the current month amount to 1,109,497 pesos and two reales and the repayments made by the Treasury, to 600,777. Accordance to the calculations of which I hereby supply a copy to Your Excellency, there remain 508,720 pesos and two reales to be paid to the Royal Exchequer."

In order to pay off his debt, and setting a precedent for Argentine civil servants to come, Liniers without much ado made use of the funds that the population had donated and that should have been shipped to Spain.

Syndic Matías de Cires denounced the viceroy in these terms: "Soon after a regular fund had been raised, the creatures and accomplices of the viceroy began to expand the scope of their affairs. The total annihilation of the Royal

Exchequer, which they themselves had caused; the low esteem in which the merchants held the viceroy on account of the deceit and bad faith he had observed in earlier loans made in the name of His Majesty; the prevailing feeling among honorable men regarding the dilapidation of the public funds; all this had led the viceroy to trample over the most sacred considerations for the sake of money, and he had no qualms about grabbing the funds raised by the subscription, borrowing them from the *Cabildo*, as can be gathered from Documents 1, 2 and 3 attached herewith, and used them to pay unnecessary wages and expenses to the total annihilation of the Royal Exchequer."

On hearing about the actions of the viceroy, the attitude of the people towards fund-raising changed drastically. "The indignation and outrage provoked by such resolution," adds Cires "beggar description, its most harmful consequence being that the people have become suspicious and have stopped sending donations, for they have evidence that these contributions will not be shipped to the Metropolis, but will be spent in a manner that everyone deplores. Who might be willing to surrender his money if, disdaining the holy cause, it shall be distributed among prisoners and vagabonds, whom the Viceroy has rewarded with the prizes and honors of the first military posts?"

In those days as well, justice was enmeshed in a network of corruption: "This is no vain fear and might not be attributed to the viceroy's difficulties in effecting his will: it has been almost a year since the viceroy made use of the funds, the dire needs of the Peninsula have grown, numberless vessels have gone back and forth, but still the money from the donations has not been returned. This behavior justifies the fear that any other donation made might follow the same path, for which reason the people, the merchants, and the *Cabildo* have decided to withhold their offers until their wish to aid the Metropolis can be fulfilled, to succor which they were all willing to make the greatest sacrifice. There exist in this city large sums collected by some corporations to alleviate the expenses of the present war, but donors are forced to hide them, finding all kinds of obstacles to secretly ship them in a country where the government does not respect public funds and where inviolability of correspondence has been made a joke of, for they intercept and open letters on the merest suspicion and for the weakest of motives."[5]

On the 12th of December 1808, however, Viceroy Liniers reverted to his old ways, as can be gathered from a letter bearing his signature. Santiago de Liniers says: "Being the General Treasury in the need of funds to pay the troops, Your Excellency shall immediately transfer to it the product of the patriotic contributions made during the past month. May God keep Your Excellency in good health."[6]

Seven days later, on the 23rd of December 1808, Viceroy Liniers thought it meet to return to the *Cabildo* part of the funds he had borrowed earlier on. These funds, however, did not belong to the *Cabildo*, but had been lent by city residents willing to favour the *Cabildo* and the government with their help. But for the moneylenders had been for two months in great worry and requested a reimbursement of

5 Facultad de Filosofía y Letras, UBA, Sección de Historia, *Documentos relativos a los antecedentes de la independencia de la República Argentina*, Buenos Aires, 1912.

6 Archivo General de la Nación Argentina, División Colonia, Sección Gobierno, sala VI, cuerpo XIX, anaquel 11, número 4.

their money. In a letter addressed to the *Cabildo*, the viceroy did his best to calm them down: "Ever since Your Excellency informed me in the letter dated October 24th about the clamors with which I am told they request a reimbursement of the quantities that under guarantee of Your Excellency some individuals of this city have provided the Royal Exchequer with, I have requested from the General Treasury the most effective means to raise funds in order to make a reimbursement; but since new expenses of an urgent nature have to be met on a daily basis, as Your Excellency very well knows, it is not possible to resort to them immediately and proceed to effect the reimbursement that Your Honor justly claims."

Since the loans made by the *Cabildo* were not enough for the hero of the Reconquest, he laid hands on the alms destined to Santos Lugares and borrowed money from the bishop. Directly or indirectly, everyone in the city had helped pay the excessive expenses of Liniers.

As a way to reduce his debt, Liniers authorized the *Cabildo* to collect money from the neighbors who owed the Customs House. "Considering the large sums that the commerce and neighborhood of this Capital owe His Majesty in the Royal Customs House, surpassing 500,000 pesos, the collection of which has not been effected in its entirety on account of the Law not being applied strictly enough, as in privileged debts, I have resolved that through the Administrator of the Customs House bills of exchange be drawn on them in favor of His Majesty, who without the rigors of the Law might be able to collect his money from them, and pay off the moneylenders under their guarantee."

*Ñoquis** à la Liniers

A report issued by the *Cabildo* of Buenos Aires dated January 16, 1809 informs that the said institution cannot continue sustaining a dual system of "civil servants: some, practicing; others on leave, emigrated, far away from their posts, or who simply do not come to work or who have never been seen at their post since their designation" because "their wages take up a large portion of the public funds. The Royal Treasury cannot afford to pay these without neglecting its main object, our defense, the consequences of which we are facing. Certainly they are creditors, but there are no funds to pay them. If their wages were reduced to a small pension for food, we would avoid present hardships."

The Creator of Bonds

A record at the General Archive of the Nation dated December 7, 1808 states that Santiago de Liniers was the creator of subcurrencies in the River Plate. They were "royal promissory notes," that is to say, inconvertible currency, unbacked paper money.

"Don Justo José Núñez, lawyer of this *Real Audiencia Pretorial*, public and Town Hall notary. I hereby certify that on the fifth day of the current month, by order of the *Alcalde de primer voto* Don Martín de Álzaga, we visited the silversmith's belonging to Juan de Dios Rivera to inquire if in point of fact he had been commissioned by the Superior

---

* **Translator's note:** ñoqui: Argentine spelling of the Italian *gnocchi*, a small potato dumpling. The word is also used to refer to state employees who only show up on the 29th, the day of the month when employees get paid and *gnocci* are traditionally consumed.

Government to work on a plate to print Royal Promissory Notes or Paper Currency, and found him engraving the Royal Arms, following other engravings he had already made at the angles, on a bronze sheet of size slightly larger than a paper quarto; and the said Juan de Dios told the procurer that he was following orders of the Superiority on the job, which he had been commissioned to finish as soon as possible, as he had been told that the said plate would be used to print royal promissory notes, and that he therefore worked relentlessly, and that in a few days he would have finished it. And by virtue of the order of the Honorable *Cabildo*, I hereby seal and sign the above on the 7th day of December 1808."[7]

Spanish laws prohibited the issue of "royal promissory notes" – quite common in Spain – in the colonies, as in this way the central authorities would lose control of the income of their dominions to the hands of local authorities, whom they had always mistrusted.

The syndic advised the *Cabildo* to do everything in its power to stop the issue and circulation of these patriotic notes.

"Honorable *Cabildo*: The syndic of this capital informs Your Honor that the news has reached him that by order of the Supreme Government a certain number of plates or moulds have been engraved with the inscription 'Patriotic Notes,' and that in the past few days a considerable number of these have been printed.

"What we have said so far proves that the creation of promissory notes is detrimental to the general welfare of these Provinces; that they would not be necessary if the

---

7 Archivo General de la Nación Argentina, División Colonia, Sección Gobierno, sala VI, cuerpo XIX, anaquel 11, número 4.

reforms suggested by the syndic in the abovementioned Representation were adopted and that finally, they are abusive since the Government lacks the authority to issue them. And what else is necessary to draw the attention of His Excellency against a practice which, without being profitable, might convulse the public peace? The sacrifices made by this Honorable Body in the preservation of the Continent despite so many public and secret efforts to separate it from the benevolent rule of our august Sovereigns only strengthen the need for further action in such a critical junction as this. Thus the syndic hopes that Your Excellency shall take measures, while account of everything that has transpired is given to the Supreme Authority of the Peninsula represented by the Royal person of Ferdinand VII, Our Beloved Monarch, and to the Gracious Town Halls of the Viceroyalty. Buenos Aires, December 27, 1808. Esteban Villanueva."[8]

A few days after the writing of this report, the house of Don Esteban Villanueva was ransacked by men in the viceroy's circle who, like in a pirates' movie, dug out a treasure that had been hidden in the "toilet" since Beresford's days, and took most of it away. Thus Villanueva lost some 240,000 pesos.

An Englishman residing in Montevideo wrote to Secretary George Canning in these terms: "Liniers, who has always been an avid and incorrigible gambler, devoid both of talent and honor, was known in Spain before I departed as a Frenchman, both by his principles and his origin. However, as far as the entrance of ships is concerned, he

---

8 Archivo General de la Nación Argentina, División Colonia, Sección Gobierno, sala VI, cuerpo XIX, anaquel 11, número 4.

has proven himself to be utterly alert, because custom duties go to the public treasure, which are now paid, as bribes for the privilege of smuggling, to a French lady, who lives with him and who regulates the entrance of the shipments that have already paid their royal duties in Montevideo, so as not to hamper their particular entrances, acquired by the intercession of his mistress."[9]

In a letter addressed to the Council of Seville dated May 6, 1809, Liniers tried to defend himself of the accusations in a manner that reminds one of Atahualpa Yupanqui's famous phrase "Your clarifying has left me in the dark":

"After peace had been declared with England, the English residing in Rio de Janeiro who had their stores overstocked with textile goods naturally tried to find an outlet for them (...) since I lack the troops to keep them at bay and, even if I did, the close relations between the two nations and the great sacrifices that the British Nation is making for our cause would force me to observe the most circumspect behavior with these allies, especially under such critical circumstances; all of these reasons have led me to somehow make the best of the situation, authorizing the entrance of textile goods to dress the troops, and of articles for the Navy Arsenals and Artillery Depots, all of which we were sorely lacking. I have granted these permits only to those who have unmistakably collaborated in the defense of the capital, and who shall nonetheless pay their dues. Thus I intend to benefit the treasury, being of necessity obliged to resort to this procedure, and for the political reasons mentioned above so as not to display against the English all the resources of violence I could deploy."

9 Vicente Sierra, *Historia de la Argentina*, Buenos Aires, UDEL, 1957.

In fact, large-scale traffic with the British had begun in 1808. John Street[10] points out that Luis Liniers, son of the viceroy, kept from his sailboat an alert eye on the traffic of His majesty's vessels into the River Plate, so that they might bypass the port of Montevideo which was controlled by the jealous governor Elío, who had his own interests and who wrote to Captain Sidney Smith in oedipal terms about "the pleasure of receiving at this seat any individual from that Great Nation which does so much good to our heroic Mother." So as to make things even clearer, Elío hosted a banquet for all British officers and merchants on occasion of His Most Gracious British Majesty's birthday, on the 5th of June 1809.

American merchant Guillermo Pío White had been Beresford's right hand during the first invasion. Confined to the frontier guards, he managed to make his escape and returned to Buenos Aires as an officer in Whitelocke's army. The government of Montevideo accused him of smuggling and had him imprisoned. Liniers rescued him, together with the records of the case, of which no evidence would be left, and when White arrived at the pier, the luxurious carriage of the "First Lady", Anita Perichón, was there to pick him up.

The Reconquest

As we said in the chapter about the May Revolution, on the night of May 25 former Viceroy Cisneros sent to Córdoba a 17-year-old boy, José Melchor Lavín, carrying letters addressed to Liniers with orders to defy the Council. The messenger reached his destination on June 30 and

10 John Street, *Gran Bretaña y la Independencia del Río de la Plata*, Buenos Aires, Paidós, 1967.

stayed at the house of Dean Funes, his former teacher at the School of Montserrat. In this way, Funes was the first to learn about the events in Buenos Aires and about the plans for resistance devised by the two former viceroys.

Funes took Lavín to the house of Bishop Orellana, and pretended to join the conspirators to gather information about their plans and report it to the Council of Buenos Aires. They were joined at the bishop's house by Santiago de Liniers and the governor of Córdoba, Gutiérrez de la Concha.

Several military proposals were made. The governor suggested gathering troops in Córdoba and then marching on Buenos Aires. Liniers, on his part, suggested that they should march north, wait for reinforcements from the troops of the Viceroyalty of Perú so as to become stronger and only then attack the capital. The dean did everything in his power to keep the conspirators in Córdoba, within the grasp of Buenos Aires. Liniers was convinced and thus the counter-revolution was set in motion. The plotters were supported by Spanish troops from Upper Perú, and money coming from Lima.

Both Belgrano and Saavedra wrote to Liniers urging him to lay down his arms, but the former viceroy answered with insults and threats.

On finding out about the deportation of Viceroy Cisneros and the judges, Liniers decided to start operations, writing about his intentions to Francisco de Paula Sanz in a letter partly written with "invisible ink": "I now find myself in possession of seven hundred armed men, three hundred with firearms, an equal number carrying spears and one hundred artillerymen, and I shall have thirteen cannons. In the improbable event of the departure of the expedition from Buenos Aires, I plan to advance on them, sending guerrilla groups and also lasso men ahead, with balls loaded with grenades of my own invention that explode as stray shots, and several kinds of fireworks, with the purpose of burning the carts and scattering the droves of oxen and horses; as soon as they approach I intend to retreat following the Potosí road up to Jujuy, in the hope that by that time the forces that Your Excellency might spare will have already joined me, and thus we will be on the offensive again. To avoid any unnecessary risks, the first half of the letter is written in ink, but the most secret fragments have been written with invisible ink of which only my friend and I have the secret."

According to a document of the time, the "noble" Liniers and Gutiérrez de la Concha tried to bribe the deserter José Santos González to burn the fields through which the patriotic army was expected to pass, and offered him 50,000 pesos if he managed to blow up the troops: "And on realizing the advantages of the project, they agreed that 8000 gold pesos would be granted to him, and promised to pay him 50,000 extra when the total destruction or incapacitation to operate offensively of the said troops was verified."[11]

Just in case, the counter-revolutionary governor of Córdoba, Gutiérrez de la Concha, withdrew from the royal coffer all the available money, which amounted to 76,761 pesos, as was registered in the records of the local treasury, where one may read about one of the forerunners in the art of discretionally using public funds: "Withdrawal for reserved war expenses."[12]

11 Carranza, "La ejecución de Liniers", *Revista Nacional*, tomo 24, capítulo XLI.
12 Archivo General de la Nación, *Archivo del gobierno de Buenos Aires*, tomo 23, capítulos LXXIX y XC.

Communication between Liniers and the reactionaries from the northern territories was cut – Chiclana tells us – thanks to Lieutenant Martín Güemes, who intercepted anyone coming from up north. In this way, he managed to capture a man called Silvestre Calancha, and get hold of the correspondence he was carrying.

The commander of the naval station of Montevideo, José María Salazar, testifies that "Mr Liniers had sent letters and proclamations to the members of the Council including all kinds of infamies and claiming that he would punish their wickedness, for in addition to the great damage they were causing, they were very ungrateful, as the Nation, Europe and the World would say that it was under his instigation that they had attempted to devastate the country."

Dean Funes managed to find out that Luis Liniers, the son of the leader of the conspiracy, had left for Montevideo to gain the support of Governor Elío. He informed the Council through his brother Ambrosio, and Luis was subsequently captured carrying valuable information in his saddlebag.

The gravity of the situation obliged the Council to send troops under the command of Ortiz de Campo and Hipólito Vieytes with orders to put down the counter-revolution and execute its leaders. Soon after arriving in Córdoba and capturing the insurgents, Vieytes, moved by the pleas of the Funes to spare the lives of the rebels, on August 10, 1810 addressed the Council in the following terms: "Your Excellency is aware that we need to win over the affection of these oppressed fellow countrymen, showing them that, contrary to all the previous sanguinary despots who would rejoice in shedding their blood, all the sweetest measures are implemented to make known the advantages of the soft and wise rule that they unanimously find in Your Excellency."

Ocampo and Vieytes did all they could to delay the execution of the insurgents, and attempted to send them to Buenos Aires. Moreno, outraged at the situation, rejected the delay and wrote a letter to Feliciano Chiclana, acting governor of Salta, dated August 17, 1810 saying: "They captured the wicked men, but out of respect for their stripes and not giving a shit about the very the precise orders of the Council, they are sending them to this city. You cannot even suspect the position they have put us in. How are we to expect great deeds from men who back away from an execution? (…) Make sure the *criollos* find out about this. Let there be no rulers except the native sons, let them learn about the advantages of this rule."[13]

Moreno made the drastic decision of removing the irresolute leaders and replacing them with Castelli, Balcarce, and French, with orders to wipe out the uprising once and for all.

The order of the Council, signed by the president, the secretaries and all the aldermen except Alberti, who being a priest excused himself, read: "The Council orders the execution Don Santiago de Liniers, Don Juan Gutiérrez de la Concha, the bishop of Córdoba, Dr Victorino Rodríguez, Colonel Allende, and the royal official Joaquín Moreno. Immediately after each or all of them are captured, this resolution will be carried out without any delay that might make room for pleas. This punishment shall be the cornerstone of the stability of the new system."

"You go," said Moreno to Castelli, "and I hope you will not fall prey to the same weakness as your general. If this

13 Biblioteca de Mayo, tomo XVIII, Buenos Aires, Senado de la Nación, 1966.

decision were not carried out, Alderman Larrea, who I believe is not lacking in determination, will go; finally, I shall go myself if it were necessary."

But it wasn't necessary. Castelli, whom Viceroy Cisneros called derisively "of men the most interested in novelty," strictly complied with the orders of the Council, and Liniers and his accomplices, with the sole exception of Bishop Orellana, whose life was spared, faced the firing squad at Cabeza de Tigre, on the 26th of August 1810. Domingo French was in charge of finishing Liniers.[14]

In a letter, Nicolás Rodríguez Peña tells his friend Vicente López: "Castelli was neither fierce nor cruel. Castelli acted in that way because we had all committed ourselves to acting that way, we had sworn to act that way, and men of our caliber could not back out. Were we cruel? Some charge indeed! We saved the country the way we thought we should save it. Were there other means? There might have been: we neither saw them nor believed that by other means we would have been able to do what we did." And anticipating the critics, he challenged them thus: "You may blame us and enjoy the results, we will be the executioners, you will be free men."[15]

Matheu says in his *Memoirs*: "The members of the Council had committed themselves to eliminating anyone who opposed them, and had they not acted that way, they would already be six feet under."

A resolution of the Council written by Moreno established that the books belonging to the conspirators were to increase

---

14 Alberti, for his being a priest, was the only member of the Council that did not sign the decree of execution of Liniers and the rest of the insurgents.

15 Letter from Nicolás Rodríguez Peña to Vicente Fidel López.

the patrimony of the Public Library: "Without affecting the embargo placed on the properties of the conspirators of Córdoba and their main accomplices, aimed at recovering the amount taken from the Royal Exchequer to finance their rebellion, Your Honor will see to it that all the books in the library of Bishop Orellana, and all the books belonging to the other criminals, should be crated and delivered to the public service."[16]

On September 9 Moreno wrote about the execution in *La Gaceta*. He began by claiming that the conspirators were delinquents whose "existence we have not been able to preserve." As in every piece that he wrote, he made use of the circumstances to give his opinion on the political situation, thus becoming the main propagandist of the revolution. He stressed the double standard by which the absolutists judged the incidents in Spain and those in America: "Since we are as free as the people of the Península, we must consider we have the same rights as they; and if they were able to create councils, and remove their magistrates from the capitals of Spain, an equal authority cannot be denied to the capitals of America."

Moreno continued by exposing the real political goals of the conspirators: "It must be noticed that the leaders of Córdoba did not reproach us our excesses, a reformulation of which might have led to conciliation; they were appalled at any minor deviation from the old system. They wanted to exterminate the Council, regardless of how fair the motives for its creation might have been, and they had sworn to the ruin of the people, if they persisted in the effort of

---

16 Mariano Moreno, *Escritos Políticos*, Buenos Aires, La Cultura Argentina, 1915.

standing for their rights and looking for a guide other than the blind impulses of their corrupt leaders. Such effort (clearly manifested in their correspondence) dooms America to perennial slavery, and so we appeal to the judgement of noble souls, that they might justly appraise the crime of six men who wanted to suffocate with armed force the most sacred rights and the most positive happiness of the numberless inhabitants of this vast continent.

"In the face of such considerations, and extolling the rage of justice, we have ordered the sacrifice of these victims for the health of so many millions of innocents. Only fear of death may set the example for their accomplices. The commendable qualities, employment and services which should have never authorized their wicked projects, have not gained them an immunity that would have made the rest more insolent. Terror will dog those who persist in following their plans, and ever escorted by the horror of their crimes and the fear that possesses criminals, they will abandon the reckless schemes they have connived."

Perhaps, when proposing the sentence, Moreno remembered the words of Liniers in his letter to Cisneros: "Our wisest legislators, on the crime of treason, spare magistrates the formalities attending upon the death penalty applied to traitors."

Castelli and Monteagudo:
Túpac Amaru's Avengers

*Let us stop preaching maxims, let us preach
with examples: let our feelings unite us in a single heart,
and we will see the tyrants cry like children
and tremble like criminals whom a terrible
judge has condemned to death.*

BERNARDO DE MONTEAGUDO
La Gaceta de Buenos Aires, February 28, 1812

The May Revolution had to make its way. No one really believed in "the mask of Ferdinand VII," and it was threatened by the royalists on every front. In the north, Lima and the capitals of Upper Perú, the leading political and military centers, were getting ready to avenge the execution of Liniers and his accomplices, and to put down the last stronghold of anti-Hispanic resistance on this part of the continent.

The Sate Secretary and Secretary of War of the Revolution, Mariano Moreno, had to make a decision that, he knew, would determine the final defeat or triumph of the revolution, and his own life as well – to secure the Revolution through the force of arms, he had to dispense with his two main political allies: Juan José Castelli and Manuel Belgrano.

Manuel Belgrano, of all the Revolution's cadres the most lucid and better prepared to govern, was sent on an impossible mission to Paraguay. This was, unquestionably, one of Mariano Moreno's greatest tactical mistakes, celebrated nonetheless by Saavedra's supporters, for whom it paved the way to get rid of a dangerous enemy. For men like Moreno and Castelli, Upper Perú had a double meaning. On the one hand, it represented the most serious threat to the survival of the revolution. But, on the other hand, it was the land where they had become intellectuals. It was in the classrooms and libraries of Chuquisaca that Mariano and Juan José first came into contact with the works of Rousseau, and it was in the streets and the mines of Potosí where they first came into contact with human exploitation at its highest and most perverse degree, as was admitted by the viceroy, the Count of Lemus, one of the men responsible for the massacre: "The stones and minerals of Potosí are steeped in Indian blood and if the money obtained from them could be squeezed, more blood than silver would ooze out."[1] It was there that they had also learnt about an epic silenced by the official history of the Viceroyalty: Túpac Amaru's great rebellion. The Indians told them of the all-too-brief period when they had enjoyed dignity and freedom, and of how they cherished these memories as they would a treasure or an heirloom that should pass from father to son, so that no one would ever forget what the "despots" wished had never occurred.

After Castelli put down the Córdoba insurrection, Moreno had no doubts about the man, realizing he would not hesitate to defend libertarian ideals, so it was only natural that, when the time to make justice in Upper Perú arrived, he would trust him with the mission.

The departure of his comrades left Moreno in dangerous isolation, a circumstance his enemies swiftly turned

---

1 El Conde de Lemus a Su Majestad, "contrarréplica a Victorián de Villava", en Ricardo Levene, *Ensayo histórico sobre la Revolución de Mayo y Mariano Moreno*, Appendix, Buenos Aires, El Ateneo, 1961.

to their advantage. They would eventually overthrow him and do everything in their power to destabilize Castelli and Belgrano, seriously jeopardizing the future of the revolution.

Castelli's army leaves for Upper Perú with what little is at hand, followed by the poor, and with a revolution to carry out. He is headed towards the territory Túpac Amaru and Micaela Bastidas had not been able to liberate; he is going to make justice, to prove that each part of the torn bodies of the *Tupamaros* blossomed into red flowers in every usurped village. One of the few cannons in Castelli's army is called Túpac Amaru; and he intends to aim it at the core of Spanish power in these territories.

There Goes the Revolution

Following Liniers' execution, Juan José Castelli returned to Buenos Aires for a secret rendezvous with Mariano Moreno. After congratulating him on the decision and patriotism shown during the suppression of the counter-revolution in Córdoba, Moreno appointed him, on the 6th of September 1810, representative of the Council, with ample powers to put an end to the "despots" of Upper Perú.

The most significant items in the set of instructions he received were the following:

• He should strengthen the trust the people from the provinces had placed on the government.

• He should establish a strict discipline among the troops.

• He should incorporate all the patriotic soldiers from Buenos Aires that he might find in Chuquisaca, where they had been taken [in 1809] by Nieto.

• He should keep his decisions secret, his measures should always be a mystery known solely by their effects, for this was the surest means for a general to become respectable in the eyes of his troops and fearsome in the eyes of his enemies.

• President Nieto, Governor Sanz, the bishop of La Paz and Goyeneche were to be executed wherever they were found.

• Cañete, Terrazas, Orihuela, the Zudáñezes, Ibarguren and Areta should be transported to Buenos Aires; those who dared show their hostility towards the Council should come in chains, the rest were to be brought under the pretense that the Council was in need of their sapience.

• He should conquer the will of the Indians, sending them emissaries to make them understand that the expedition was meant to assist them. He should be especially careful in replacing the members of every *cabildo* with people they could trust.

Moreno made his goals clear: "Since one of the main objectives of the expedition is to surprise the peoples of Perú before reinforcements from Lima can arrive and fortify them in their defense, it will perhaps be convenient that a division of 400 men under the command of Mayor Balcarce, with four convoys and 100 horsemen, should be sent ahead to Tupiza, where they will remain until the main body of men arrives. The distance between Potosí and Tupiza will prevent this force from being attacked, provided they take the precautions and the fortification measures taught by the art of war."

The four provinces that formed Upper Perú – Potosí, Charcas, Cochabamba and La Paz – were shocked at the news about drastic changes arriving from the capital of the Viceroyalty. Reactionary leaders were ready to resort to force and increased repressive measures to prevent the sparks from turning into a blaze.

In view of this serious situation, the president of Chuquisaca, Don Vicente Nieto[2] called a meeting attended by all the "high dignitaries" of La Paz and Potosí. They decided that all the men taking part in the expedition from Buenos Aires should be sentenced to death and that the provinces of Upper Perú were to remain under the protection of the viceroy of Perú, Abascal, who was only too willing to have the revenue from the Potosí mines filling his coffer once again. He also issued a manifesto stating: "Americans were born to be slaves; nature has doomed them to vegetate in darkness and dejection."

The next day, something odd happened: someone left three sacks in the main square of the city of Lima, one filled with salt [SAL], another one with beans [HABAS] and the third one with lime [CAL]. Taken together, they spelled "SAL HABASCAL" ("Abascal, go home"). One of the viceroy's supporters must have deciphered the pun and ordered the removal of the bags. Mariano Moreno, on his part, gave a more straightforward answer: "Without being vain, we may safely claim that, man to man, we are by far the better men. It should also be noticed that it was the ancient government

2 Marshall Vicente Nieto – president of the Audiencia of Chuquisaca – had been appointed by Viceroy Cisneros as acting governor of Buenos Aires on July 21, 1809. Nieto remained in office for only ten days. He had been born in Spain in 1769, had joined the army in 1791 and had obtained the title of captain during the war against France. After the Treaty of Basel was signed in 1795, he was sent to America. He returned to Spain in 1808 to fight the French once again. That same year he was designated president of the Audiencia of Chuquisaca, and as such he savagely put down the uprising that took place in the city. In 1810 he was promoted to Field-Marshall "on merit."

that doomed us to vegetate in darkness and dejection, but since nature has made us for great deeds, we have started by clearing the land of so many ignorant and abusive rulers, whose only brilliance was that of the stripes their guardian angel had deigned conceal their vices and miseries with."

Nieto did not trust his troops, which had come from Buenos Aires in 1809 to stifle the rebellions of Chuquisaca and La Paz. Without a second thought, he disarmed the *Patricios* and *Arribeños* and sent them in chains to Potosí, where they were received by the mayor and mine exploiter Francisco de Paula Sanz, who without further ado threw them into the mine shafts of the Cerro de Plata as slave laborers. A month later, at least one third of them were dead.

In this context, the Quito uprising went off like a bomb behind Abascal's back, and the whole Argentine north was shaken by the defeat of Liniers' counter-revolution. The defeat of the forces commanded by José de Córdova, which were to join Liniers, at the hand of the patriotic forces led by Balcarce, on the 7th of November 1810 in Suipacha, further complicated the situation.

The day following the first victory of the revolutionary forces Juan José Castelli joined the troops and began to receive messages from the rebels who had joined the American cause in various regions of Upper Perú.

Castelli's address to his troops made the political and military objectives of the expedition clear: "Citizens, soldiers, friends, brothers, comrades: Virtue and heroism cannot go unrewarded, as crime cannot go unpunished. I share my glory with you, for the life of the Fatherland and the extermination of our impenitent, hardened and envious rivals."

At a short meeting, Castelli and Balcarce agreed on creating a special task force, with a specific mission – the capture of Nieto, who, true to his principles, had fled after the defeat of Suipacha. Castelli suggested that the group should be integrated mainly by those *Patricios* who had survived the forced labor of the Potosí mines and who had been reincorporated into the patriotic army with full honours. Castelli explained that he entrusted them with this mission because "it was interesting to give the survivors the opportunity of righting their wrongs on the person responsible for inflicting such miseries." The group would be guided by a party of Indians who were familiar with the territory, and would take a shortcut through terrain impassable on horseback and thus "guarantee the swift capture of the murderer Nieto."

The natives were the first to reach the village of San Antonio de Lipes, near Oruro. There they run into a group of fugitive Spaniards, who were taking a rest. They took away their horses and waited for the arrival of the *Patricios*, to which the Spaniards led by Nieto – the coveted trophy – surrendered. A few days earlier he had said: "I have reports in my power concerning the orders and regulations proclaimed by the revolutionary Council of Buenos Aires which I have not yet put to their appropriate use because I expect to have the satisfaction of feeding them to these dirty and vile insurgents, who preposterously sent them to me as Representatives of Sovereign Power." In his communiqué – which he now would have to feed to himself – Nieto dreamed of attacking Salta, Santa Fe and Buenos Aires: "The troops shall punish Salta, keep Tucumán and Santiago del Estero under control, and shall assist the province of Córdoba as Your Excellency sees fittest. Once Santa Fe is overpowered, and this shall be one of my main objectives, only Buenos Aires shall remain, with its enclosure and its vast and useless pampas, and so it shall be brought to its knees, without forgetting to punish the authors of so much evil. I know we can count on the Commander of the Navy (of Montevideo), who by means of a blockade shall prevent large overseas ships from entering Buenos Aires, and shall effect a blockade on the firewood, the coal and tallow coming down the Paraná Rivers, without which they cannot subsist, and all this shall greatly vex the revolutionary government."

"The Party Most Interested in Novelty"

Meanwhile, Bernardo de Monteagudo was confined in the Royal Prison of the Court of Chuquisaca for "the abominable crime of disloyalty to the cause of the King;" he had been one of the leaders of the revolution of the 25th of May 1809 against the abuses of the viceregal administration and in favor of a local government.

Marshall Nieto had sent all available forces to fight the patriots, in support of Captain José de Córdova. The University City was almost completely bereft. Monteagudo, eager to join the approaching patriotic army, devised a plan of escape. Claming that he was "having tea with some important ladies" at the garden adjoining the prison, he was granted the key that would allow him to make his escape.[3]

Thus, escorted as usual by beautiful ladies, on the 4th of November 1810 Bernardo de Monteagudo regained his freedom. He left for Potosí and put himself at the disposal of the revolutionary army, which under Castelli's command had taken control of the strategic city on November 25. Well aware of the record of the young *tucumano*, Castelli appointed him his secretary. The tandem alarmed both

---

3 Original documents owned by G. René Moreno. Cf. Mariano A. Pelliza, *Monteagudo, su vida y sus escritos*, Buenos Aires, Lojouane, 1880.

royalists and Saavedra's supporters, who saw them as "the henchmen of the Robespierre-inspired system of the French Revolution."

Monteagudo knew that he was in the right place when he witnessed Castelli carry out Moreno's harsh orders without hesitation: "Since only the Europeans have been a challenge to our army, we cannot but expel them from Potosí, to the extent that not a single one should remain in the village."

Thus on the 13th of December 1810 the first fifty-three Spaniards were banished to the city of Salta. The list was personally drawn by Castelli, who explained his decision as follows: "The peace, quiet and public safety of this great village, which are the concern of the Superior Government of the Province, require some sacrifices and mortifications which cannot be avoided without jeopardizing the future of our work. By this principle, I took it upon myself to qualify the subjects of this neighborhood who were suspected for their previous behavior, so that they are driven out of its bosom, whence they might attempt to infuse new life to ideas of uncertainty, causing greater damage than the one already caused by their imprudent and obstinate behavior."

Following this, he briefed Chiclana, at the time governor of Salta, on the CV of some of the unwanted guests he was sending him: "Dr Otondo, presbyter; he is a haughty and arrogant hypocrite, who takes advantage of the consideration that his title allows him; he dared appeal to the privileges and rights to thwart my order of elimination; my command must have hurt his pride, as I threatened to send an escort if he failed to comply with my orders, warning him that all the privileges and rights are bound to political law, and that if his title gained him some consideration on my part, it certainly did not grant him immunity; I have destined him to the Bethlemite Convent, where he will make his lodging, without the right to hear confession, because by means of this and by his public preaching, he has managed to foster the party of despotic revolution. As for the rest, none are any good, and Your Excellency should without delay deal with them as the Superior Government sees fittest."[4]

Castelli submitted his decision to the approval of the Council, not knowing that it had been renamed Great Council (*Junta Grande*) and that Mariano Moreno, its former political leader, had been forced to renounce. Things were changing for the worse. Domingo Matheu, alderman of the Council and a Spanish merchant, was concerned about the future of two of the Spaniards deported by Castelli – whom he had commercial ties with – and used his influence to obtain a revision of the order, alleging that Castelli had not been properly advised, misled by groundless slanders and accusations.

To protect his commercial agents, Salvador Tulla and Pedro Casas, Matheu succeeded in nullifying the expatriation of the entire party, and on the 28th of January 1811 he informed Chiclana about the suspension of the order: "(…) we are positive that they never acted against our cause, and for this reason we ask the Governor of Salta to rescue them immediately from their banishment at Orán, remaining in that city under your orders until Castelli calls them to Potosí with the purpose of inquiring if they have committed any offenses, and if that were the case, they should be punished accordingly or at your discretion. I am not partial to any one in particular, and therefore I ask nothing, in favor or against any of them."

4 Archivo General de la Nación, *op. cit.*, tomo II.

In answer to a letter sent by Chiclana, Matheu exulted in his success: "(...) I have been witness to the joy the revocation of the confinement in Orán has provoked; it would have been a shame if because of four sloppy drunkards a cause as great as the one we are to crown should begin to totter (...)".[5]

But these Spaniards, pardoned, at Matheu's request, by the Council led by Saavedra, were not four sloppy drunkards, but rather dangerous counter-revolutionaries, as doctor Juan Madera, member of Castelli's army, testifies: "Having the *Cabildo* of Potosí requested that the European enemies be expatriated, Juan José Castelli complied, but they were then pardoned and sent to Potosí by order of the government of Buenos Aires, against the opinion of all good patriots, and to the detriment of the public cause; as very soon, in May 1811 they entered a horrific conspiracy, and were surprised while meeting at the place called the Copacabana Community House, and they made fire and resisted, and these individuals were not punished, and the same thing happened in Charcas with the enemy European expatriates, and the same thing would have happened with the insurgents Nieto, Córdova and Paula Sanz had not Don Juan Xastelli executed them following orders. For immediately after Moreno left and the new council members were incorporated, an urgent missive was sent pardoning the criminals and ordering Castelli not to execute anybody else."[6]

5 Domingo Matheu, *Memorias*, tomo II, Buenos Aires, Biblioteca de Mayo, 1966.

6 Declaración del Dr. Juan Madera en el juicio de residencia iniciado a Saavedra por la Asamblea de 1813, Biblioteca de Mayo, "Sumarios y expedientes", Buenos Aires, Honorable Senado de la Nación, 1960.

This unilateral decision, the first of a long list, was aimed at eroding Castelli's prestige and power, disliked by the conservatives now ruling the Council of Buenos Aires.

Irrefutable evidence of a long series of decisions made to that purpose is the designation of the Spaniard Matías Bernal, suspect of having collaborated with Goyeneche, as governor of Potosí. Dean Funes, who masterminded Saavedra's party, justified the designation by saying: "His being a *chapetón*,[7] speaks of the government's integrity." The *Cabildo* of Buenos Aires answered that it was extremely serious to place "the key to Perú in the hands of a military leader whose very birth bespeaks suspicion and mistrust."[8]

In a letter to Chiclana, the president of the Coucil himself expressed his satisfaction at the political changes that had taken place after Moreno's departure: "Things have changed; following the reunion of the Provinces of the Viceroyalty, it is only logical that resolutions should also change, that is to say, that the rigors be moderated and mitigated. The system based on Robespierre's ideas, that some groups wanted to implement among us, and the imitation of the French Revolution which was to set the example, have thank God all but vanished; now we are ruled by the same principles constituting the core of the instructions you communicated to your successor in Salta, which have received the applause and approval of this Council."

Castelli and Monteagudo were the survivors of *Morenismo*, and therefore all the political maneuvers of the Council, led by Dean Funes and Saavedra, were aimed against them.

---

7 Spaniard.
8 Acuerdos del Cabildo de Buenos Aires, tomo IV, p. 439.

Revolutionary Justice

Marshall Nieto soon received pleasant company at his Potosí prison. The governor of Potosí, Francisco de Paula Sanz, had attempted to flee with 300,000 pesos in gold and silver belonging to the State, but he was captured, and so was his comrade, Mayor General Córdova.

Instructions from the Council read: "President Nieto, Governor Sanz, the bishop of La Paz, Goyeneche, and whoever was an important leader of the Expedition are to be shot wherever they are found." Captain José de Córdova[9] was not mentioned because prior to the instructions he had not taken a role as active as the rest. But his arrogant behavior at the Battle of Suipacha, where he dared wave the black flag with the skull and crossbones to symbolize his intention of exterminating the rebels, lost him.

His defeat took him down a peg or two and, shoving his pirate flag out of sight, he showed himself willing to consent to any transaction that would spare his life, including going over to the patriotic side with all his troops. Without any attempt at disguising his treason, he said: "(...) Yesterday I was hostile to the Council, which has established its own government, and today I yield to it, and recognize its authority (...), my dear Balcarce: we were friends first, then

9 Córdova had been born in 1774 on the Island of León (Spain). While still young he enrolled in the navy and participated in several battles both in the Pacific and Atlantic Oceans. He participated in the Sardinia Campaign, in the Gulf of Parma, and collaborated in the conquest of St Peter and St Antioch Islands. In 1801 he was posted at the naval station of Montevideo. In 1806 he participated in the defense of Buenos Aires under the orders of Liniers, and was promoted to captain. In 1808 he was transferred to the army of Marshall Nieto, with the title of Mayor General.

we became enemies, and now we are friends again. You have triumphed in combat and now I am giving orders to gather what the unworthy President has scattered. I acknowledge the Council, I yield to it; and so does this navy and so will the troops that I have commanded."

After reading the letter, Castelli sent the following message to the Council: "(Córdova) has offered to join us in the attack against the exalted army that Viceroy Abascal is preparing and that Goyeneche[10] will command; he guarantees victory in Perú and request that the life of his troops be spared. Is Your Excellency in need of more? Can you believe this? Read so yourself in the note sent by General Córdova on the 8th of this month, and you will marvel at the extraordinary contrast between this one and those of his preceding messages I am also sending for Your

---

10 Manuel José de Goyeneche had been born in Arequipa, Perú, in 1775. While still young he moved to Spain to complete his military career, and participated in the defense of Cádiz against the English. Goyeneche became a friend of Manuel Godoy, the "Prince of Peace" who paid his expenses for a trip across Europe to familiarize him with the art of war. He studied in Berlin and Prussia, under the supervision of Wilhelm of Prussia, and in Vienna, under the tutelage of the Archduke Charles. Finally, he also studied in Brussels and Paris, under the orders of Napoleon Bonaparte himself. He was able to visit England, Switzerland and Italy, Holland and Saxony. In 1808 following the Napoleonic invasions, Goyeneche was appointed brigadier and ordered to sail to the River Plate. On August 23 he arrived in Buenos Aires, where he was appointed acting president of the Audiencia of Cuzco. On the 25th of October 1809, after defeating the La Paz revolutionaries led by Pedro Domingo Murillo, he carried out a fierce manhunt which included torture and executions. In May 1810, he received the command of the army and the order to reconquer the provinces of the River Plate.

Excellency's best intelligence. When you compare them you will see that the last one is as courteous and respectful, down to the envelope and its official character, as the previous ones were unmannerly and insolent."

In his memoirs, Beruti gives a semblance of the imprisoned counter-revolutionaries: "(...) they were sentenced to death for not having obeyed this capital, for having spent public funds to raise an army to oppose our arms and our just cause, for seceding from the authority of this capital and joining the Viceroyalty of Lima, forcing the provinces under their command to recognize the Viceroy of Lima as captain general and viceroy, interrupting communication with this capital, both active and passive; and even though Córdova had no superior command in these provinces, he was executed as the leader of those opposing our ideas, as the general who fought ours, and as having hoisted the black flag with skulls, in token of giving our troops no quarter should victory be his."[11]

On the 14th of December 1810 Castelli signed the death sentence of the enemies of the revolution. They were lodged in individual rooms so that they "could prepare to die a Christian death."

On the 15th, at the Plaza Mayor of the imperial village, between 10 and 11 in the morning, the sentence was publicly read to the criminals, who were kneeling before the regimental flags, and carried out.

Among the spectators surrounding the gallows, there was one that anxiously followed the proceedings. Bernardo de Monteagudo, who had seen the massacres perpetrated

---

11 Juan Manuel Beruti, *Memorias curiosas*, Buenos Aires, Emecé, 2000.

by Paula Sanz and Nieto barely a year ago in Chuquisaca, would never forget the scene being played before his eyes: "O illustrious shadows of the dignified citizens Victorio and Gregorio Lanza![12] O you who rest in your lonely sepulchres! Rear your heads: I have seen them expiate their crimes and have approached with satisfaction the scaffolds of Sanz, Nieto and Córdova to examine the effects of the wrath of our dear Fatherland and bless it with victory."[13]

Castelli sent a letter to the Council saying: "The execution has been of an imposing character on account of the military apparatus, its punctuality and observance."

Thus two of the tree officials who had arrived in Perú to serve their king died by the hands of the "rabble" of Buenos Aires, for which they had felt so much hatred and contempt. The third one, José Manuel de Goyeneche, managed to escape and lived on to harass the patriotic forces for many years to come.

Back in Chuquisaca

On December 25 Castelli left Potosí, heading for Chuquisaca. Twenty-two years earlier he had left the city with his law degree. The city had changed a lot in his absence, but he was still the same. He now was the representative of the Council, for whom the *Cabildo* provided lavish hospitality and lush lodgings. Castelli, however, preferred to stay, at his own expense, in a humble inn he had known since his student years.

12 Names of the revolutionaries murdered by Nieto and Paula Sanz.
13 Bernardo de Monteagudo, "Ensayo sobre la Revolución del Río de la Plata desde el 25 de Mayo de 1809", *Mártir o libre*, Buenos Aires, 1812.

A Te Deum was offered in his honor at the Cathedral, and although Castelli had planned to sit at the centre of the Church in the company of his deputy Balcarce, Balcarce's chair never showed up. Castelli sent someone to find out what had happened, and learnt that a member of the *Audiencia* had ordered not to pay the deputy the same honors as the Council representative. The rage of the orator of the revolution could hardly be restrained. He ordered that the *Audiencia in toto* present their excuses to Balcarce and appointed him honorary president of the corporation "so that those who did not want to see him at the Cathedral, now have to see him presiding over the *Audiencia.*"

When the party was over, Castelli got down to work. There was much to do, many wounds that needed healing, many wrongs to set right. One of his first tasks was the creation of a progressive legislation thanks to which the native inhabitants could recover their freedom and properties. Castelli's dispositions included:
- the emancipation of the peoples;
- the freedom of settlement;
- free trade;
- the distribution of the lands expropriated from the enemies of the revolution among the workers of the mills;
- the total annulment of the Indian tribute;
- suspension of personal services.

Also:
- He placed Indians and *criollos* on the same legal standing, declaring the former apt to fill any position at the State;
- he translated the main decrees of the Council into Quechua and Aymara;
- he opened bilingual schools: Quechua-Spanish and Aymara-Spanish;

• he removed all Spanish civil servants from office, executing some, deporting others, and imprisoning the rest.

The regulations were undoubtedly revolutionary, and it wouldn't be long before they unleashed the rage of the wealthy – both Spaniards and *criollos* – who benefited from the exploitation of the Indians. A contemporary witness set down what follows: "Under the power of political and ecclesiastical hierarchy, the interests of the people amounted to zero – and that is all they were – in the computation of colonial administration, from what follows that the things and people who attempted to alter a system devised to satisfy both the natural greed of the Spaniards and the vanity of the *Limeños* met with enormous resistance."[14]

My Beloved Buenos Aires

In Buenos Aires some drastic changes had taken place. Thanks to the incorporation of new Council members, Saavedra and Funes had achieved two much longed-for objectives: that the followers of Moreno be in the minority, and that Mariano Moreno himself renounce, which he did on the 18th of December 1810.

The news reached Chuquisaca in the correspondence distributed on the 5th of January 1811. It was clear to everyone that this incident meant the end of the policies carried out so far, and the termination of Castelli's severe instructions.

Communiqués like the one signed by Moreno before his resignation would not be seen again: "The Council approves of the system of blood and rigor that Your

14 Ignacio Núñez, *Noticias históricas,* Buenos Aires, Jackson, 1957.

Excellency has been practicing on our enemies, and orders that not a single European – soldier or civilian – who ever took arms against the capital remain in Perú."[15]

The change was evident in the letter that Saavedra addressed to Castelli on the 11th of January 1811: "We have approved of the behavior of Your Excellency, but attending to the change in circumstances it is advisable that Your Excellency avoid the capital punishment, which should be commuted for a pecuniary penalty or of any other kind, giving written account of the causes and of the exact value of confiscated property."

Despite the threat of Saavedra's supporters, Castelli, on personal conviction and in homage to his deposed leader, continued his revolutionary work. On the 5th of February 1811 he issued the following manifesto, addressed to the Indians of Upper Perú: "The proclamation that on October 26 of the last year your Viceroy addressed to you, compels me to oppose its principles, before your simplicity fall victim to deceit and your future and your children's into the hands of error. I am concerned for your happiness not only because of my temperament, but also due to long hours of reasoning, and reflection, and I would be failing my obligations if I consented to truth being concealed or lies being disguised (...) It is high time you thought about yourselves, and suspected the false and luring hopes by means of which they intend to secure and guarantee your servitude.

"These are the Viceroy's intentions when he offers to clear for all of you the path to instruction, honor and employment, which he never believed you deserved. You

---

15 La Junta de Buenos Aires to Castelli, December 3, 1810, Archivo General de la Nación, tomo II, p. 74.

may ask him, since when does he deem you worthy of such elevation? Is it not true that you have always been looked down on as slaves, and treated with the utmost contempt, for no crime but that of inhabiting your own Country and with no right except that of force? Have you ever enjoyed any of those positions and honors that are now being offered to you, or any of the goods that your own soil has granted you and that nature entitles you to with absolute dominion? (...) The history of your ancestors and your own experience should reveal the venom and hypocrisy behind this recent Plan that your Tyrants with such pomp announce: you very well know that their language has never been that of truth, and that their lips never speak their hearts. Today they flatter you with advantageous promises, tomorrow they will ransack your homes, upset your families, and add more links to the chain you are already dragging.

"Take notice of your master's behavior in this: tell me if they have ever kept their promises, which they so frequently and in such an artificial manner make; and compare their behavior to that of the most excellent Council on whose orders I and all my officers act: we never fail to carry out our promises (...) The Council of the Capital considers you their brothers, and will treat you as equals: this is all there is to their plan, and my behavior will ever be in accordance with it, despite what, to seduce you, the wickedness of you chiefs may publish to the contrary."

While Castelli was trying to kindle revolutionary fire, the *saavedrista* Council appointed Lorenzo Córdova and José Calvimonte, both open enemies of the revolutionary movement, as co-judges to the Royal *Audiencia* of Chuquisaca.

Outraged, the president of the *Audiencia* of Charcas wrote to the Council of Buenos Aires as follows: "These two men, scandalously hostile to our cause, have merited the hatred and contempt of the general." His only reply was the guilty silence that confirmed the two counter-revolutionaries in their posts.

The *saavedrista* faction wanted to take control of the Army of the North and eliminate Castelli and Balcarce, who openly supported Moreno.

In secret meetings and discussions, they began to weave the threads of their conspiracy. On the 7th of March 1811, in Oruro, several officers met at the house of Luciano Montes de Oca. Among those attending the meeting were José María Echaurri; an aide of the Dragoons Regiment, Casco; José León Domínguez; Matías Balbastro, a priest, Manuel Antonio Azcurra, and sergeant-mayor Toribio de Luzuriaga.

The confederate agreed unanimously to kidnap Balcarce and Castelli, transport them to Buenos Aires to be put on trial, and hand over the command of the army to one of Saavedra's most fervid supporters, Colonel Juan José Viamonte.

A delegation of the group formed by Montes de Oca and Luzuriaga sought Viamonte to acquaint him with the plan, but he deemed it untimely and bound to fail, although he did not turn in any of the conspirators, who continued to plot against Castelli and Balcarce until they managed to destabilize them.[16]

Chaplain Fray Manuel Azcurra stood out for his zeal in favor of Saavedra. This is how Dr Diego Paroissien remembers the incident: "(...) Captain Juan Antonio Argerich commented that various officers had gathered in Oruro with the purpose of capturing J.J. Castelli and

16 Archivo General de la República Argentina, *Sumarios y expedientes*, tomo XII, Buenos Aires, Senado de la Nación, 1962.

General Balcarce, and that Fray Manuel Azcurra was the leading agent and spokesman."[17]

In his statement of the 9th of July 1813 at the *causa de residencia* (inquiry) carried out by the 1813 Assembly, the abovementioned Juan Madera provides us with a curious version regarding the animosity that this friar entertained against Moreno: "(...) being the deponent in Oruro in March 1811, he overheard father Azcurra thanking God for the removal of Dr Moreno and as if foretelling his death in the following manner: 'He is already embarked and soon will be dead.'"[18]

How could he have known about Moreno's murder, which had been committed on the fourth of the same month and which would only be made known in Buenos Aires in October 1811? Was he a clairvoyant, as well as a priest?

During the second week of May, there arrived at Castelli's camp the news about the April 5 and 6 Movement that had removed Moreno's supporters from the Council, had confined them to the hinterlands and had declared press censorship and embarked upon the persecution of everyone who opposed Saavedra. The position of Moreno's supporters could not be worse: Moreno had been murdered; Rodríguez Peña, Vieytes, Larrea, Donado and French had been confined; Belgrano had been prosecuted. Only Juan José Castelli, the voice of the revolution, was still on his feet, and against him were leveled all the energies of the reactionaries, who had taken over the dreams of the revolution and turned them into dirty business, shameful proposals to foreign monarchies and secret pacts with the enemy.

---

17 Archivo General de la República Argentina, *op. cit.*
18 *Idem.*

The news irritated the officers, who "full of energy and love of freedom, found out about the news and gathered at the door of Castelli's lodging, claiming that since this was how the men who had led them on the path of happiness were treated, they could no longer tolerate so much abuse, that they were ready to sacrifice themselves in revenge, that the Desaguadero should soon be attacked and Buenos Aires after it: they all swore to die a thousands deaths rather than admitting another crown in America. In unison they shouted that they had abandoned their homes, parents, wives and sons for their and their country's freedom; that they only had one life and that they were willing to sacrifice it to defend their independence."[19]

Saavedra's supporters feared that, following Monteagudo's invitation, Moreno's remaining supporters would march on Upper Perú, secure their political and military power and then march on Buenos Aires to take power. Funes admitted "we do not know what will happen if those who have been banished take over Perú, since we know that Castelli is not glad about the news." And he began a campaign of slander and defamation that eventually would yield its fruits: the prosecution and imprisonment of Castelli and Monteagudo. Perfectly aware that raising false testimony was a capital sin, the dean nevertheless wrote a letter stating: "The plan devised by the confederate could not have been more detestable: the annihilation of religion was part of it. Castelli behaved like a libertine. I wish he were soon taken care of, as I fear what may come."[20]

19 Ignacio Núñez, *op. cit.*

20 Dean Funes to his brother Ambrosio, Buenos Aires, April 8, 1811.

Saavedra accused Castelli of having induced Vieytes, Peña, Larrea and Azcuénaga to escape the places where they had been constrained to live: "(...) he had no qualms about writing to them under cover of Don José de Paz, Mail Administrator of Córdoba, telling them to take the byroads and reach his army that was willing to aid them. It is apparent that the friend of the offenders chose their friendship over the welfare of his country, assuring them that once victory had been secured at the Desaguadero, he would declare war on the capital, and that with twenty thousand men he would overpower it and put his friends back in office."[21]

While civil war was breaking out, the one with the Spaniards proceeded slowly but steadily, and the royalists devised a plan to take over Potosí. The attack was to take place on April 21. That night, the conspirators prepared to mingle with the faithful in a procession, arms concealed under their *ponchos*. The meeting points were the temples of Copacabana and San Bernardo. But a patriot found out about the scheme before it was too late and gave the alarm. Castelli's agents captured the confederate before they could do anything. No one was left to tell about the plan they had connived.

The Fragility of Peace

Following the Council's orders, Castelli had begun secret negotiations with the enemy leader Goyeneche with the purpose of reaching a truce. Domingo Tristán, governor of

---

21 Instructions given by Don Cornelio Saavedra to his agent Juan de la Rosa Alba during the *juicio de residencia*. Dated in San Juan de la Frontera, August 3, 1814.

La Paz and cousin of Goyeneche, played a crucial role in the negotiations and finally the armistice was signed on the 16th of May 1811. It established:

- the stand-by for the positions of both armies;
- good faith, permanent peace and mutual security for 40 days;
- hostilities could only be resumed 48 hours after both parties were notified about the dissolution of the negotiation;
- the term was due on June 25.

Differences deepened within the patriotic ranks, now inactive. The campaign of slander fostered by Saavedra and Funes was yielding its fruits and the political and military power of Castelli was trickling like water through his fingers.

In spite of all this, Castelli would not stop dreaming, believing in a project which in the years to come his friend and comrade Monteagudo would pass onto his chief José de San Martín: South America united in a single nation.

"In the future, the whole of South America will be but a large family which through fraternity might equal the most respected nations of the ancient world." And he dreamed on: "I believe that if we pave the way to Lima, there is no reason why the whole of Santa Fe de Bogotá shall not join us and the three, together with Chile, shall form an association with general courts to set the principles of government."

Apotheosis at Tiahuanaco

While the pro-Saavedra Council was sending Castelli orders as preposterous as the following, unprecedented in military history, orders whose sole purpose was the dispersal and defeat of an army that jeopardized the interests of the capital: "You are not to enter combat unless entirely assured of success," the first anniversary of the revolution was approaching and Castelli decided to celebrate it as he saw fit: with a revolutionary deed. He called all the native communities of the province of La Paz to a meeting before the ruins of Tiahuanaco, only a few feet away from Titicaca, the sacred lake of the Incas, birthplace of the founders of the empire of the sun, Manco Cápac and Mama Ocllo. And there they gathered, hundreds of Indians and soldiers of the Army of the North, waiting for the speaker to address them. Castelli began by paying homage to the memory of the Incas and inviting them to avenge their deaths at the hand of the Spanish oppressor. "The efforts of this government," he said in Spanish, giving the interpreters time to translate into Quechua and Aymara, "have been aimed at achieving the happiness of all classes, among them the natives of this district, for so many years neglected, oppressed and disappointed in their rights and even denied the condition of men." Castelli concluded his harangue by saying: "I at least do not believe that the viceroy or his accomplices are entitled to decide upon the fortune of a people whose fate does not depend but on their consent alone, and for this I see myself in the obligation of conjuring these provinces so that, making use of their natural rights, they might make their will known and decide freely upon the course of this affair, crucial to every American."

As for Bernardo de Monteagudo, the remarkable Paraguayan historian Julio César Chaves says: "Perhaps young Monteagudo was at that point pondering over the cabalistic date of his existence: the 25th of May. Four years earlier, on the 25th of May 1808, he had read his dissertation before the Caroline Academy. On the 25th of May 1819, he had declared the revolution in the streets and squares of Chuquisaca. On the 25th of May 1810, he awaited sentence in jail, while far from there, his future was being decided for him. On the 25th of May 1811, in Tiahuanaco, he witnessed the redemption of the Indian."[22]

The Nazi-fascist Argentine writer Gustavo Martínez Zuviría (1883-1962), better known by the not-so-nationalistic pseudonym of "Hugo Wast," shows that the Argentine ruling classes were, more than 130 years after the fact, irritated by Castelli's defense of the Indians in Tiahuanaco, which Martínez ridiculed in these terms: "One day he decides to organize an assembly of Indians in the region of Lake Tiahuanaco (*sic*). Picture, if you can, in such a setting and before such an audience, Castelli's drivel about popular sovereignty and the rights of man, given in the unintelligible and wordy style of the Jacobins! Imagine Castelli saying all this and concluding with this interrogation: 'That is the government of tyrants. This is the rule of the people. You tell me what you want,' and the Indian throng answering: 'Rum, sir!'"[23]

It should be noted that the National Library of the Argentine Republic decided to "honor" this propagandist of racism by naming one of its halls after him.

Mister Wast was wrong when he called Moreno's supporters Jacobins, as Moreno, Castelli and Belgrano had gone beyond the Jacobin followers of a Voltaire who could claim: "I believe we do not agree upon the concept of the people that you believe worthy of being instructed. By people, I mean he who has but his arms to survive. I do not think that this kind of individual will ever have the time or capacity

22 Julio César Chaves, *Castelli, el adalid de Mayo*, Buenos Aires, Leviatán, 1957.
23 Hugo Wast, *El año X*, Buenos Aires, Peuser, 1947.

to be instructed. I find the existence of the ignorant and poor essential. If you worked the land, if you owned a plough, you would agree with me. It is not the peasant that should be instructed, but the bourgeois, the city dweller."[24]

Belgrano, Moreno and Castelli did everything in their power to dignify the inhabitants of these provinces, using the most powerful weapon, and the most dreaded by the tyrants at that: education for all.

Meanwhile, in Buenos Aires the anniversary of the revolution was being celebrated in accordance with the tastes and ideas of Funes and Saavedra. A contemporary witness wrote "at four o'clock in the afternoon, there appeared in the Square an American and a Spaniard, marching two by two. Then they stopped and positioned themselves at the centre of the *Cabildo*, and began the counterdance. In this great party, the cheers for freedom and boos to tyranny had been forbidden, and only the cheers for the captive King Ferdinand VII were allowed. When President Saavedra found out that a group of men from the 3rd Regiment was preparing a short play that would conclude with the words 'Long Live freedom!,' he ordered their mayor to omit that exclamation and any other reference to independence."[25]

The Mother of All Battles

Saavedra's supporters knew that the one thing that could finish Castelli off was an utter rout in the battle against Goyeneche, and so began plotting to bring it about. Saavedra, who had signed instructions ordering Castelli to negotiate with Goyeneche, would now deprive him of authority in a

24 Voltaire to his friend Daminaville. Letter, April 1, 1766.
25 Ignacio Núñez, *op. cit.*

letter sent to his ally and confident in the Army of the North, Juan José Viamonte. Dean Funes corresponded with Domingo Tristán, who was waiting to see how events developed to defect to his cousin Goyeneche's side. The latter had taken advantage of the truce to position himself at the Desaguadero River, which allowed him to receive daily reports on the exact position of the opposing army.

Goyeneche was just waiting for an opportunity to launch a surprise attack. The *Porteño* government, giving proof of a very remarkable imagination when it came to new ways of destroying the Army of the North, ordered Balcarce to attack the hostile army whenever he saw fit, without waiting for Castelli's orders, and authorized him to decide on promotions, without the intervention of the representative of the Council.

As was to be expected, on the night of the 6th of June 1811, Goyeneche's troops broke the truce and a force of 500 men unexpectedly attacked the patriotic army. Goyeneche claimed that the patriotic troops had been the first to violate the truce.

Both armies had kept vigil over their arms on opposite banks of the Desaguadero River, near the village of Huaqui. The troops of Castelli, Balcarce, Viamonte and Díaz Vélez, which were stationed on the left bank of the river, numbered 6000 men. On the opposite bank, Goyeneche had managed to gather 8000 men. At seven o'clock on the morning of the 20th of June 1811 the Spanish army launched a surprise attack. The divisions under the command of Díaz Vélez and Balcarce responded promptly, while Viamonte, one of Saavedra's men, ordered his 1500 men, amidst this chaos, to engage on a series of military exercises less than a mile away from the battlefield. His lack of cooperation became apparent. Díaz Vélez repeatedly asked Viamonte to send reinforcements, but the latter refused to lend him any of his men. Military historian General Bassi says: "Once again Viamonte's division failed to take part, and being at a short distance from the field busied itself with a purposeless parade."[26] Díaz Vélez, seeing that his troop was decimated and exhausted after four hours of intense combat and sorely lacking in ammunition, and noticing that not even under these circumstances did Viamonte answer his request, ordered the retreat. Goyeneche's expertise and the disorderly scattering of soldiers did the rest. It was a total rout.

Defeat

After defeat at Huaqui, on the 18th of July 1811, Castelli did not give up and issued the following communiqué: "If the people are the source of all authority, and the magistrate but a precarious economist of their interests, it is his duty to divulge the motives behind his actions. In the light of these considerations, I would like to inform the Patriotic Army and all the Provinces of the River Plate, of the just and urgent reasons that motivate me to go into a combat that would certainly be fatal to our enemies and fortunate to our armies (...) A heart breeding on intrigue and accustomed to crime cannot hide the poison feeding it for long, and although the outburst of its wickedness is sometimes delayed, at last its developments are revealed. Thus it happened on the night of the 6th of the current month, when vanished the phantom of pretense under whose shadow America's most dangerous abortion had been concealed.[27] Our army was peacefully

---

26 Juan Carlos Bassi, "La expedición libertadora al Alto Perú", en *Historia de la Nación Argentina*, tomo V**, Academia Nacional de la Historia, Buenos Aires, El Ateneo, 1961.
27 Evidently alluding to Goyeneche.

resting, safe in the guarantee of good faith offered by that general, so prone to boast of the dignity of his word, when between ten and eleven in the evening, 1000 men attacked our advance party at Juraicoragua (...) The evils of war are now inevitable, and nothing could ever justify my behavior, if I allowed the violation of our arms to go unpunished and the safety of our territory exposed to the incursions of that horde of slaves. It is fair, it is necessary to exterminate the murderers of our country's freedom, to humiliate our rivals, to teach them to respect our arms and to destroy, once and for all, the immediate source of the dangers looming over our territory. Consequently, I declare the armistice ended and announce that our legions of armed citizens are ready to fulfill their duties rescuing the Country from this last conflict it must face (...) Death will be the greatest reward for my toils, death after having seen all the enemies of the Fatherland dead, for then my heart will desire nothing else and my hopes will rest in endless apathy, seeing that freedom of the American people is secured for ever."

Castelli met with Balcarce and his secretary Monteagudo and decided to face up to defeat. For a while, he wanted to forget about so much misery, the cries of the wounded, the hunger for food and justice that surrounded him and that he himself felt. Upper Perú was a living hell and in Buenos Aires the Council was plotting against him. He imagined Saavedra's supporters discussing the war and deciding on their fate without even knowing where Huaqui was or how to find it on the map, as Castelli ironically expressed in a letter addressed to the Council: "Your Excellency seems to have better knowledge at a distance than myself on the spot."

It was clear that his internal enemies would do everything in their power to get rid of them, humiliate them and even imprison them. Maybe it was during those nights of endless talk in the Andean Valleys that they conceived the political plans that Moreno's surviving supporters would deliver at the Patriotic Society, and it is very likely that there and then Bernardo de Monteagudo might have written the first drafts of the most modern and just constitutional project of the time, which he would publish in *La Gaceta de Buenos Aires* only a few months later. This illustrious *tucumano* would say: "The tribunes will have neither executive nor legislative power. Their sole duty will be to protect the freedom, security and sacred rights of the people against the usurpation of government by a corporation or individual party; but making this known in their assemblies and councils, where they – with the government's license – will be allowed to summon the people. But since the government might refuse permission, since no one wants his usurpations to be known and thwarted by the people, it will be established that every three months the people will gather on the first day of the corresponding month to decide by suffrage upon the issues which the Constitution makes their concern, and only then might the tribunes expose what they deem necessary and fitting, unless the affair be so urgent that it require the immediate assembly of the people.

"The State is a moral persona composed of many peoples whose life consists of the union of its members. Its most important concern is its own preservation, for which it requires a compulsive force to deal with each part in a manner most convenient to the whole (…) Sovereign and legislative power resides in the people. This, by nature, is incommunicable, and therefore it cannot be represented by anyone other than the people themselves. It is also inalienable and indispensable, for which reason it cannot be granted to or usurped by anyone.

"Thus the modern and improper name of Representatives of the People is extinguished, by means of which, because of their ambition, the deputies vainly refer to themselves; they will be called Commissioners, and they will depend entirely and compulsorily upon the will of the people and will be subjected to the Superior Government like the rest of the citizens.

"The Aldermen of the Superior Executive Government and the Secretaries will be replaced every three years and so will the aldermen of the provincial councils; each province will elect by majority of vote one or two men possessing all the sublime qualities required for the position of Alderman of the Superior Government, and Buenos Aires will designate two or four in the same manner. When the three-year period be over, or when the government changed, they will be chosen by public ballot (...) Thanks to this wise procedure, the purchase of votes will be avoided and the ambition and greed usually mediating in elections and suffrages will be checked."

The Revolution at the Dock

Everybody knows it. Defeat is not its own end. There must be somebody to blame. The *Porteño* Council washed its hands off the affair and delayed for as long as it could the news about defeat at Huaqui. In the meantime, it ordered the detention of Castelli and Monteagudo and had them conveyed to Buenos Aires.

On his arrival at Tucumán, the ex-representative of the Council was informed that by order of the Superior Government he was to leave for Catamarca. Castelli stated that he could not afford the journey because he was penniless and that, far from making money in his commission, "he had sacrificed the whole of his moderate fortune, and had not even fifty pesos left to go to Catamarca." He couldn't even sell his possessions, as they had been stolen on the road. On the 30th of October 1811, the Council granted him 500 pesos to travel to Buenos Aires and sit at the dock.

Castelli turned himself in at the Regiment of the *Patricios*, at the time under the command of his cousin Manuel Belgrano. A jury was selected, but it was tinged with partiality and Castelli refused it. One of the prosecutors, Vicente Anastasio Echeverría, had been one of Liniers' main collaborators.

The days passed and no one really knew what the charges were. Finally, on the 5th of December 1811, a jury was put together, presided over by Dr Tomás A. Valle.

The government's contempt for the accused became apparent in the unnecessary delays and legal chicanery, denounced by Castelli on the 6th of February 1812. "The detention, confinement and, arrest and privations I have been subjected to since August 17 for no clear reason, not even to inquire into the cause that justifies the suspension of the rights of man in society."

On the 14th of February 1814, the witnesses began with their statements. The records of the case leave no doubts as to the partiality of the trial. Here are some examples:

> Question 11: *Whether there existed any disagreement between the chiefs and officers of the army; whether the troops of Upper Perú were scorned, especially those from Cochabamba; whether it was claimed that they would be successful, even against the will of God; whether Dr Castelli was a part of all this.*
> Captain Suárez: No disagreement existed, except with Viamonte after the arrival of the communiqué announcing the banishment of Rodríguez Peña and the rest. As for the troops of Cochabamba, I only know that some officers mocked them and made them the object of scorn, whereupon an order was issued by the command to put an end to this behavior (…)

Captain Antonio Argerich: That in the Village of Oruro a council was formed with the purpose of overthrowing Dr Castelli and General Balcarce. That once the Council was dissolved a delegation was created to inform Colonel Viamonte, but the latter did not acquaint Dr Castelli and General Balcarce with what had happened; who learnt about the incident many days later and who had irrefutable evidence proving that all the operations had been directed by an agent of Juan José Viamonte, Friar Manuel Azcurra.

Bernardo de Monteagudo: Of course there were quarrels, but these were promoted by Colonel Viamonte, who, particularly after the incidents of April 5 and 6 did nothing to conceal his support of Saavedra's party, utterly upsetting all the chiefs and officers.

Colonel Juan José Viamonte: That there never existed any quarrels among the chiefs and officers or among the troops.

Question 14: *Whether loyalty to Ferdinand VII was in question, in an attempt to induce the system of liberty, equality and independence. Whether Dr Castelli knew about this.*

Captain Suárez: In a conversation about the various systems of government I overhead Dr Castelli say that no crowned head should be recognized. In official ceremonies the name of Ferdinand VII was used.

Question 15: *Whether Dr Castelli disregarded the law, without rewarding merit or punishing crime.*

Captain Alvariño: On the contrary, delinquents were punished, since many deserters were executed.

Question 16: *Whether there existed the intention of obeying government authority by organizing in Potosí the Congress of the provinces of Upper Perú.*

Captain Figueroa: Following the episodes of April 5 and 6, I heard the officers say that once the show at the Desaguadero River was over, Buenos Aires was to be attacked (...)

Question 17: *Whether Dr Castelli received bribes for conferring employment or for any other reason. Whether he received presents or gifts in cash or any other kind of gift during the time of his commission.*
Professor Carrasco: Quite the opposite. In Potosí and Charcas he refused the offer of the *Cabildos* to pay his expenses. I was commissioned to notify the town halls about his negative myself. In Cochabamba he did not accept the presents offered him and in La Paz he refused a horse with gold harnesses and a key, also made of gold, which he requested be granted to the city.
Dr Monteagudo: I am positive that he did not receive any bribes or gifts from the authorities or from any particular individual, except a silver card presented to him by the University of Charcas.

Question 18: *Whether he engaged in communication or carnal intercourse with women. Whether he surrendered to the vice of drinking or gambling, in a way that might have shocked the people.*
Friar Cuesta: Dr Castelli has not incurred in any of the defects mentioned in the question, for I did not know about it and he could not have concealed this from me since I knew him intimately.

It is clear that none of the witnesses confirmed the charges brought against him by the enemies of the revolution. Bernardo de Monteagudo set the tone when, asked "Whether loyalty to Ferdinand VII had been attacked, in an attempt to induce the system of liberty, equality and independence. Whether Dr Castelli knew about this," he replied, proudly, honoring his comrade: "The illegitimate rule of the Spanish sovereigns was formally attacked and Dr Castelli attempted through every mean, direct or indirect, to propagate the system of equality and independence."

Silence

But by then Castelli was facing a trial more terrible than this legal one. An untended cigar burn on his tongue had started a cancerous tumor that would prove fatal.

On the 11th of June 1812 the revolution began to lose its voice. A surgeon amputated Castelli's tongue who could thereafter only defend himself in writing: "I am not escaping the trial; Your Excellency very well knows that I requested it, for I have no crimes to hide." Perhaps during those terrible days Castelli remembered the phrase of his admired Socrates: "Those who serve their countries should be glad if before they have statues erected to them they do not have scaffolds erected."

Few are the friends who visit him: Bernardo de Monteagudo, who is in charge of his defense, and his cousin Manuel Belgrano, who "busted a few horses" in his haste to reach and embrace him.

According to the death certificate issued at the Parish of la Merced, on the night of the 11th of October 1812, he received the extreme unction. He asked for some paper and pencil to write: "If you see the future, tell it not to come." Ironically enough, he died in the early hours of October 12, Columbus Day.

Manuel Moreno says: "Castelli died a poor and persecuted man. The evils that dug his grave before his natural time were not the excesses of his life, as the slanderers said, but ingratitude and affliction."[28]

On December 8, 1812, a notice appeared in the *Grito del Sud* announcing the selling in auction of "the house and the possessions of the late Dr Castelli, on the coast of San Isidro." In 1814 his widow María Rosa Lynch, almost a pauper by then, began the task of claiming the salaries owed to her husband in these terms: "Following the death of my husband the citizen Juan José Castelli in October 1812, with the cause of the *Residencia* followed him left pending and no steps taken to resume it, on account of the order in which the incidents took place, and the inexcusable delays systematically observed in this affair by the Triumvirate of that day."

Salaries and travelling expenses owed to Castelli totalled 3378 pesos. They were paid thirteen years later.

28 Manuel Moreno, *Vida y memorias del Dr Mariano Moreno*, Buenos Aires, Eudeba, 1972.

So Much Fire: Mariano Moreno's "Mysterious" Death

> *Saavedra and the rogues like him*
> *are the ones who are benefiting,*
> *and not precisely for the good of the country,*
> *because what you and the other patriots*
> *have achieved is lost already.*
>
> LETTER SENT BY
> MARÍA GUADALUPE CUENCA DE MORENO
> TO HER HUSBAND dated April 20, 1811

When those who wield power and own history want to conceal their crimes, they shroud them in mystery, plant misleading clues, and accuse those who suspect them of entertaining "conspiracy delusions," resorting to the old trick of charging the victim with the crime. Thus, according to this discursive strategy, both the victims and those who will not resign themselves to repeating the lesson written by their officious scribes, become suspect.

Moreno's death is in this aspect paradigmatic. It is difficult to find another episode where all the evidence leads us to conclude that this was a murder case, although we are expected to ignore this certainty on behalf of national unity or some similar entelechy.

Mariano Moreno was murdered, and what is more, he is murdered everyday when his ideas are adulterated and he is described as a terrorist, an English agent, an *Unitario*, a centralist, or a forerunner of Rivadavia. As Borges said, "the only real death is oblivion," and that is the goal of those who feel indicted by what Mariano Moreno did, thought, dreamed and wrote back in 1810.

Between Rousseau and Túpac Amaru

Mariano Moreno had been born in Buenos Aires on the 23rd of September 1778. He was 21 when he arrived in Chuquisaca. There he was befriended by Terrazas, a clergyman whose illustration went beyond the strict limits of the theological and scholastic learning of his day. Terrazas gave Moreno access to his library and welcomed him into his circle of friends and disciples.

Of all the authors that he frequented in that library, Juan de Solórzano y Pereyra and Victorián de Villava made the deepest impression on him. Solórzano demanded that *criollos* were granted equal rights. Villava, a famous attorney at the *Audiencia* of Charcas who defended the Indians and translated the physiocrat Genovesi's *Lessons in Commerce*, denounced, in his *Discourse on the Mita of Potosí*, the brutal slavery the Indians were subjected to in the mines: "In mining countries all one sees is the opulence of a few based on the misery of the many." The thinker that most influenced Mariano Moreno as a student, however, was Geneva-born Jean-Jacques Rousseau (1712-1778), of whom he would later say: "This immortal man who excited the admiration of his century, and who will continue to marvel us throughout the ages, was perhaps the first to dissipate the darkness through which despotic rulers have shrouded their usurpations, and to bring the rights of the people to the light."

In 1802, when he was about to be awarded his degree in law, he visited the mines of Potosí and was deeply moved by the degree of exploitation and misery to which the Indians were subjected. At about the time of Victorián Villava's death, and in homage to his teacher, on his return to Chuquisaca Moreno wrote his doctoral dissertation and called it *Legal Dissertation on the Personal Service of Indians*, where he said, among other things: "From the moment of the discovery malice has had its sway, persecuting men whose only crime was to have been born in a land made by nature rich in opulence, men who have preferred to leave their villages rather than suffer the oppression and service of their masters, their judges and their priests. Over and over again, these miserable men are torn from their home and country to become the victims of a veiled immolation. They are forced to crawl through narrow, underground tunnels carrying on their shoulders the food and tools needed for their labor; to remain underground for many days, and then carry out the metals they have dug out on their backs, which is a flagrant infraction of the law prohibiting even voluntary transport of such loads; all these torments, together with the abuses they must suffer, cause that less that three quarters of the Indians that leave the *mita* ever make it back home."[1]

Chuquisaca had a population of about 18,000 and was the seat of one of the most prestigious universities in America, in which, in addition to Moreno, Juan José Castelli and Bernardo de Monteagudo would study. Fresh in the area were the memories of the rebellion led by Túpac Amaru and his successor, Túpac Catari, who managed to frighten the *encomenderos* and all those who benefited from the system of exploitation built up by Spain, and revealed how cruel the powerful can be when they feel threatened. The descendants of the 100,000 dead the repression left in its

1 Mariano Moreno, *Escritos*, Buenos Aires, Estrada, 1943.

wake preserved the story the murderers had tried to silence forever. Moreno became interested in Túpac Amaru's ideas and related them to Rousseau's, who had written in *The Social Contract*: "Man is born free, but everywhere he is in chains."

In 1804, while visiting a shop, Moreno was stunned by the beauty of a young lady portrayed in a cameo. He asked if that lady existed and was told that this was the case – she was fourteen years old and her name was María Guadalupe Cuenca. Moreno did not pause until he found her. They looked into each other's eyes and Guadalupe, whose mother had destined to the nunnery, found in her love for Moreno the most convincing argument against being confined in a convent. They got married on the 20th of May 1804 and a year later their son Marianito was born. Between 1803 and 1804, Moreno had undergone his professional training at the office of Agustín Gascón, taking up the defense of several Indians against the abuses of their masters. In his allegations, he accused the mayor of Cochabamba and the mayor of Chayanta. The situation of the Morenos in Chuquisaca was getting difficult. Pressure increased and Moreno decided to return to Buenos Aires with his family in 1805.

Moreno and Rivadavia

Soon after arriving in Buenos Aires, Moreno began to work as a lawyer and was appointed court reporter of the *Audiencia* and assistant to the *Cabildo* of Buenos Aires.

One of the first cases he had deal with involved young Bernardino Rivadavia, who had filed a complaint before the *Cabildo* because he had been denied his designation as second lieutenant, for which had been recommended by his friend Liniers. It would be helpful if the so-called Argentine liberals and the right-wing nationalists – traditionally, historical partners in every military coup – who always attempt to put Moreno and Rivadavia in the same bag, had the following excerpt in mind, where Moreno describes the future father of the foreign debt: "May Your Excellency be so kind as to take note of the behavior of this young man: he has already opened an office, although he is not a lawyer; he already affects the air of the wise, although he has never set foot in a classroom; no sooner does he pretend to be a judge than he is introducing himself as a wealthy merchant, and all these roles are the unfortunate consequence of the tenacity with which he affects to excel in all careers, when in fact he has not even taken the first step in any. He has no career, no faculties; he is a young man without training or merit or any other of the qualities that are respected in this town."[2]

Making the Revolution

The writing in 1809 of *The Representation of Landowners*, where Moreno revisited Manuel Belgrano's ideas of promoting agriculture and manufactures, gained him the goodwill of the revolutionaries, whose activities had been developing since the English Invasions, and from which he had so far kept at a prudent distance. Perhaps this is the reason why, according to his brother Manuel, his appointment as Secretary to the *Primera Junta* (First Government Council) surprised him so.

Mariano Moreno's role during the May Week was low-key at first. Unlike Castelli, he did not speak at the famous

2 Mariano Moreno, *op. cit.*

Cabildo on May 22, nor did he linger round the Square with French, Beruti and their *chisperos*. Only on the 25th of May 1810 did he come to center-stage, when he took up office as War and Government Secretary of the First Council, and gave his inaugural speech: "The present change should not be reduced to the substitution of public officers while emulating their corruption and indolence. It is essential that we eliminate the abuses of the administration, display an unprecedented activity, remedy the evils that affect the State, excite and direct the public spirit, educate the people, destroy its enemies or put them in check, and give new life to the provinces. If the government turns away from work, follows in the steps of its predecessors, pledging allegiance to corruption and disorder, it will betray the just hopes of the people, and will not be worthy of the high destiny entrusted to it." Once in the Council, Moreno put all his revolutionary ideas into practice. Thanks to his impulse, the Council opened several ports to foreign commerce with the purpose of fighting "the smugglers' monopoly," lowered the tax on exports and wrote trade regulations with the aim of improving tax collection and the economy in general.

"Contraband," he wrote, "was exercised so shamefully in this city, that it appeared to have lost all its deformity, and complicity became the norm. Why, we should blush at the memory of those governments, which allowed for the luxurious existence of criminal men whose sole income derived from the contraband they protected."

Moreno took an active role in the creation of a public library, and personally promoted education, for "there is nothing as deserving of the attention of the magistrates as the improvement of public education by all means," to which purpose he collaborated in the writing and publication of a text-book featuring all the "new ideas" and commissioned the *Cabildos* to "distribute it free of charge among all the poor children in school and command the children of wealthy parents to buy them at the printing house."[3] With regard to education, he established a pension for teachers, "offering them the support of the government for any of their undertakings." He promoted education among the military because "in addition to surprising the enemy with his courage, the officer of our army must win the support of the people through the irresistible lure of his instruction. He who is deprived of these qualities must redouble his efforts to acquire them, and not feel ashamed of gently surrendering to the lessons imparted to him, for in a new country we are all beginners, and only different in our good or bad wishes. He who does not feel urged to learn and excel in his career should abandon it in good time, and not be exposed to the sure shame of being thrown out in ignominy: he should seek shelter in a land of barbarians or slaves and escape our great Buenos Aires, which will not accept among its children men foreign to virtue."[4]

Moreno vindicated his dear friend Manuel Belgrano when he opened the longed-for School of Mathematics, which had been boycotted by the spokespersons of the Consulate.

On June 7[5] he created the official medium of the revolutionary government, *La Gaceta de Buenos Aires*, where he wrote: "The people have the right to know about the behavior of their representatives, and the honor of the latter desires that everyone know how contemptuously

---

3 Mariano Moreno, *op. cit.*
4 *Ibid.*
5 Because of this, June 7 has been established as Journalist's Day.

they look at the schemes and mysteries devised by power to conceal its offenses. The people should not be contented with their chiefs doing good, they should demand that they never do wrong. To fulfill such just desires the Council has resolved that a new weekly periodical with the title *La Gaceta de Buenos Aires* be printed."[6] In it he published – in the manner of the newspaper serials popular in Europe at the time – his admired Rousseau's *The Social Contract*, to acquaint as many citizens as possible with this work. As he was aware of the alarming percentage of illiteracy, he ordered the reading of Rousseau from the pulpits of the churches, upsetting some counter-revolutionary priests. In his prologue to the work he wrote: "If the people are not educated, if their rights are not vulgarized, if every man does not recognize what he is worth, what he is capable of and what he knows, new illusions will replace the old ones, and after hesitating for some time between a thousand uncertainties, it will be our lot to change tyrants, without destroying tyranny."[7]

For strategic reasons, Moreno suppressed the last chapter of *The Social Contract*. It would not have been wise to clash with the Church, given that many of its members supported the revolution. Moreno justified his censorship of the fragment by saying: "As the author had the disgrace to talk nonsense when discussing religious matters, I have suppressed the chapter and the main passages referring to them." One of the passages censored by Moreno read: "Religion in essential to the people and to the chiefs of state; no empire

6 In every number, *La Gaceta* included the following quote by Tacitus: "They are times of a rare happiness, when one can feel what one wishes and licitly say so."

7 Mariano Moreno, *Escritos políticos*, Buenos Aires, La Cultura Argentina, 1915.

ever existed without it. But religion should not be mistaken for its ceremonial. The cult demanded by God emanates from the heart; and the heart, when it is honest, is always uniform. It is therefore vain to believe that God concerns himself with the manner in which the priest is dressed, the order of his words, his gestures at the altar, or his genuflexions."[8]

As Boleslao Lewin points out, Moreno, who was a practicing Catholic, agreed with all of Rousseau's ideas, even the religious ones, as he stated in one of his first writings, where the influence of Rousseau is evident: "The external forms of worship have no intrinsic relation to their object; in our day to bend a knee is an act of reverence, tomorrow it might be a sign of mockery or disrespect."[9]

La Gaceta was destined to be much more than the government's official medium, it was a platform through which, for the first time, the citizens of the ex viceroyalty would have access to the modern ideas that would slowly wake them from the nightmare of backwardness that almost 300 years of scholastic education had produced.

Meanwhile, former viceroy Cisneros and the members of the *Audiencia*, whose salaries and personal safety had been guaranteed by the new government, began to prepare the counter-revolution, attempting to escape to Montevideo and join Governor Elío – who had not recognized the authority of Buenos Aires and had managed to be appointed viceroy – but, as we mentioned earlier, they were all arrested and sent to Spain on a British vessel.

Playwright Cernadas Lamadrid has Cisneros pronounce the following speech before boarding the ship: "If I represent

8 Boleslao Lewin, *Rousseau y la independencia americana*, Buenos Aires, Eudeba, 1965.
9 *Idem*.

what you despise, finish me off! Display my head in the square, stamp your freedom with the seal of my blood. But do it! Otherwise *your* blood will run for the benefit of others. Pay the price of freedom. Let the arm you have raised to strike come down. If you do not finish me off, you will never finish anything. You will only pretend to. O those who grow on borrowed roots! Hundreds of viceroys with a thousand costumes will come to enslave you. And what is worse: you will become your own viceroys."

In July 1810, the Council commissioned Moreno to write a plan aimed at unifying the goals and strategies of the revolution. Moreno, who wrote it together with Manuel Belgrano, presented it before the Council in August, and as an introduction, he told his readers that they should not "be shocked at my phrasing – cutting heads off, shedding blood, sacrifice at all costs. To achieve the revolutionary ideal, one must resort to very drastic means."

In the plan, Moreno suggested starting an uprising in the Banda Oriental and the south of Brazil while continuing to feign loyalty to Ferdinand VII – so as to buy time and guarantee neutrality, that is to say, England's and Portugal's support – expropriating the wealth of the Spaniards and using those funds to create sugar mills, factories, and promote navigation. He recommended the observance of "the cruellest and most sanguinary behavior towards the enemy" to achieve the final goal: complete independence.

Those who would see Moreno as an English agent have evidently not read the text published in *La Gaceta* on the 6th of September 1810: "The people should always look after their interest and rights, and should only trust themselves. The foreigner does not come to our country to work for our benefit, but to make as great a profit as he can. Let us welcome him kindly, let us learn from the improvements of his civilization, accept the works of his industry and give him access to the fruits that nature has granted us so bountifully; but let us listen to his advice with caution and let us not make the mistake of those peoples who, enchanted by colorful beads and trinkets, are wrapped in chains instead. Let us learn from our fathers and may no one ever write about us what has been written about the inhabitants of ancient Spain and the Carthaginians that ruled them:

> *Happy, free independent Spain,*
> *Welcomed the Carthaginians in their folly:*
> *Only to see these traitors*
> *Arrive as friends to become masters,*
> *Start by selling to end by ruling.*[10]

In the same sense, we should take note of the irritation felt by the British ambassador in Rio de Janeiro, Lord Strangford, on finding out about the execution of Liniers and his accomplices in Córdoba: "The recent procedure of the Council with regard to Liniers and his comrades, in stark contrast to the moderate spirit that governed your first measures, has led those who initially pronounced themselves in your favor, to change their minds. I would like to believe that while on my part I strive to preserve the harmony existing between these two countries, you, on your part, will not do anything that might taint it or raise concern or alarm."

Moreno's acts and ideology couldn't but distance him from the president of the Council. Moreno embodied the ideas of the groups that wanted to go beyond administrative

---

10 Mariano Moreno, *Escritos políticos, op. cit.*

transformation and who were willing to make deeper political and economic changes. If he believed that the revolution should be controlled from Buenos Aires, it was because the provinces were still under the control of the most conservative groups, in alliance with the previous government. He claimed that "it was the ancient government that doomed us to vegetate in darkness and dejection, but since nature has made us for great deeds, we have started by clearing the land of so many ignorant and abusive rulers."

Cornelio Saavedra, on the other hand, represented the interests and ideas of the conservative elite, who was striving to maintain its privileges and consequently, had to preserve the ancient social order, in which, as Moreno argued, "some people seem to believe that we have made a revolution so that the native sons may now enjoy the posts from which they were previously excluded; as if the country were less unfortunate in knowing that misrule was now in the hands of her sons."

An incident further complicated the relationship between the president and the secretary. Through a political maneuver, the reactionary groups in Buenos Aires attempted to appropriate the glory of the patriotic army's first victory, at Suipacha – present-day Bolivia – on the 7th of November 1810. Thus, on the evening of December 5 a celebration was held at the Regiment of the *Patricios*, the stronghold of Saavedra's supporters. The gathering was so exclusive that not even the Council's Secretary of War, Mariano Moreno, could get in, a sentry barring his way at the gate. Moreno found out that one of the guests, Captain Atanasio Duarte, who had drunk a little too much, had proposed a toast to "the first King and Emperor of America, Don Cornelio Saavedra" and had offered Doña Saturnina, Saavedra's wife, a sugar crown that lay on a cake.

Moreno got carried way by his revolutionary passion, falling for his enemies' provocation. That same night he ordered the banishment of Atanasio Duarte,[11] arguing that "a citizen of Buenos Aires cannot, be he drunk or asleep, make statements against the freedom of his country," and wrote the remarkable Decree for the Suppression of Honors, whose sole addressee was the president of the Council, deprived by it of all the rights and privileges inherited from the viceroys.

The text was extremely harsh, and began as follows: "Useless would be the publication of liberal principles by this Council, leading the people to appreciate the invaluable gift of their freedom, if it allowed for the continuity of those privileges invented by tyrants to disgrace humanity and stifle natural feelings. The many, being deprived of the necessary intelligence to value things rightly, prevented by the nature of their labor to follow their meditations beyond their first needs, used to seeing the magistrates and chiefs shining with a luster that astonishes and sets them apart from the commonality, end by mistaking the incenses and ceremonies for the authority of those who enjoy them; and never pause to judge the chief by his merits but by the trinkets and stripes they have always seen him adorned with. It so happens that the usurper, the despot, the murderer of his country is followed by a large worshipping crowd, while at the same time he is burdened with the execration of the philosophers and the curse of the good citizens; and it so happens that at the sight of such exterior apparatus, as sure a sign of forthcoming punishment and violence as any, the

11 Atanasio Duarte was arrested and confined to prison until April 6, 1813.

oppressed tremble with fear and are frightened of themselves, if they were at some point led, by the excess of oppression, to secretly wish to put a remedy to their situation." Saavedra signed the decree as if he were signing his adversary's death sentence.

One of Moreno's last decrees, dated November 26, 1810, further infuriated the *porteño* reactionaries: "The Council has resolved that the current Capuchin abbess be removed, as a nun caught keeping correspondence with the enemies that are blocking us is not worthy of remaining in office. Thus this Council hopes that Your Illustrious Holiness provide this monastery with a new prelate as you see fit."

To get rid of Moreno, his enemies, led by Dean Funes, the deputy for Córdoba and Saavedra's main political operator, connived a scheme consisting in the incorporation of the deputies from the provinces, who were beginning to arrive in the capital, directly into the Council, that is to say, into the executive power, and not into the projected Constitutional Congress, or legislative power.

Funes publicly owned up to his reactionary intentions: "By making the deputies take an active role in the government we have banished the secret of its workings, its celerity of action and its harshness," thus thwarting the rule of those who "were mindlessly distributing the legitimate riches of wealthy citizens."

Moreno did not oppose the incorporation of the deputies from the provinces. What is more, he had proposed a selection criterion, and therefore a representation criterion, much more inclusive than the one projected by Saavedra. While the president argued that only the capitals of the provinces should elect delegates, Moreno wanted a greater number of provincial cities to be represented; and wrote: "For the community to feel bound to the acts of a representative, it is necessary that he be elected by all, and has ample powers to perform his task."

In this sense, Moreno's opposition to their incorporation stemmed from his clear perception of Funes' scheme, aimed at undermining his power. Moreno was concerned about the conservative tendencies of the chosen representatives of the provinces and suspected their legitimacy, and as they began to arrive he realized that their influence would negatively affect the development of the revolution. Furthermore, Moreno knew that the object of this maneuver was to endlessly postpone the General Constitutional Congress, which according to his ideas should not be reduced to electing provincial authorities at the president's convenience, but should fulfil the duty of creating a modern and fair Constitution for the provinces, still ruled by the medieval Hispanic legislation. Moreno was positive about the existence of many competent people in the provinces, friends of the revolution who could represent their province with dignity, but he did not have the contacts or the power to outweigh the political machinery of Saavedra's supporters, who did everything in their power to manipulate the elections and designate the men most hostile to the changes promoted by Moreno and his supporters.

As an example, here are the CVs of some of the deputies whom certain historians are wont to consider the forerunners of federalism: José Tomás Sánchez, deputy for Salta, accused of bankruptcy and embezzlement of the Royal Tobacco Agency; Francisco de Acuña, for Catamarca, Spanish commander and official of the Royal Treasury, leader of the counter-revolutionaries in his province; Juan José Lami, for Santiago del Estero, a confessed enemy of the revolution. Moreno managed to contest their diplomas, but Saavedra's supporters succeeded in designating men of a similar background in the majority of the provinces.

Moreno, the "*Unitario*"

Some shortsighted people want to see in this dispute the origin of the opposition between *Unitarios* and *Federales*, branding Moreno as the father of the *Unitarios* and offering Saavedra as the progenitor – our history being so fond of finding "fathers" – of Federalism. This is odd, for Saavedra, who was not very prone to philosophy and writing, never jotted a line including the words "Federalism" or "federation," whereas Moreno, the "*Unitario*", devoted several passages of his work *On the Goals of the Congress Recently Convoked* and *State Constitution* to this question. He argued: "The leading principle of a federation lies in that the individual states, retaining part of the sovereignty necessary to the prosecution of their internal affairs, endow a supreme and national authority with a part of their sovereignty that we may call eminent, for the management of general affairs, in other words, for all those matters that require to be dealt with as a nation. Therefore, while in regard to particular affairs and within its territory a member of a federation acts independently as his own legislator, in regard to general matters he is subjected to the laws and regulations issued by the national authority that they all have constituted. Despite opinions to the contrary, this form of government has the advantage of the influence of general accord: it resembles the harmonies found in nature, where diverse actions and forces converge to a common end, with the purpose of balance and not of opposition; and since it is practiced in the most uneducated societies, it cannot be said to be difficult. This is, perhaps, the best system ever created by men."

On the 18th of December 1810 the voting concerning the incorporation of deputies took place. Moreno opposed the conservative coup, but was largely outnumbered, his only support being that of his friend and comrade Juan José Paso. Saavedra admitted that this was an illegal procedure, but voted in favor of the inclusion alleging that "despite it not being according to law, he accepted the incorporation for public convenience," setting a serious precedent, so useful to future generations of politicians, through which public convenience and the law are always at odds.

Moreno decided to resign, stating his position clearly: "I believe the incorporation of the deputies into the Council to be contrary to the law and the well-being of the State." An he added: "Since the continuation of a discredited magistrate cannot be beneficial to the public, I resign, but do not regret the December 6 Act (Decree of Suppression of Honors) which has gained me the present discredit; I hope that some day I will enjoy the gratitude of the same citizens that have now persecuted me, whom I forgive with all my heart, and look upon their misguided behavior with some kind of pleasure, for I would like to see the people begin to concern themselves with the government, even if they make mistakes they will later remedy, and regret having wronged the men who have defended their rights with pure intentions." Miguel Ángel Cárcano rightfully argues that Moreno's "deficiency as a statesman was not to secure the support of the army. A revolutionary without a military force is at the mercy of his own guard."

Cárcano is referring to Moreno's decision of sending two allies as irreplaceable as Manuel Belgrano and Juan José Castelli away from Buenos Aires on a military mission, following the desertion of the *saavedrista* military commanders, like Ortiz de Ocampo and Viamonte.

Ignacio Núñez, a friend of Moreno's, said: "The disorder caused in the organization of the primitive government by the incorporation of the deputies and the proscription of

Dr Moreno was as alarming to Representative Castelli as it had been to General Belgrano: they disapproved of it not only because they were left with no political operators in the capital, but also because of the spirit that had guided the whole affair. There existed a clear determination to extinguish the people's revolutionary fire, which the primitive government had drawn on directly in order to give an unexpected boost to the general cause in only six months. Espionage, treason, and threats were used against those who dared oppose or question the government's procedures."

Bernardo de Monteagudo agrees with Núñez: "Saavedra knew that many deputies were rascals ready to prostitute his mission, and he was not mistaken. Conceivably, each step taken by the deputies beyond the object for which they had been appointed would be dangerous and illegal: the people had granted them power only to legislate and set the constitution of the State; until the Congress was assembled, they had no proper task nor no right to take part in the provisional system. But let us leave this controversy and pay attention to the evils that their incorporation has brought."[12]

On the 24th of December 1810 Saavedra signed the decree appointing Moreno representative of the Council before the governments of Rio de Janeiro and London. Moreno's mission was to strengthen the bonds between the Council and each of these governments through a series of pacts and agreements against the common enemy – France. Accompanying him on a mission that everyone thought rather impracticable and therefore suspicious went his

12 Bernardo de Monteagudo, *Escritos políticos*, Buenos Aires, La Cultura Argentina, 1916.

brother Manuel and Tomás Guido as secretaries. Moreno also carried a letter of recommendation written by McKinnon, the leader of the British merchants in Buenos Aires, to hand to Wellesley.

On Christmas Eve, celebrations were held at the leading mansions of Buenos Aires. The conservatives congratulated themselves on the overthrow of Moreno. The Marquis de Casa Irujo, Spanish Ambassador in Rio, wrote to the Portuguese minister that Spain celebrated the removal of Moreno, described as "a wild Jacobin, with a great talent for evil." In a letter to Chiclana, Saavedra made a similar remark: "I have achieved what I had set my mind on – expelling that demon from hell."

Cornelio Saavedra was now surrounded by the most conservative groups of the former viceroyalty, who had obtained their first victory in setting the counter-revolution in motion.

Months later, Saavedra himself admitted to this in a letter to Viamonte, his ideological partner: "For a long time now, the Council of Buenos Aires has not concerned itself with general welfare. Does happiness consist in adopting the most coarse and unpolitical democracy? Does it consist in men doing what their whims or interests dictate to them? Does it consist in trampling over every European, stealing his properties, killing him, finishing and exterminating him? Does it consist in furthering the system of terror that was beginning to rear its head? Does it consist in freedom of religion and in being able to say 'I don't give a shit about God' and do whatever I want? (...) If you remember Moreno's iniquities and believe that what we have done in Buenos Aires is but to tear out by the root the seed planted by this perverse man, which was rapidly growing wild, your suspicions will be undoubtedly allayed, for, my friend, you are free to believe what I am telling you, or not, but it is the whole truth."

Moreno had been defeated and, facing various threats against his life, he accepted – perhaps with the intention of buying time for his friends to revert the situation – a mission to Europe with the purpose of purchasing arms. Saavedra gave his version of the incident in a letter to Chiclana dated January 15, 1811: "This low-life scoundrel, a revolutionary by temperament, and cold in the extreme, who tried to have me arrested and even murdered, took me aside and begged me to send him to London as a deputy: I conceded and gave him my word; I got him everything he asked for: he has been allotted 8000 pesos per year for the time of his stay, he has been given 20,000 pesos to cover expenses, he has been granted permission to take his brother and Guido, both as good a piece of work as he, with two years advanced salary and an extra 500; in brief, I have consented to every one of his demands." The letter concluded with an odd request: "If you have the time, please buy me or order four dozen sets of silver cutlery and send me the bill, which I will pay it later." It appears that the president was preparing some kind of celebration.

Saavedra's scornful language and passion for defamation omitted what the money was for: Moreno had to buy three tickets to London, pay his and his secretaries' expenses for two years, set up a secretariat and pay the rent. In 1812, exasperated by slander, María Guadalupe Cuenca, Moreno's widow, addressed a letter to the Triumvirate saying that "the money is neither on mine nor on his account, because he never was in possession of such a sum."

Manuel Moreno, Mariano's brother and biographer, comments on the threats to his brother's life and how he reacted to them: "The enemies of the system fingered him as the first victim of their revenge. This did not prevent Dr Moreno from behaving as modestly as he had always behaved (...) He would leave the palace of government very late at night, despite the risk of being assaulted by the discontented (...) Many times the commanders of the guard urged him to take an escort home, but his answer was always: 'I'd rather take the risk of being murdered for serving my country, than walk the streets with the trappings of tyrants.' (...) He would always carry a pair of small pistols with him, and when he retired at night, two or three friends, but never soldiers, would walk him home."

In a report dated January 4, 1811 the Council no longer integrated by Moreno warned him that "given the circumstances the departure of an emissary was unsafe," and that "the diplomatic mission was at his discretion."[13]

With the Serenity of Socrates

On the 24th of January 1811 Moreno embarked upon the British schooner Mistletoe, which was to take him to the English frigate Fame, hired by Saavedra's agents. There, his two secretaries are waiting for him: his brother Manuel and Tomás Guido. Moreno thinks he is going to London. A few men know that he is going to his death.

Soon after embarking, Moreno, who had never enjoyed very good health, fell ill and told his companions: "This journey is ill-omened." He devoted the few hours he felt relatively well to translating from the English a curious book: *Travels of Anacharsis the Younger in Greece* by Jean-Jacques Barthelemy. Anacharsis, a Greek philosopher from

13 Revista *Ilustración Histórica*, 1st of November 1909.

the 5th century B.C., had said: "Wise men propose, and fools dispose." The opening of Manuel Moreno's account of his brother's death is also related to Greek Philosophy: "Dr Moreno saw the proximity of death with the serenity of Socrates." It should be noted that in 399 B.C. Socrates had been accused of rejecting the gods worshipped by the State, of introducing new deities and of corrupting youth. In *The Apology of Socrates*, Plato tells that the death sentence was passed by a divided jury and a difference of a few votes, but when in his argument the great philosopher offered to pay a paltry sum for his life, because, in his opinion, that was what a philosopher was worth to the State, the jury felt offended and sentenced him to take hemlock by an overwhelming majority. Socrates' friends, his great disciple Plato among them, suggested he escape, but the master preferred to comply with the law and be poisoned.

While Moreno's suffering continued at sea, on the 9th of February 1811 – that is to say, fifteen days after Moreno's departure – in Buenos Aires the *porteño* government led by Funes and Saavedra signed a contract with a certain David Curtis from Forest sending him on a mission identical to Moreno's, with the purpose of furnishing the burgeoning national army. The fifth article of the document established that "to act on the agreement Mr Curtis shall first come to an understanding with the emissary of this Council in London, Dr Mariano Moreno, whose approval will be a prerequisite for Mr Curtis to obtain the authorization of this Council." The sixth article stipulated that payment of his fees should be certified by Dr Moreno. But here comes the best part: the eleventh article specified, with a foresight unprecedented among our statesmen, that "if Dr Moreno passed away or for some unforeseen accident were not in

England, Mr Curtis shall deal with don Aniceto Padilla on the same terms as he would have with Dr Moreno."

Padilla, who had cooperated with Beresford's escape in 1807, was chosen by the Council in September 1810 to buy arms in London. He was Curtis' business partner and together they planned an illegal operation to purchase arms through the French trafficker Charles Dumouriez – whom Saavedra had introduced to Padilla – given that England could not be caught selling arms that were to be used against Spain.

When Moreno embarked, the deal had already been closed. In a letter addressed to Saavedra, Dumouriez asked him to trust Padilla entirely and "avoid designating new agents that far from benefiting our business here would hinder it" and asked him to remember that "in a country where money is the key that opens all doors, it is essential that you give Padilla discretionary credit limit on the London bankers to face obligations, or cover unforeseen or secret expenses."

Without any doubt Moreno would object to the economic terms of the deal and the bulky commissions paid to the intermediaries, as his brother Manuel did on his arrival in London, calling Padilla "a rascal, miserable parasite and a conspirator." The number of persons who did not want Moreno to reach his destination was growing by the minute.

The aldermen of the *Cabildo* of Buenos Aires issued a decree saying that "the reading of Roussseau's *Social Contract* ordered by Dr Moreno is not only useless but also rather detrimental" and declared the "purchase of 200 copies of the work as superfluous."

"Before embarking," Manuel Moreno continues, "Dr Moreno's health was greatly affected by the permanent weariness caused by political affairs. Recent grief had considerably abated his spirit and the notion of ingratitude would constantly creep upon his imagination, so forcibly that it could not but damage his physical constitution. Ineffectively, reflection would try to alleviate the strong impression caused upon his honor by the unfair attack leveled at him by the shameful passion of his adversaries. His extreme weakness made the shadow of absurd irregularity that had been attributed to his operations seem unbearable."

"Not being able to minister to him any of the remedies of the art," Manuel Moreno carries on, "our only hope was set on the swiftness of the voyage; but unfortunately this was extremely slow, and our entreaties to the captain to land in the Janeiro [Rio de Janeiro] or the Cape of Good Hope, were disregarded."

The captain of the Fame, whose name has been mysteriously omitted by the scriveners of official history, usually thorough in these matters, proved to be hostile throughout the journey and refused to pay heed to the humanitarian entreaties of Moreno's secretaries, who asked him to land in the nearest port. In view of Moreno's constant request for painkillers, and of the absence of a doctor on board, the captain secretly administered Moreno drops of a mysterious alleged medication, but under this treatment Moreno's condition only got worse. Finally, on the night of the 4th of March 1811, the unidentified captain offered him a glass of water containing four grams of tartar emetic (antimony potassium tartrate).

In his book *Pharmacology*,[14] Dr Manuel Litter explains that antimony is a heavy metal resembling arsenic, and the

---

14 Manuel Litter, *Farmacología*, Buenos Aires, El Ateneo, 1961.

ingestion of a 0.15 gram dose might be lethal. Moreno was administered forty times this measure. Dr Litter observes that the symptoms provoked by antimony poisoning are similar to those caused by arsenic.[15]

In 1836, by then a diploma-carrying physician, Manuel Moreno recalled this incident as follows: "The fatal accident that took his life was caused by an excessive dose of an emetic administered by the captain in a glass of water one afternoon when he found him alone and prostrated in his study. It is a serious circumstance that he said to the patient that it was a light and vitalizing medication without explaining what it was or informing the rest of us before presenting it to him. If Dr Moreno had known that he was being given such quantity of the substance, he would have not taken it, for in view of the damage that it caused him, and once the fact was revealed, he said that his constitution did not admit the fourth part (of the dose) and that he reputed himself dead. Doubts remain as to whether the quantity of the drug was larger or whether it was another corrosive substance that was administered to him, the circumstances of the incident not allowing for an autopsy."

"This was followed by a terrible convulsion," Manuel Moreno continues, "which hardly gave him time to bid farewell to his country, family and friends. In spite of our efforts to stop him, he left his bed while already in this state and with visible agitation lied on the chamber floor, and then struggled to make an admirable exhortation about our duties in the country we were about to enter, and instructed us in the manner we should, in his absence, fulfill our

15 Eduardo Durnhofer, *Mariano Moreno inédito*, Buenos Aires, Plus Ultra, 1972.

assignments in. He asked his friends and enemies to forgive him; he called the captain and commended our persons to him; particularly and most vividly, he entrusted me with the care of his innocent wife, using this word to refer to her on several occasions. The last concept he uttered were the following words: 'Long live my country although I perish!' He died on the 4th of March 1811, at dawn, twenty eight degrees and seven minutes south of the line, at the age of 32 years, 6 months and one day. He could speak no more."

Thus ended his days one of the first Argentine revolutionaries. His corpse was thrown into the sea. It would be the first in a long list.

A Few Complaints

On the 9th of March 1813 the General Constitutional Assembly made an inquiry into government procedures. In the cause concerning Moreno's death one can read that an Officer from the War Office, Pedro Jiménez, stated that he had suggested Moreno to seek shelter in a safe place because "there were rumors that he was going to be murdered." The prestigious Dr Juan Madera, who introduced the smallpox vaccination in the country and who was Dean of the School of Medicine and Surgery, stated: "In Oruro in March 1811, he overheard father Azcurra thanking God for the removal of Dr Moreno and as if foretelling his death in the following manner: 'He is already embarked and soon will be dead,' and that lately, because of this piece of information, given so blatantly in advance of the arrival of news about Moreno's death, which was to be known in the month of October, and because of the report that his brother Manuel wrote about the illness, the emetic, and the dose that the British Captain administered him, and the guarded behavior of the latter towards the said brother and Guido, who were accompanying him, as if admitting to the administration of a large dose, the deponent is positive that Dr Moreno was murdered by order of his enemies."

Thus the file ends. So far, no court has been able to bring in a verdict. As we know: Argentine justice tends to be rather slow.

Guadalupe's Letters

Soon after Moreno's departure, his wife Gaudalupe Cuenca, who had received an anonymous package containing a black fan, a veil, a pair of black gloves and a note saying "Dear lady, as I know you are soon to be a widow, I am taking the liberty of sending you these articles that will soon fit your new state," began sending dozens of letters to her husband.

She wrote:

"Moreno, if it is not detrimental to you, please try to come as soon as possible or send for me because I cannot live without you. I don't like to think that you are sick or sad and that your wife and son are not there to comfort you and share your afflictions. Or perhaps you have already found an English lady to replace me? Don't do it, Moreno, if you are tempted by an English lady remember that you have a faithful wife whom you will be offending, after God (...)" (March 14, 1811).

"They have been banished; Azcuénaga and Posadas to Mendoza; Larrea to San Juan; Peña to the farthest tip of San Luis; Vieytes, to the same place; French, Beruti, Donado, Dr Vieytes and Cardoso, to Patagones; I am sending you the manifesto so that you can see for yourself how these rascals lie. Poor Castelli they have covered in slander, they say that he has robbed, that he is a drunkard, that he is a criminal, they don't know how to incriminate him, they have even said that he didn't allow Nieto and the rest who were executed in Potosí to confess; it is clear that those who have made the greatest sacrifices are the ones who are worse off, as you yourself are the best example of, and those poor men who are suffering after all they have done, and this is the whole truth, my dear Moreno, because Saavedra and the rogues like him are the ones who are benefiting, and not precisely for the good of the country, because what you and the other patriots have achieved is lost already, for they only care about their personal interest; as soon as this commission is over we will drag our bones where no one can mess with us and we will enjoy the peace and quiet we were wont to" (April, 20, 1811).

"Ah, Moreno of my heart, I do not have a life without you, my soul has fled and this soulless body cannot live and if you want me to live, please come soon, or send for me. I only find comfort in the promises you made on the days before parting to never forget me, to try and come back soon, to love me always and be faithful, because as soon as you start loving some English lady, good-bye Mariquita, she shall no longer be in your heart, and I will be crying as I am crying now, and suffering because you are not here, which is like death to me, exposed to the hatred of our enemies, and you, you will be enjoying yourself with your English lady; if that happens, as I think it will, I will have to go to you even if you refuse, to get in your way; but to quit suffering I will stop writing these things, I will pretend I have dreamed, and please don't get mad at me for saying these stupid things" (May 9, 1811).

"Your enemies never tire of promoting hatred against you, nor does that scraggy cat of Saturnina (Saavedra) tire of speaking against you at the law courts and blaming you for everything" (May 25, 1811).

"Our Marianito remembers you always, thinks about you a lot and misses you everyday; so my dear Moreno come home soon, if not for me do it for our son, and remember the promises you made before embarking, don't be deceived by any women, remember you are only Mariquita's and she and no one else will love you till death do us part" (July 1, 1811).

"You can figure out for yourself how much this separation hurts, and if you don't mind me saying so, it hurts me more than it hurts you, because I have always known that I love you more than you love me; forgive me my dear Moreno, if I offend you with these words" (July 29, 1811).[16]

This is the last letter that Guadalupe wrote to Moreno. A few days later she finally received an answer to them. It was a letter from her brother-in-law Manuel, dated in London on the 1st of May 1811, telling her that her beloved Mariano had died on March 4.

Saavedra could not conceal his relief and spoke his famous phrase: "So much fire could only be put out by so much water."

Several months later, armed with her immense dignity, Guadalupe addressed the members of the Triumvirate in these terms: "I have just lost my husband. He died on March 4 on the British ship that was carrying him; guided by

16 Enrique Williams Álzaga, *Cartas que nunca llegaron*, Buenos Aires, Emecé, 1967.

enthusiasm for his country, he did all kinds of services and took all kinds of risks; to it he sacrificed his talent, his work, his comfort, even his reputation; in the middle of the ocean he sacrificed himself and put an end to his life's career as a victim of his own misfortune.

"A small child of seven years of age and a sorrowful widow implore the aid of the Fatherland, certain that neither the latter nor its fair government could be indifferent to our misery or be insensitive spectators of our bitter tears, and of the ruin and damage that the most unblemished patriotism have caused us; we appear before Your Excellency with the purpose of asking for a moderate pension as a compensation for so much suffering, this is all we ask. I wish my helplessness were not so great, that I could avoid making a request that so mortifies me."[17]

María Guadalupe received a pension of 30 *pesos fuertes* per month. The salary of each of the members of the Triumvirate was of 800 *pesos fuertes,* but this should not surprise us, for, as Socrates said, to some States, thinkers are not worth much.

[17] Enrique Williams Álzaga, *op. cit.*

The Son of the Fatherland

*I am far from being a true
father to the Fatherland.
I'd be happy, on the other hand,
to be a good son to it.*

MANUEL BELGRANO

Official history has decided that Manuel Belgrano be someone else. Belgrano has not been assigned a day on the official calendar. The anniversary of his death is commemorated as Flag Day. And I need not point out how little that patriotic symbol has come to mean to us beyond football celebrations and chauvinistic declamations. We have not been taught to love our flag with positive examples. It has been violated and usurped by genocidal governments which have abused its use. We must reclaim it for ourselves, an essential but difficult task. In the meantime, however, Belgrano is not remembered as he ought to.

Manuel Belgrano, one of the most remarkable Argentine thinkers, forerunner of national journalism, promoter of popular education, national industry and social justice, among other things, has been condemned to become a Brave Little Tailor of sorts.

The plan is simple enough. He was an ideologist of American subversion and it is not convenient for children to learn to honor the memory of intellectuals, innovators and revolutionaries, particularly those who had the unusual idea of matching their words to their deeds.

The Argentine wealthy – which have profited at the country's expense, and by the hard work of its sons – like to remind us that Belgrano died a poor man. According to their ideas about obedience and example, there is nothing as inspiring – for the rest of mankind – as to die in poverty. Learning to die as one is born, without contending for the oak coffins, the gold fittings, the costly obituaries and the exclusive lot in a private cemetery, is highly rated by those who live off the highs of the stock market.

Magnanimity, unselfishness, and abnegation are a few of the virtues that our patrician families purport to admire in others, rather than practice in themselves. Because the members of these families will be, in dying, much richer than when they were born, as the rest of the Argentine people will be much poorer. It's nothing but applied arithmetic. A ruler's rule.

Of course they forget to mention that Belgrano was born a rich man and that he invested all his economic and human capital in the revolution. They conceal the fact that Belgrano would not accept to die a poor man and that right up to the end he claimed his share: his unpaid salaries, and the putting of the 40,000 gold pesos, which he had donated for the construction of schools and which had been stolen by the crooks in public administration, to their proper use.

They also seem to forget that Belgrano would never tire of denouncing them and would not mince words to describe them. He called them "parasites," "loafers," "speculators" and "partisans of themselves," among other things. And Belgrano's standards – honesty, coherence, humility and dignity – continue denouncing them today.

The following pages do not purport to be a detailed biography of Don Manuel but a brief examination of the least known aspects of his ideas and work.

In Revolutionary Europe

Manuel Belgrano, the first Argentine economist and one of the most lucid intellectuals of the May Revolution, was born in Buenos Aires on the 3rd of June 1770. He studied at the School of San Carlos and then in Spain, at the universities of Valladolid and Salamanca.

Young Manuel arrived in Europe when the French Revolution was at its height, and closely followed all ensuing discussions and debates. "Given that in 1789 I was in Spain, and that the French Revolution had changed ideas, particularly in the men of letters I frequented, I was taken over by the ideas of freedom, equality, security, property, and could only see as tyrants those who opposed the fact that man, no matter where he lived, did not enjoy the rights that God and nature had granted him, and that even societies had agreed to establish directly or indirectly."[1]

Owing to his outstanding grades and his position as president of the Academy of Roman Law, Forensic Politics and Political Economy of the University of Salamanca, he requested and obtained an authorization from Pope Pius VI himself to "read and hold all and any books written by condemned and even heretic authors in any way that they had been prohibited, taking care they would not fall into the hands of others and excluding astrological predictions – which contain superstitions – and those which deliberately deal with obscene matters."

Thus he managed to get acquainted with the ideas of Rousseau, Montesquieu, Adam Smith and the physiocrat Quesnay.

1 Manuel Belgrano, *Autobiografía*, Buenos Aires, Carlos Pérez, 1968.

He was particularly interested in physiocracy, which proposed land as the main source of wealth, and in the liberalism of Adam Smith who, back in 1776, had argued that "the wealth of nations" originated primarily in the labor of its inhabitants. Belgrano believed that both theories were complementary, particularly in a country with so many natural riches to exploit.

In 1794 he returned to Buenos Aires with a degree in law and an appointment as first secretary to the Consulate, granted by King Charles IV. The Consulate was a colonial institution aimed at promoting and controlling economic activities. In that position, Belgrano took it upon himself to put his ideas to work. He was well aware of the importance of promoting education and training people to learn crafts and be able to use them for the benefit of their country. He created schools of technical drawing, maths and navigation.

Education: A Powerful Weapon

Belgrano believed that in order to build a more equitable country, the first task was to drastically transform the colonial educational system: "It is true, children look upon school with dislike, but this is because the school forces them to do the same thing over and over again; they are merely taught to read and write, but they are forced to perform these activities for six or seven hours per day, which makes the memory of school repugnant to them; were it not for the promise of Sunday, this baneful theater where their curiosity and thirst for truth is forever oppressed would be even more repulsive. What a sad state our past and present education is in! The child is punished and chastised in the classroom, scorned in the streets and deceived at home. If attempting to satisfy his natural curiosity he should ask any question, he is looked down upon with scorn, or deceived with two thousand absurdities which will be with him till his final day."

Don Manuel believed in the total equality of opportunities for men and women. He believed that "the woman instils in her children the spirit of the future citizen;" therefore an ignorant woman is a poor generator of citizens, for she will breed retarded, unproductive and incompetent citizens for a democratic nation.

Bu he did not believe that mere words or formal changes could make any real difference. He knew that if the system was not transformed, if wealth was not distributed more equitably, all hope was lost. "There are many books containing discoveries and experiences carried out in agriculture, but these books have never reached the ploughman or peasant."

In 1798 he wrote the first project for a state-supported, public and compulsory education: "How can we expect that men love their work, that habits be changed, that honest behavior spread, that virtue dispel vice, and that the government collect the fruit of its care, if there is no education, and if ignorance is passed on from one generation to the next? Elementary schools should be built at the expense of the Cities and Villages in every Parish under their jurisdiction, and especially in the Countryside where, truth be told, the main contributors reside, those who more justly deserve a compensation. The Judges should compel the Parents to send their children to school, using all the means that good sense may suggest."

He enthusiastically supported the study of History because, he argued, "the study of the past teaches man to deal with his present and future affairs (...) It is of no value to learn about the lives of a certain class of men who have devoted all their efforts and work to themselves, and have not even spared a moment of their lives to think of others."

Industry, Agriculture, Commerce and Internal Market

Belgrano's innovating ideas were reflected in his annual reports for the Consulate, through which he endeavored to promote industry and change the prevailing production model.

He suspected the easy fortunes derived from cattle-grazing because it employed few men, did not foster creativity, discouraged population growth and concentrated wealth in a few hands. His obsession was to promote agriculture and industry.

He offered practical advice for the better use of the land, suggesting that it should not left to fallow since "true rest lies in the rotation of crops." He approved of the system used in Germany at the time, where parish priests guided and assisted the peasants who, in turn, thanks to the knowledge gained, carried our experiments of real value, since they were taught state-of-the-art practices.

Belgrano, the most Catholic of all our national heroes, believed that these were responsibilities belonging to the priests since, "the most effective way to eliminate beggary and misery is to prevent it and tend to in the cradle." He suggested we should follow European practice in giving rewards to those who planted new trees, "granting a prize for each tree that took root."

The secretary of the Consulate proposed protecting the local crafts and industries through a "fund allotted to the ploughman both at sowing and at harvest time." Because, "the importation of merchandise that replaces and prevents the consumption of those produced in the country, or hampers the development of its manufactures, necessary entails the ruin of a nation."

In his view, this was the only way to avoid "the large monopolies existing in this capital, controlled by men who, deprived of love towards their fellowmen, only worry about their particular interest and do not care if the class most useful to the State, the productive class of society, lives in poverty, a poverty which is the consequence of these procedures so abhorrent to nature, religion and the law." Until then, no one had given a better description of the *Porteño* ruling class and its total lack of concern for the progress of the country and its inhabitants.

As far as monetary issues were concerned, Belgrano formulated a pointed critique of Spanish mercantilism, which would base the wealth of nations on a worship of metal for its own sake. On one of his reports he wrote: "Currency, in itself, is not wealth but a bill of exchange that must be paid to the bearer in exchange of the fruits of Agriculture or the works of industry. If these fruits or these works be missing, there will be poverty with a lot of money; if they are abundant, there will be wealth with little money; thus, a nation might be poor even in possession of a large quantity of metals, while another might flourish without other resources than those provided by its agriculture; but until not so long ago, it was believed that states were made rich by the mines they possessed."

In *Memo to the Consulate 1802*, he presented his argument for industrialization: "No educated nation wishes that their raw materials leave the country and be manufactured abroad; on the contrary, they strive not only to give them new shape at home, but also to attract raw materials from other countries, transform them and then sell them."

But Belgrano's innovating ideas could not go beyond theory, for they met with great opposition among the other members of the Consulate.

"I can hardly begin to convey my surprise when I learned the names of the men appointed by the king for the Consulate. Except the odd fellow, they were all Spanish merchants; they cared for nothing other than their monopolist commerce, that is to say, to buy at four and sell at eight. My spirit was abated, and I realized that nothing would be done for the benefit of the provinces by a bunch of men whose personal interest outweighed that of the general public. However, because of the responsibilities of my position, I could talk and write about such matters, so I decided to sow the seeds that would yield fruit some day."

In one of his last articles for the *Correo de Comercio* (*Commerce Courier*), he insisted on the need of creating a strong internal market, as a prerequisite for a more equitable distribution of wealth: "Our love for the country and our obligations demand that we direct our concerns to the essential objects of agriculture and industry in order to profit through domestic trade, making the country rich in turn; for the country will never leave its present state of misery if the objects of exchange are not valued; at present, far from speaking of revenues, they not only lose their capital, but also the wages they deserve. Only domestic trade is capable of furnishing the said objects with their proper value, increasing the capital and with it the funds available to the Nation, because by searching and facilitating an outlet for them, their prices are kept at a competitive price, both for the producer and the consumer, necessarily resulting in an increase of useful labor, which in turn brings about abundance, comfort and an increase of the population."

Manuel, the Subversive

As the following report well shows, Belgrano's ideas had a high level of social awareness: "It grieves me to say that, without even leaving this capital, I have seen a large number of idle men whose only possessions are misery and privation; a large number of families whose only subsistence derives from the fertility of the country, which is constantly denoting the wealth it possesses, that is, its potential abundance; and only with difficulty may one find a family applied to a useful job, exercising an art or employed in such a way as to make their lives more comfortable. These miserable ranchos where the children reach puberty without ever having been anything but idle, must be dealt with straight away." But he would not be contented with expressing his disapproval, and offered solutions: "Wool, cotton and other raw materials we possess, or may possess through industry, may offer a thousand means of subsistence to these unfortunate people who, used to living in idleness, as I have said, from an early age, find work very taxing in adult life, and become thieves or beggars."

Belgrano was the first man to propose, in the region and towards the end of the 18th century, a comprehensive agrarian reform based on the expropriation of uncultivated lands, and their allotment to the dispossessed: "It is essential that those who are now almost ashamed of appearing before their fellow men on account of their privation and misery are given the means to enter the order of society, and this shall be possible only if property be given to them (...) Those who possess uncultivated land should be forced to sell it, or at least half of it, if after a certain period of time the proprietors do not cultivate the same; and even more so those whose land is not made to produce in any way, and are adjoining our countryside towns, whose inhabitants are surrounded by great proprietors, and who neither individually nor communally have any of the rights stipulated by the law – for this reason, they do not make progress."

On the 1st of September 1813 *La Gaceta*[2] published an article written by Belgrano a few years earlier, which had failed to pass the censorship of the colonial period. It is an invaluable, extraordinary document, displaying a sense of political awareness unthinkable in any other intellectual of the time. Don Manuel Belgrano wrote: "There are two very different classes of men; the first class disposes of the fruits of the land while the second one is only called to assist through its labor in the annual reproduction of these fruits and riches or to employ its craftsmanship in order to offer proprietors comforts and luxury items in exchange for what they can spare (...) There exists an everlasting struggle between these two classes, but since their force is unequal, the ones must invariably submit to the Laws imposed by the others. The benefits obtained by the class of Proprietors from the labor of the men without property seem as essential to them as the land they possess; but favored by competition and the urgency of their needs, they become arbiters of the value of their wages, and while this reward is enough to cover the daily needs of a frugal life, no combined insurrection ever upsets the exercise of such authority. The power of property is what reduces the majority of men to a life where only basic needs can be met."

---

2 José Carlos Chiaramonte, *Ciudades, provincias, estados: orígenes de la Nación Argentina (1800-1846)*, Biblioteca del Pensamiento Argentino, tomo I, Buenos Aires, Ariel Historia, 1997.

The Journalist

In 1801 Belgrano participated in the foundation of the first periodical edited in our country, the *Mercantile, Rural, Political, Economic and Historiographical Telegraph of the River Plate*. Some of it leading collaborators were Domingo de Azcuénaga, José Chorroarín, Juan Manuel de Lavardén, Pedro Antonio Cerviño, Gregorio Funes, and Juan José Castelli, Belgrano's cousin and friend.

The *Mercantile Telegraph* came out twice a week and featured very diverse articles, from serious political opinion pieces to scatological sonnets about piles: "Why o why, treacherous piles / after deceiving us with wiles / into believing you are gone / will you come back anon? Why do you irritate the peace / of our gentle orifice / and mar, without fail / the pleasure of its travail?"

Irritated by the political tenor of the publication and by the ever-extending range of its influence, Viceroy Del Pino closed it down on the 17th of October 1802 alleging that the publication was "indecent."

In March 1810 Belgrano returned to journalism and edited the *Correo de Comercio (Commerce Courier)* where he took up his search of, as he put it, "the happiness of the majority of the citizens." He persisted in the idea that the country had to be industrialized: "Neither agriculture nor commerce would be, in themselves, enough to attain the happiness of a people if obliging industry did not come to their aid. There can be no development if this vitalizing sector does not come to add value to the raw productions of the first, and matter and structure to the permanent variation of the other."

In an article published on August 11, Belgrano defended the freedom of the press as the cornerstone of public illustration. "This faculty is as just," he wrote, "as that of thinking or speaking, and oppressing it would be as unfair as tying the intellect, the tongues, the hands and the feet of all the citizens. It is essential to public instruction, to the improvement of the rule of the Nation and to its civil freedom, that is to say, essential to avoid the tyranny of any government that might be established (...) Only those who enjoy ruling despotically might oppose the freedom of the press, so that, although a fact be known, no one would be able to mention it; or those who are dumb and, not knowing the evils of the government, do not suffer the torments of those who are aware of them and cannot remedy them for lack of authority; or those who are very shy, and are frightened of the bogeyman of freedom, because it is a new thing and they have not seen its strength, and are not sure about the principles that make it kind and useful (...) But to deprive us of the benefits of the pen and the press because they can be abused is an apparent contradiction and an unforgivable abuse of authority, and indicates the desire to keep people in ignorance, which is the source of all our evils, and the tyrant's most reliable weapon to control the whole of Europe. Without that freedom, let us not believe that any blood shed or any work done will bring us any good."

Tossing Viceroys Out of the Window

During the first months of 1810, the meetings at the soap shop of don Hipólito Vieytes were very frequent. Those who attended were Belgrano and his cousin, Juan José Castelli, Mariano Moreno, Cornelio Saavedra, Domingo French and Antonio Beruti, among others. On finding out about the fall of the Council of Seville – last bulwark of

Spanish resistance against Napoleon – the group designated Belgrano and Saavedra to meet Mayor Lezica and request that an "open" *Cabildo* be called. The *Cabildo* finally took place on May 22 and discussion began about the future of the colony. But Viceroy Cisneros devised a scheme and on the 24th formed a council presided over by himself. Belgrano lost his usual composure and declared before the Council: "I swear to my country and to my comrades that, if by tomorrow afternoon at three o'clock the viceroy has not resigned, we will toss him out of the fortress window." That wouldn't be necessary. Cisneros renounced on the 25th and the First Council of Government was formed, led and composed mainly by *criollos*, and with Belgrano as one of its aldermen.

The First Draft of a Constitution Our Country ever knew

While his cousin Juan José Castelli, a supporter of Moreno's ideas just like himself, decreed the freedom and equality of the Indians and the end of tribute and personal services in Upper Perú, Belgrano was doing likewise with the native inhabitants of Misiones. On his way to Paraguay, he laid the foundations of the first constitutional project in the River Plate: *Principles for the Political and Administrative Regime and Reform of the Thirty Towns of the Missions*, signed on December 30 at the camp at Tacuarí. The text was used by Juan Bautista Alberdi in 1853 as one of the bases of our National Constitution.

Belgrano made his point in the introduction to this extraordinary text: "As a consequence of the Proclamation issued to let the Native inhabitants of the Towns of the Missions know that I came to restore their rights to freedom, property and security, which for so many generations they have been deprived of, and which have only served for the benefit of their rulers, as the evidence proves, not being one single family who could claim, 'I have inherited these properties from my elders.' (...) My words are not aimed at deception or delusion, through which the unfortunate Native inhabitants have been held under the iron yoke, treated worse than beasts of burden, until they were buried in misery and unhappiness, which I am seeing with my own eyes in their helplessness, their wan demeanor, and the scarcity of resources for survival they have been left with."

Among other things, the remarkable document established:

• Freedom to all the native inhabitants of the Missions: they shall enjoy their properties and use them as they see fit, provided it is not against their fellow men.

• Suspension of tribute for ten years, until they are able to produce and live with dignity.

• Creation of free elementary schools, and of schools of arts and crafts.

• Promotion of trade with the products of the communities.

• Equality between *criollos* and native inhabitants.

• Access to all posts, even military and ecclesiastic.

• Expropriation of the properties of the enemies of the revolution.

• Free distribution of those lands among the native inhabitants.

• Provision of seeds and farming instruments until they are able to obtain them on their own.

• This disbursement shall be covered with the fines on cattle-rustling.

• As the weights and measures had been modified to steal from the native inhabitants, the same weights and measures as in the great capital of Buenos Aires would be used.

• Those that went on stealing from the native inhabitants would be penalized, including the loss of property.

• The product of these expropriations would be used to create a fund for the construction and maintenance of schools.

• Election of a deputy per town to attend the future National Congress, whose living expenses would be covered by the Royal Exchequer "in view of the state of misery these people are in."

• Creation of a popular militia called "Patriotic Militia of the Missions," which would be integrated both by the native inhabitants and Spaniards[3] who had come to live to the towns, considering that these honorable positions are no longer sold or offered in return for favors as the despots of the ancient Government were wont to."

• Defense of ecology: "Maté trees cannot be cut down under penalty of a fine of ten pesos each, to be divided into equal shares: half to the informer and the other half to the school fund."

• Labor rights: "The horrid excesses perpetrated against the native inhabitants, whose labor is appropriated without pay, are made worse by the application of scandalous punishments;" all workers shall receive their wages in cash – promissory notes and vouchers are not accepted. The employer who did not comply "shall be fined 100 pesos the first time,

3 In those days it was common to refer to the *criollos* as "Spaniards born in America."

500 the second time, and the third time his properties shall
be confiscated and he shall be banished, giving half the
value to the claimant, and the other half being donated to
the school fund."

• Death penalty to those who apply physical punishment to their workers: "They will be forbidden to impose
any kind of punishment to the native inhabitants, as I know
they have done with overwhelming iniquity, for they
should appeal to their judges if they had something to complain about; and if this abhorrent behavior continue and
they use the stick against the native inhabitants, they will be
deprived of all their possessions, which shall be done in the
aforementioned manner, and if they use the whip, they will
be punished with execution."

Do not Wave Flags at Me

Towards the close of 1811, Spanish attacks against the
coast of the Paraná River had increased, directed by the
Spanish governor of Montevideo, Pascual Vigodet. In face
of this situation the Triumvirate ordered Belgrano to leave
for Rosario with an army corps on the 24th of January 1812.
General Belgrano managed to control Spanish aggressions
and established, on the bank of the Paraná River, a battery
which he called Liberty. Belgrano requested and obtained
permission for his soldiers to wear a rosette. By a decree
dated February 18, 1812, the Triumvirate created, following
the design proposed by Belgrano, a "national rosette for the
United Provinces of the River Plate, of two colors, white
and light blue, abolishing the red one formerly used to
identify them."

Belgrano got carried away and replied to the Triumvirate,
saying that on the 23rd of February 1812 he had handed

the rosettes to his soldiers to "show our enemies that we are determined to sustain the independence of America." He was one of the few who in those days dared speak of independence.

By contrast, the Triumvirate, and especially its secretary, Bernardino Rivadavia, did not want to upset Great Britain, which was at this point Spain's ally and had let the Triumvirate know through its ambassador in Rio, Lord Strangford, that at present it would not approve of any attempt at independence in this part of the continent.

But Belgrano was determined to follow the path to freedom. On the 27th of February 1812 he inaugurated a new battery, which he called Independence. Far from the saccharine version classroom history feeds us, Belgrano did not stare at the sky to wait for the ideal cloud to pass and so obtain the colors of "our patriotic ensign," but made his troops line up in front of a flag sewed by María Catalina Echeverría, a neighbor from Rosario. The flag had the colors of the rosette and its creator ordered his officials and soldiers to pledge allegiance saying: "Let us swear to defeat our internal and external enemies and South America will be the Temple of Freedom and Independence."

Rivadavia objected to this and in a furious letter ordered Belgrano to put that flag away and continue to use the Spanish one: "The demonstration in which Your Honor inflamed the troops under your command by hoisting the white-and-blue flag is, in the eyes of this government, capable of destroying the grounds on which our operations are based and the protestations we have so frequently made, which in our foreign affairs constitute the main political principle we have adopted. This government has resolved that you make the hoisting of the white-and-blue flag pass for a fit of enthusiasm, furtively conceal it and replace it with the

one sent herewith, which is the one used at the fortress; ˎ
taking care in the future not to disobey the decisions of the
government in such important matters. The government
leaves the redress of such tremendous disorder to Your
Honor's judgement, but must warn you that this is the last
time it will sacrifice the respect owed to its authority and the
interests of the nation that it presides over, which can never
be opposed to uniformity and order. By return of post Your
Honor will give a thorough account of what you have done
to comply with this superior resolution."

But Belgrano only heard about this resolution several
months after it had been issued and continued to use the
national flag, which on the 25th of May 1812 was blessed
at the Cathedral of Jujuy by the priest Juan Ignacio Gorriti.

In July he finally received the notification from the
government and replied indignantly: "I will cut it into shreds,
so that no memory of it will remain. And if someone asks,
I will say that it is being saved for the day of a great victory,
but since that day is still very far off, everyone will have
forgotten about it." Thus Belgrano concluded his letter to
the Triumvirate on the 18th of July 1812, with manifest pain
and indignation.

Apparently, the first flag displayed two vertical, blue-
and-white stripes, like the flag of the Andes Army, which
San Martín would use in his independence campaigns.

As from 1813, however, in Buenos Aires and the Littoral,
the flag would change its shape and color. It would display
three horizontal stripes: light blue, white and light blue.
These were the colors of the Royal House of the Bourbons,
to which Ferdinand VII belonged, so that the use of these
colors was in fact a demonstration of loyalty towards the
captive King.

With the Ruins of the Northern Army

At last, Belgrano managed to gain command of the Northern Army – if that group of disarmed, underfed and underdressed men could be called one – which had been under the orders of Pueyrredón until then. The outlook was bleak: out of the 1500 that had survived, almost 500 were wounded or sick. There were 600 rifles and 25 bullets for each. But the general managed to reorganize them, spruce up the relaxed discipline and, thanks to the aid of the population, supply it with what was necessary to launch an attack.

Sadly, throughout the Twentieth Century, Belgrano's notions about the army were forgotten by most Argentine generals: "Subordination of the soldier to his commander is strengthened when it begins at the head, and not the feet, that is to say, when commanders are the first to set the example; for this to be so it suffices that the General be subordinated to the government, and so will the rest in the line of command. Fortunate is the army in which the soldier does not see honesty and obligations gainsaid by all those who are in command."

The troops led by Belgrano, as all the troops of our wars of independence, spent months or even years without receiving their pay, went poorly dressed and had to face all kinds of hardships. Belgrano had the idea of allotting a plot of land to each regiment for cultivation, so all the corps had a garden with vegetables and legumes and, in addition, everyone had their needs covered and the team was entertained, for the remaining products were sold for the benefit of all the soldiers who had grown them.

The image of a slightly "soft" Belgrano does not correspond with reality at all. He applied military discipline with rigor, even in the case of the Bishop of Salta, whom he ordered to leave that capital within 24 hours after intercepting a letter he had written to enemy commander Goyeneche.

The Exodus of the People of Jujuy

On the 29th of July 1812, facing the imminent advance of a powerful Spanish army led by Pío Tristán from the north, Belgrano issued a communiqué ordering a general retreat. Belgrano's order was strikingly clear: the land was to be devastated before the arrival of the Spaniards – neither houses, nor food, nor beasts of burden, nor iron objects nor mercantile articles should be left for them to use.

Belgrano was wary of the local oligarchies, which he described as "the denaturalized men and women who live among us and who would not give up any opportunity to abuse our sacred rights of liberty, property and security and see us once again enslaved." He had been informed that the local oligarchy had already made contact with Spanish troops with the purpose of making profitable deals with the prospective new authorities, who had promised to respect their properties. Belgrano left them no choice: either they burned everything and joined the exodus, or he would have them executed. The rest of the population collaborated fervently, losing what little they had, which was everything.

Belgrano exhorted them: "Since I set foot on this land to be in charge of your defense, I have spoken from the heart (...) Time has come for you to demonstrate your heroism and join the army under my command if, as you have often said, you want to be free."

This impressive operation began in the first days of August 1812. The people took everything they could transport in carts, mules, and horses. The furniture and household goods were loaded and the cattle were driven. The fire devastated the crops and in the city streets the objects that could not be carried were burned. A wasteland was all that was left for the Spaniards to find.

Diáz Vélez's voluntaries, that had gone to Humahuaca to watch Tristán's arrival and had returned with the news of an imminent invasion, were in charge of protecting the rearguard. Because of the proximity of the enemy, retreat had to be achieved in record time. 155 miles were covered in five days and very soon the human tide arrived in Tucumán. On their arrival, the people from Tucumán formally requested Belgrano to stay and stand up to the royalists. For the first and only time Belgrano disobeyed the authorities – who wanted him to go to Montevideo to fight Artigas – and on the 24th of September 1812 obtained the crucial victory of Tucumán. Encouraged by this triumph, Belgrano and his men chased the royalists all the way up to Salta, where they once again defeated them on the 20th of February 1813.

Belgrano knew he was on the right path, and knew who his allies and who his enemies were. He pointed this out to his close friend, the brave strategist from Salta, Martín Miguel de Güemes: "You are right to disdain doctors; their empty words are blown away by the wind. The only object of my concern is general welfare, and guided by this notion I do not pay heed to those wicked men who are trying to divide us, for what should rulers be if not the business agents of society, arranging and directing these matters in agreement with public interest? Let us work hard then, and if present generations are ungrateful, future ones will revere our memory, which is the reward that patriots should hope for."

Belgrano's Schools

As a reward for the victories of Salta and Tucumán, Belgrano was granted 40,000 pesos in gold by the 1813 Assembly, requesting that the money be used for the construction of four public schools in different parts of the country. To justify his donation he said: "To the honest man, to the true patriot deserving the trust of his fellow citizens in the management of public funds, there is nothing as despicable as money and wealth; these are an obstacle to virtue, which in the shape of a reward are capable not only of exciting selfishness in others – making people subordinate public interest to personal welfare – but also of encouraging a passion as abominable as greed. In accordance with what behooves my honor and the desire to see my country thrive, I have deemed it fit to allot the forty thousand pesos that were given to me as a reward for the victories of Salta and Tucumán to create elementary public schools."

True to his habit of seeing things to their end, Belgrano wrote down for these schools a set of rules[4] in which can be noticed the influence of the Swiss pedagogue Jean Henry Pestalozzi (1746-1827) – establishing, among other things:

- Provision of sufficient funds for the supply of paper, ink, and books for all students.
- Decent wages for teachers.
- Competition for posts as opposed to personal designation.
- Teachers were to revalidate their post every three years, demonstrating the capacity and qualifications to continue in office.

4 The original is in the *Archivo Capitular* of Jujuy (vol. 2, book IV), dated May 25, 1813.

• Students are not allowed to attend school wearing clothes that denote ostentation or luxury.

• The teacher is like a father of the fatherland and as such should be given a place of honor at the local *Cabildo* during celebrations.

Whatever Happened to the Money Donated by Belgrano?

Belgrano's donation was accepted by the 1813 Assembly, which established an annual interest rate until the construction of schools could actually begin.

Facing the inertia of the central government and after five years without anyone lifting a finger, in 1818 the beneficiary provinces filed a collective complaint to Director Rondeau. In 1823, Minister Rivadavia astoundingly replied that he had not been able to locate the funds. Ten years later, the governor of Buenos Aires, Juan Ramón Balcarce, officially admitted that the phantom funds were now part of the huge debt of the province of Buenos Aires, which was tantamount to saying "you might as well ask God to pay you."

In 1858, Amadeo Jacques brought up the subject once again, pointing out that the money had been deposited by Belgrano in the Provincial Bank, created by the Martín Rodríguez-Bernardino Rivadavia tandem. The famous rector of the National School of Buenos Aires tried to make further enquiries but in the end all he got were slanders from the official press.

Only in 1870 did the provincial state publicly acknowledge that the funds and the accumulated interest were under the jurisdiction of the Council of Public Credit of the Province of Buenos Aires, but were not available.

In 1882, the province of Buenos Aires was reorganized and given a new capital – La Plata – and a new financial administration. A pardon of sorts was issued for previous governors and Belgrano's funds were transferred to an account wittily called Primitive Public Funds. Marta Dichiara, a researcher from Tucumán, found the record of the funds and also evidence of the fraud: for forty five trimesters the bank belonging to the farmers of Buenos Aires had made use of the resources donated by Belgrano without paying any interest.

Sleeping dogs were let lie until 1947, when Evita and Juan Domingo Perón laid the foundation stone of the School of Tarija (Bolivia). For twenty years the stone slept undisturbed, until some official of the military government remembered the affair and saw the opportunity of making business with the Bolivian government, which at the time was getting ready to assassinate Ernesto "Che" Guevara.

By a decree of the National Executive Power signed by Dictator Juan Carlos Onganía in April 1967, 430,000 dollars were granted to finish the work. A bidding process was followed – suspected of irregularities – and trouble occurred at the Bolivian Customs House with regard to the entry of the cement and iron sent from Argentina. The school was inaugurated on the 27th of August 1974 during Perón's third administration, who christened it Argentine School Manuel Belgrano, and sent 356 school desks through the Air Force. The school has a capacity for 600 students at pre-primary, primary, intermediate and middle levels. It is a two-story building and it is set on a plot of more than 25,000 square meters.

The school in Santiago del Estero was inaugurated by Governor Felipe Ibarra with provincial funds in May 1822 and closed down in 1826.

Initially, the province of Jujuy was the one that better fulfilled Belgrano's legacy, without waiting for the funds to be sent from Buenos Aires. Work began punctually in 1813 but a few months later had to be stopped because of the advance of the royalist army coming down from Perú. On the 3rd of January 1825, during the inauguration of the humble school financed entirely with provincial funds, the *Cabildo* of Jujuy thanked Belgrano's gift and declared in an official document: "The gratitude of future generations will be eternal. In time, this philanthropic establishment will give good fathers to families, good citizens to the Republic and illustrious soldiers to the Fatherland." But the civil wars that ravaged the North allowed the school to function for barely three years before it was closed in 1828.

In 1998, the government of Jujuy gave 700,000 dollars to a building company to finish the work which as for today remains unfinished.

But the most pathetic case is Tucumán's, precisely one of Belgrano's[5] most beloved provinces, where his General Headquarters of Ciudadela functioned for years, where he fell in love with María Dolores Helguero and where his daughter Manuela was born.

In 1976, the governor of Tucumán, none other than General Antonio Domingo Bussi, decided to desecrate Belgrano's legacy by creating the School of the Fatherland, and for this purpose a commission with negligible funds was created to "honor the memory of our national hero." Besides the fact that if Belgrano had risen from the dead in

---

5 In a premonitory letter Belgrano wrote: "I loved Tucumán as if it had been my birthplace, but everyone has been so ungrateful to me here."

the Tucumán of 1976 he would have rejected categorically any kind "homage" from the perpetrators of the genocide, the project of Bussi and his civilian partners became a new opportunity to pull off illegal business deals. As of 1981, the site, located in La Rioja Street in the 600s, inaugurated by the general with great pomp, circumstance and a foundation stone, was as empty as the dignity of the commander of the murderous and genocidal "Operation Independence" of the last military dictatorship. Not even the stone remained; someone had stolen it.

Predictably, President Menem, holder of the Guinness Book record for broken promises, took up the matter, commissioning Minister Decibe to build some of the schools our national hero had dreamed of.

Governor Miranda, Bussi's successor in the government and a few other things, faced up to the challenge. Eventually, the school was built. But it was much smaller and much more expensive than expected. In particular, as Pablo Calvo explains in an exhaustive dossier published in *Clarín* on the 14th of March 2003, "no one knows what became of the 299,033 pesos that make up the difference between the sum sent by the National Government and the amount actually paid by the province to build the school. Attention has been drawn to this matter again, at the request of the Anti-Corruption Prosecutor of Tucumán Esteban Jerez, and the National Bank has been invited to explain where the money has gone. There have been no answers yet."

In sad, painful Tucumán province, where children die of starvation, in the so-called "Garden of the Republic" turned into an early grave, 300,000 pesos disappeared, that is to say, thousands of doses of medication, and thousands of food rations, as it appears in an internal report of the Minister of Education which, in addition, states that the government of Tucumán ignored its *repeated demands for an explanation*. "By 14th of February 2003 no information updating the case has been sent," read the ministerial report. And everything was done in the name of Manuel Belgrano.

Prosecutor Jerez found out that the funds had been transferred to a "unified account of the Provincial State" where Governor Miranda grouped the special items of his budget. "The account," Carlos Calvo points out, "identified as 'Z 05' like in an espionage film, was closed last year for alleged irregularities."

The supporters of former Governor Antonio Bussi and the followers of the Peronist Julio Antonio Miranda put the blame on one another which, at this state, is not surprising.

History's Biggest Fraud

Prosecutor Jerez intends to make further legal inquiries with regard to the black hole in Belgrano's inheritance. "My intention is to prepare a more specific file, because some sort of *legalized misappropriation* of the funds of the donation might have taken place."

To assist Your Honor, here we present the amount updated to March 2004, considering:

• that in 1813 the 40,000 pesos equalled 176 pounds of gold;

• that according to the current price of gold, the original capital amounts to 4 million current pesos;

• and that, with a humble 5% annual interest rate, which was what the 1813 Assembly had set until the schools were built;

• if we add the capital to the interests accumulated during the past 191 years, the total in pesos is 133,121,281,257,438, that is, one-hundred and thirty-three billion, one-hundred and twenty-one thousand two-hundred and eighty-one millions, two-hundred and fifty-seven thousand four-hundred and thirty-eight pesos.

The School of the Fatherland, quite a symbol, was never completed in line with the wishes of the Commission of Belgrano's Legacy functioning in the province and that, believe it or not, is run by Governor Miranda. By contrast, the National Ministry of Education has declared that it had done its share and stated that "the premises that were erected suffice to honor the memory of the hero." Evidently, the memory of the hero was not worth much to the tenants of the Pizzurno Palace (the ministerial seat) in those days of March 2003.

But the wise people from Tucumán believe that the homage was inadequate and in the early days of March 2003 a demonstration demanding the proper conclusion of the work and the construction of twelve new classrooms took place, led by teachers, students and students' parents, chanting "Belgrano is a patriot for all, so stop breaking his balls."

Vilcapugio, Ayohúma, Europe and Tucumán

Encouraged by the victories in Salta and Tucumán, Belgrano's troops entered Upper Perú, but the royalists received reinforcements and defeated the patriots in Vilcapugio on the 1st of October 1813, and in Ayohúma on the 14th of November. Belgrano, who had caught malaria, had to retreat with what little remained of his army. At the post house of Yatasto, Salta, he handed over the command of the Northern Army to José de San Martín. From that moment on, they would be united by a genuine friendship and mutual admiration.

In September 1814 the Directory entrusted Belgrano and Rivadavia with a difficult mission in Europe – obtaining the approval of European powers to the declaration of our independence. But it was not the right time: Europe was witnessing Napoleon's downfall and the defeat of the ideals of the French Revolution. The Kings, Ferdinand VII among them, were returning to their thrones, and it was therefore not a good time to speak of independence. The mission was a complete failure.

When Belgrano returned to the country in the last days of March 1816, the Congress of Tucumán had already begun its sessions, and thither he went. He participated in the declaration of independence and when discussions about the form of government began he seconded the majority of deputies who proposed a monarchy; he did not, however, suggest looking for a prince in Europe, but instead recommended offering the throne to a descendant of the Incas as a means to right the wrongs perpetrated by the conquerors against American cultures.

Belgrano's proposal, which was supported by San Martín and Güemes, was rejected, and some deputies, such as Buenos Aires-born Anchorena, mocked him and accused him of attempting to crown a king "of the caste of the chocolate-skinned."

Soon after, Belgrano resumed his military career by once again taking over the Northern Army, which was out of control after defeat at Sipe-Sipe and the disastrous and corrupt leadership of José Rondeau. While the soldiers wallowed in the direst misery, Rondeau lived like a *pasha*, in the words of a Swedish traveler who visited him at his camp in Jujuy the day before the disaster that would entail the definitive loss of Upper Perú: "I visited General Rondeau at his camp in Jujuy on the eve of the day he was expecting to be attacked. He received me in his tent which was set up in the oriental style, with all the comforts of a seraglio. Surrounded by women of all colors, he offered me sweets saying that in such a devastated country and on the eve of a day of battle, I should excuse him if he could not offer the comforts that could be found in a general headquarter in Europe. Shocked at the ostentation of his affected luxury, I replied that, on the contrary, I was quite surprised at what was displayed before my eyes."[6]

By contrast, Belgrano lived like any of his soldiers. He had donated half of his salary and as his dear friend José Caledonio Balbín said about him, "he was always short of funds, so that many times he was forced to borrow from me 100 or 200 pesos to eat."

Belgrano would constantly send dispatches describing the state his troops, that is, the men who braved the recent campaign against the Spaniards, were in: "Misery has no limits: there are men who carry their weapons on their own flesh, and to the greater glory of the Nation, we have seen some men take off their ponchos to prevent their weapons from getting wet, and suffer it with delight." The corrupt authorities of Buenos Aires, who assigned generous funds to destroy Artigas and who distributed among themselves the profit from the monopoly of the port and of the Customs House, would not even deign to answer. Until Belgrano could stand it no more and sent the following dispatch: "The men sitting on sofas or on pretty chairs, enjoying all kinds of comforts, might say what they like while we poor devils do all the work: beset by the smoke of food and cigars alone, they cut, evaluate and destroy the enemies with the

---

6 Jean Adam Graaner, en Vicente Sierra, *Historia de la Argentina*, Buenos Aires, UDEL, 1957.

same effortlessness with which they raise their glasses (…)
If the army cannot be assisted, if you cannot afford what it
consumes, then it should be let off."

Solitude and Oblivion

In January 1820, already a very sick man, the general
left on his last mission: to pacify the province of Santa Fe.
But only a few days later his health forced him to relinquish
his leadership and head for Buenos Aires.

In addition to syphilis, which had been detected in 1796,[7]
he was afflicted with malaria and an acute dropsy, which
prevented him from walking and riding.

Once in the capital, on April 13 he wrote to governor
and former friend Manuel de Sarratea informing him about
his "poor health," and attached a chart to the message listing
the salaries the State owed him. They amounted to 13,000
pesos. Sarratea would not deign answer. On the 19th of
April 1820, he repeated his request, and the governor sent
him a paltry sum. Belgrano had no valuable objects left to
sell and had to pay his physician, Dr Readhead, with his
watch. He told his friend Celedonio Balbín who visited on
his deathbed: "Dear friend, I am not well, I will not live
much longer, I await death without fear, but there is
something upsetting me: I die such a poor man that I have
no means to pay back the money you have lent me. But

---

7 When he began working at the Consulate, customary medical
examination was carried out by doctors Miguel O'Gorman, Miguel
García Rojas and José Ignacio de Aroche, who wrote in the medical
report: "We have evaluated the state of health of Don Manuel
Belgrano, Secretary of the Royal Consulate of this Capital, whom, we
have agreed, suffers various ailments caused by a syphilitic vice, and
complicated by other illnesses originated in the country."

you will not lose it. The government owes me a few thousand pesos in unpaid salaries; when the country settles down, they will give the money to my executor, who has been instructed to satisfy you with the first payment he receives."

The 20th of June 1820 was not just any other day. At the height of civil war, the city had three different governors on the very same day and without anyone noticing, Manuel Belgrano died. His last words were: "I hope that the good citizens of this land will work to remedy its afflictions. O my dear country!"

According to one of his most exhaustive biographers,[8] when Dr Readhead carried out the autopsy, he noticed that Belgrano's heart was larger than average.

Only one newspaper in Buenos Aires, *El Despertador Teofilantrópico*, run by Father Castañeda, made a reference to Belgrano's death. It said: "The sad, poor and somber funeral that the illustrious citizen General Manuel Belgrano has received in a Church by the river is a dishonor to our country and an ingratitude abhorred by Heaven."

Neither *La Gaceta*, which was the official newspaper, nor *The Argos*, which boasted of having a hundred eyes to see reality, noticed or mentioned Manuel Belgrano's death. For them, it was not news.

8 Bartolomé Mitre, *Historia de Belgrano y de la Independencia argentina*, Buenos Aires, Lojouane, 1887.

Incas, Kings and Traitors:
the Vicissitudes of Political Independence

*The most noticeable flaw in the inhabitants
of these lands is the habit of leaving for tomorrow what
should be done today – a habit confirmed by the colonial
system, which suffocated all energy and progress in their
inceptions. Tomorrow, tomorrow, tomorrow is the common
answer to any request, from the most trivial to
the most crucial; it is like a millstone hanging round
their necks, hampering them, and constituting
a serious impediment to any undertaking. When will they
understand that tomorrow never comes?*

JOHN PARISH ROBERTSON
British merchant, 1816

Before Tucumán

Following the incorporation of the deputies from the
provinces, towards the end of 1810 the First Council became
the "Great Council." This brought about Mariano Moreno's
resignation, and the quarrel, in the new government, between
Saavedra's and Moreno's supporters. In addition to the
defeats suffered by the Northern Army, which jeopardized
the success of the struggle against the royalists, the need to
make quick decisions led to the concentration of power in
a few hands.

The creation of a three-member Executive Power, the
Triumvirate, took place on the 23rd of September 1811. The
triumvirs Juan José de Paso, Feliciano Chiclana and Manuel
de Sarratea, and the secretary Bernardino Rivadavia, believed
that the demands of war called for a strong government and
dissolved all provincial Councils, including the Great

Council. These measures caused power to be concentrated in Buenos Aires, and deprived the provinces of all their representatives.

At the beginning of 1812, there arrived in Buenos Aires several Argentine officers coming from Europe, San Martín and Alvear among them. Soon after his arrival, San Martín visited his Masonic contact in Buenos Aires, Julián Álvarez, who put him in touch with the faction opposing the Triumvirate, led by a political and military organization clearly aligned with Moreno, the Patriotic Society, which had been founded by Bernardo de Motenagudo. At the same time, San Martín and his traveling companion, Carlos Alvear, founded the Lautaro Lodge, a secret society aimed, like the Patriotic Society, at obtaining independence and establishing a Republican Constitution.

San Martín and his comrades were ready for action and on the 8th of October 1812 marched with their troops, including the *Granaderos*, into Victory Square (present-day Plaza de Mayo) and demanded the resignation of the triumvirs for, as San Martín pointed out, "the troops are not always willing to support tyrannical governments." Thus a second Triumvirate was formed, this time aligned with the Lodge and the Patriotic Society, integrated by Juan José Paso, Nicolás Rodríguez Peña and Antonio Álvarez Jonte.

One of the crucial achievements of the Second Triumvirate was the concretion of the Constitutional Congress, pending since 1810. On the 24th of October 1812 elections were called for to choose the deputies that would represent the provinces at the Constitutional General Assembly. Among other things, the document stated: "Spain cannot justify its behavior in appearing before the court of impartial nations without, in spite of itself, acknowledging the justice and sanctity of our cause (...) the eternal captivity of Don Ferdinand VII has done away with their last rights, together with their former duties and most innocent hopes."

The Assembly began to hold meetings in the last days of January 1813 and declared itself the representative of the United Provinces of the River Plate.

Its goal was to declare independence and adopt a constitution establishing the republican form of government and the division of powers. Unfortunately, these objectives could not be met.

However, the work of the Assembly was crucial, for it produced a declaration of principles that set the precedent for future constitutional projects.

Although the struggle between the caudillo of the Banda Oriental, José Gervasio Artigas, and the authorities of Buenos Aires had already started, the Assembly caused a further rift between the two parties when it dismissed the deputies of the Banda Oriental, who carried a truly popular and revolutionary agenda, including the immediate declaration of independence, a republican constitution, civil and religious freedom, equality among all citizens, the central government's respect for provincial authorities, the establishment of the capital outside Buenos Aires and the encouragement of a fairer social system. The local bourgeoisie, represented by one of its wealthiest and most prominent members, Carlos de Alvear, found most of these items unacceptable. Oddly enough, the dismissal of the Banda Oriental deputies was based on "defects in the election process," when in fact they were the only ones in the whole Assembly to have been elected in a truly democratic manner. Evidently, they were rejected for no other reason than their representing the ideas for change fostered by the great revolutionary caudillo José de Artigas.

The illusion of independence encouraged by the meetings of the 1813 Assembly, manifest in the National Anthem, the patriotic symbols and the establishment of a local currency, was soon disappointed by the measures taken by its president, Carlos María de Alvear, who obtained two invaluable victories for the reactionary forces: the dismissal of the deputies supporting Artigas' ideas and the indefinite postponement of the declaration of our independence.

In this last matter, British interests played a crucial role, and as the British were allied with Spain against Napoleon, they opposed revolution in Spanish America. Fear of upsetting that great power – the leading buyer of the products of Buenos Aires and the sole supplier of the manufactures consumed in the city – marked the politics of those years.

Once again resorting to the excuse of an external threat, the Assembly dominated by Alvear took another step to further the concentration of power. It created a one-person executive power – the Directory. Alvear recalls this incident in his *Memoirs*: "I immediately noticed this big flaw (an executive power of various members) and being a member of the Constitutional Assembly, I advanced the idea of concentrating power in one person (...) There was no time to lose; the circumstances demanded we changed the form of government. Colonel San Martín had been sent to replace general Belgrano, and the departure from the capital of a man who had always expressed his opposition to the concentration of power, gave me the opportunity to tackle this great task."

Gervasio de Posadas, Alvear's uncle, was the first supreme director of the River Plate. Posadas, a kind of 19th century De la Rúa,* admitted to a friend: "I was not expecting this designation. After discussing the matter with men of my counsel, I accepted to carry the cross until I could put it down

* **Translator's note:** Fernando de la Rúa, president of Argentina 1999-2001, called "the autistic president" for his passivity and ineptitude, was ousted by a general uprising of exasperated citizens.

with decorum." Years later, he wrote in his *Memoirs*: "I ruled without being ruled. I meditated rather than slept; I worked and discussed affairs with experienced men; and most fervently I desired to make the right choices and endeavored to do so. If, despite my good intentions, I made mistakes, it is only human to err – I discussed everything with the secretaries, I actually read the documents before signing them and returned those I disliked."

With the support of the Assembly led by Alvear, Posadas took a number of important measures: after defeat in Vilcapugio on the 1st of October 1813 and Ayohúma on the 14th of November 1813, he substituted Belgrano for San Martín in the Northern Army, declared Artigas "traitor to the country" and ordered the creation of a war fleet commanded by Guillermo Brown, who immediately instituted a naval blockade of the city of Montevideo, thus completing the land siege laid by Rondeau.

The antagonism between Alvear and San Martín was apparent, and San Martín's assignment in the north was in fact a way of getting rid of him, rather than an acknowledgement of his well-known military virtues.

Posadas designated his nephew as commander of the Northern Army. This engendered much discontent, forced Posadas to renounce and, to make matters even worse, Alvear himself was to replace him. It was all in the family, but the maneuver was considered a provocation and the new director became even more unpopular.

Alvear's Brief Dictatorship

The new director had sent Manuel José García on a diplomatic mission to meet the British ambassador in Rio de Janeiro, Lord Strangford, and offer him the United Provinces as a protectorate of the United Kingdom.

Anticipating the ideas of so many civil and military rulers who came after him, General Alvear believed that the prosperity of his class relied on some kind of "carnal intercourse" with the hegemonic power of his day, and so wrote to Lord Strangford as follows: "These provinces wish to belong to Great Britain, receive its laws, obey its government and live under its powerful influence: they surrender unconditionally to the generosity and good faith of the English people. I am determined to support such a fair request in order to free them from the evils that afflict them. It is necessary that opportunities be seized, that troops come to rule unruly spirits, and that there be a fully authorized governor to shape the country as the King sees fit."

King George III of England, to whose rule Alvear submitted so tenderly, was as mad as a March hare, but not so mad as to accept these provinces and deal with our Southern temperaments. George III (1738-1820), King of Britain and Ireland, suffered a mental collapse soon after the beginning of his reign. His mental state was such that in 1788 a Regency Bill was introduced, but it was not passed until 1811, when the King was overcome by mental illness. He talked nonsense, would run up and down the halls of his castle naked and with a vacant look and, to the horror of the court, would relieve himself in any corner. It was not exactly the best example of superiority that Western and Christian civilization could possibly present to the barbarians of the rest of the world. His son, who would later be crowned George IV, acted as Regent until the 29th of January 1820, when his father finally died, raving mad, at Windsor Palace.

When Alvear's colonialist offer was known, protests erupted everywhere. Outraged at the news, San Martín decided to resign his position as governor of Cuyo, but an "Open" Cabildo reinstated him before the arrival of the replacement Alvear had promptly sent. Useless were the dozens of summary detentions, the application of the death penalty against opponents, or press censorship. On the 3rd of April 1815 the troops he himself had sent to fight Artigas revolted in Fontezuelas under Ignacio Álvarez Thomas. The leader of the uprising issued the following communiqué: "When a brave, generous, and virtuous country is abused, oppressed, and degraded by the small fraction of immoral and corrupted men who at present constitute and are the agents of the government General Alvear represents, it is the sacred duty of its sons to free their brothers and fellowmen from the horrors they are suffering. These and other reasons have led us to, unanimously, refuse obedience to the present government of Buenos Aires while directed by General Alvear or by any other who belong to that abhorrent faction; and we state that we shall not lay our weapons down until the people have freely elected their government."[1]

Al last, Alvear realized that he had no choice and, prompted by the English mediator appointed by the *Cabildo*, Commander Percy, announced his resignation. Percy put him on board a ship that took him straight to Rio, to get him away from the public protests which might have not stopped short of execution.

Soon after landing in Rio, Alvear appeared before the Spanish ambassador Villalba and handed him a letter saying: "It is difficult for an honorable Spaniard of noble descent and who has attempted to defend the Nation, to try to vindicate a behavior which resembles that of a criminal or

1 Julio B. Lafont, *Historia de la Constitución Argentina*, Buenos Aires, El Ateneo, 1935.

of a rebel hostile to his king. I would have gone far from men to hide my shame if I did not hope to make my procedure excusable or if I were not familiar with the clemency of the Sovereign and the indulgence of his ministers, thoroughly schooled in disgrace."

Treason was complete when he handed over to the Spanish minister confidential plans and documents including very precise details about the state and situation of the patriotic military forces, information about the next steps to be taken by the rebels, about the number of men, weapons and ammunition and their exact location throughout the territory of the former viceroyalty. It was a miserable plea for forgiveness, an abject manifestation of regret for a rebelliousness which the claimant likened to a common crime.

A few months earlier, this very same man had offered up these lands as a colony to Great Britain, and had left his country in a calamitous state. It is the very same man to whom the city has dedicated its most expensive monument and one of the most important and elegant avenues in Buenos Aires. And it is fit that this be so, as those who hold power and wealth never forget to honor the memory of the traitors to their country.

Changes in Buenos Aires

The Assembly appointed José Rondeau as supreme director, but because he was in charge of the Northern army at the time, he had to be replaced by Álvarez Thomas.

Although Alvear's fall dragged down an Assembly dominated by his supporters, the need to organize the country and declare the independence was still pending.

The *Cabildo* of Buenos Aires appointed a Council of Observation to issue a Bill defining the functions of the central government and calling for a Constitutional General Congress. Thus the Provisional Bill was written and passed on the 6th of May 1815. Among other things, this document limited the supreme director's period in office to one year and defined pertinent legal functions.

The Bill stipulated that Director Álvarez Thomas had to call all the citizens (i.e., property owners) of the viceroyalty to elect the deputies to the Congress that would meet in Tucumán with the purpose of discussing the form of government and a possible declaration of independence.

The ratio of one deputy per 15,000 inhabitants favored Buenos Aires, which was thus entitled to seven deputies, while the province of Jujuy, for example, would only have one. The majority of the provinces rejected the Bill, which they saw as another scheme aimed at further reinforcing *porteño* centralism, but they agreed to send deputies to the Congress. The provinces under the influence of Artigas, however, refused: Entre Ríos, Santa Fe, Corrientes, and the Banda Oriental. Chichas and Mizque, both provinces of Upper Perú, were represented by exiles, since the region was at the time under Spanish rule.

To understand the rather limited legitimacy of the deputies, it is enough to bear in mind the number of effective voters in the province of Buenos Aires, at the time the most densely populated and best-informed. Although the province had more than 90,000 inhabitants, not one of the seven deputies received more than 80 votes, and the average was 60.

The Congress could only begin to sit when two thirds of the elected deputies were present – but transportation was poor and the roads were in very bad shape. This delayed the beginning of sessions until March 1816.

Buenos Aires and the Provinces

As forerunners of the revolutionary movement, *Porteños* claimed support from the other provinces. But the fact that they had been part of the same viceroyalty did not mean that the provinces would naturally accept to be ruled by Buenos Aires or that they were willing to adopt its policies. Córdoba, for instance, due to its trade and cultural relations, was closer to Upper Perú and the Cuyo region than to Buenos Aires. Cuyo felt closer to Santiago de Chile than to the ex capital of the viceroyalty, with which it maintained, nevertheless, active commercial relations. The provinces of the north were, from every point of view, closely connected to Upper Perú.

Buenos Aires wanted to take upon itself the task of guiding the revolution, and although at first the provinces acquiesced to the new situation, they never resigned their autonomy and were not willing to comply with the orders of the *Porteño* ruling class.

The war made unified leadership necessary in order to coordinate all the economic and human resources. This responsibility rested on Buenos Aires, but it didn't mean that the different regions resigned their aspiration to rule themselves

Landowners from Buenos Aires and the Littoral, indefatigable "partisans of themselves" as Belgrano had described them, seemed to be contented with the revenue obtained from the exportation of leather, jerked beef and tallow, and besides the establishment of rudimentary meat-salting plants, did not spend one single penny from their enormous profits to transform the abundant raw materials into manufactures. Had this happened, a significant saving of hard currency would have taken place, employment opportunities would have been generated and the country would have enjoyed greater autonomy from British capital, which continued to control the commercial circuit.

On the other hand, these groups did not really care about the standard of living of the popular classes: to make production costs cheaper they would always try to pay the lowest salaries possible. The gauchos were not their customers anyway – buyers were on the other side of the Atlantic. This hampered the emergence of an internal market, kept salaries low and held population growth in check.

Ferdinand VII, a Recurrent Nightmare

In 1815 Europe was very different from what it had been in 1810. On June 18 Napoleon had been defeated at Waterloo by the joint armies of Russia, England, Prussia and Austria, commanded by the Duke of Wellington. Following this victory, absolutist kings returned to France and attempted to revoke the social and economic reforms carried out during the Revolution of 1789. One by one, European kings recovered their thrones, and for this reason this period is known as the "Restoration." It was a return to the past, to the times when the wellbeing of the majority was sacrificed to the privilege of a few. In any case, things could not be exactly as they had been before the revolution. Most monarchies had to make concessions and accept the creation of parliaments limiting their power.

Among the kings returning to their thrones, Ferdinand stood out as one of the most reactionary. "The Desired One,"[2]

---

2 It is hard to understand why he was called the "Desired One," especially after reading Benito Pérez Galdós' description of the monarch: "In close scrutiny, his peregrine physiognomy combined majesty and ignobility, beauty and ridiculousness."

as the Spanish had called him while in captivity, annulled the liberal constitution of 1812 and set out to recover the colonies in America, particularly after reading a report that stated that the metropolis collected, per year: 2.5 million pesos in Mexico; 4 million pesos in New Granada; 1 million pesos in Venezuela; 15 million pesos in Perú; and in Buenos Aires, the yet unvanquished locus or rebellion, 12.5 million pesos.

The Situation in America

In America things were taking a turn for the worse. In Mexico, at the end of 1815, the execution of the revolutionary priest José María Morelos had put and end to the anti-Spanish uprising.

In Venezuela and New Granada (Colombia), a powerful expedition under the command of General Morillo had defeated the patriots and in 1815 Bolívar was forced into exile in the island of Jamaica.

In Chile, following the defeat at Rancagua in 1814, the patriots scattered and the royalists gained strength, threatening to invade the only remaining rebellious provinces, those in the River Plate, on the other side of the Andes.

By 1816, Ferdinand VII only had to win back the territories of the ex-Viceroyalty of the River Plate, the only area still resisting the Spanish onslaught. Thus, these revolutionaries had the enormous responsibility of resisting, and extending the revolution until the Spaniards were gone for good.

The Crown organized a large army, commanded from Lima by the Viceroy of Peru, Brigadier Joaquín de la Pezuela and under the orders of Marshal José de la Serna, to harass the patriots and recover these territories.

The heroic resistance put up by the gauchos of Salta and Jujuy, led by Martín Miguel de Güemes,[3] and the liberating campaigns carried out by San Martín, were crucial in putting and end to Ferdinand VII's ambition of recovering his American Empire.

Is There a King in the Room?

This grave situation made the successive administrations send diplomatic missions to Europe and America to negotiate treatises, buy arms and obtain diplomatic support. Belgrano and Rivadavia left for London and Madrid towards the end of 1814. They stopped off in Rio de Janeiro and held a meeting with the British ambassador, Lord Strangford. There they ran into Manuel José García – sent by Alvear to offer England a protectorate over the River Plate area – and managed to hold him back before he could effect Alvear's offer.

On their arrival in Europe – shaken by Napoleon's defeat and with the conservative Restoration well under way – the two *criollos* realized that there was nothing to negotiate. Manuel de Sarratea, who had been in Europe for a while, fantasized about kidnapping the Infant Francisco de Paula (Ferdinand VII's brother), bringing him clandestinely to

---

3 Martín Miguel de Güemes had been born in Salta in 1783. He followed a military career and participated in the defense of Buenos Aires in 1806 and 1807. He also fought in Suipacha. San Martín realized Güemes' great military potential and charisma and commissioned him to train irregular troops and carry out a true guerrilla warfare. Together with his gauchos, called the "Infernal Lads," he was the one and only heroic guardian of the northern frontier.

Buenos Aires and crowning him King of the River Plate, so as to placate the Europeans. But this fantastic plan would fail.

The Congress of the Free People

Our history textbooks – even those described as "progressive" – will often shamelessly state that the provinces controlled by Artigas refused to send deputies to the Congress of Tucumán or, to make it even more personal, that Artigas himself refused to send them. But they do not say why, and forget to mention the serious episode that explains the absence of delegates from the Banda Oriental, Santa Fe, Entre Ríos, Misiones and part of Córdoba, that is to say, of about half the country at the time.

When the Congress was called for, José Artigas[4] in turn called for a Congress of the Free People to discuss democratically the briefs that the deputies would carry to Tucumán. The Congress gathered in Concepción del Uruguay (Entre Ríos) on the 29th of June 1815, with delegates from the Banda Oriental, Corrientes, Santa Fe, Córdoba, Entre Ríos and Misiones. Their first measures were to swear independence from Spain, hoist the tricolor flag – light-blue and white with a red diagonal stripe – and send a delegation to Buenos Aires to achieve the longed-for unity.

While in Buenos Aires the Bill of Transit of Individuals was being passed, stating that "Every individual lacking

---

4 José Gervasio de Artigas represented the interests of the hinterlands and was the first to advocate federal ideas for the River Plate area. He combined the ideas for political change that had been promoted by the May Revolution with the will to carry out economic and social changes, and achieve a more equitable distribution of wealth and power.

legitimate property will be reputed a servant, and will be forced to obtain papers from his employer and have them endorsed by a judge. Those who do not have these papers will be reputed as vagrants and will be arrested or incorporated into the army," Artigas issued his Bill for the Improvement of the Countryside, which established the expropriation of the lands belonging to "émigrés, bad Europeans and worse Americans," and their distribution among the dispossessed to "populate the countryside with useful arms."

This alarmed the authorities of Buenos Aires who, while receiving Artigas' delegates, were secretly preparing to invade his territories. To divert the attention of the representatives of the caudillo, a show was staged acknowledging his position and honors and begging him to take part in the Congress.

When delays became unjustifiable and the imminent invasion of one of the provinces belonging to the League of the Free People could no longer be kept a secret, Director Álvarez Thomas decided to kidnap the representatives, as he later admitted in a letter addressed to Artigas where he informed him about the invasion: "I have sent forces to Santa Fe with instructions as manifested in the proclaims I enclose herewith. The deputies of Your Excellency have been sequestered from their activities for, being informed of the said measure, I feared they might persuade Your Excellency to resist that which should be carried out with the calm and composure befitting to all." To all, except the people from Santa Fe, one might add.

The man who was taking this illegitimate measure was Álvarez Thomas, who would have never risen in revolt against Alvear had he not counted with the loyal support of Artigas' forces in Santa Fe.

As José Luis Busaniche points out, the invasion of Santa Fe meant that the glorious oligarchy of Buenos Aires had resolved to draw the limit of the new State on the Paraná River, preserving the province of Santa Fe with its port and Customs House, and seeking either to liberate the area from Artigas' influence, or to surrender those territories to Portugal. What mattered to them was to make Artigas, his gauchos and his revolutionary project disappear. Between August 25 and 30, 1815, the cities of Santa Fe and Rosario were devastated by the troops led by Viamonte, who appointed Juan Francisco Tarragona – a puppet of the *porteño* authorities – as new governor. But Artigas' popular army would soon put and end to this farce, regaining power for the Protector of the Free. Following these episodes, and seeing that the Congress of Tucumán would be dominated by the *porteño* followers of the director, and after discussing the matter with the delegates of the different regions, Artigas decided, at last, not to send his deputies to the famous Congress.

What was Tucumán Like in Those Days?

The city of Tucumán had been chosen because it was situated at the heart of the Viceroyalty and because the provinces refused to allow Buenos Aires to become the sole protagonist in a situation where all were concerned. Fray Cayetano Rodríguez explained to a friend the motives behind the choice of Tucumán: "Now you seem to find a hundred reasons against the Congress taking place in Tucumán. But where would you like it to be held? In Buenos Aires? Don't you know that they all refuse to come to a place which they see as the oppressor of their rights, and aspiring to subdue them? Don't you know that here the bayonets set the law and frighten even thoughts away? Don't you know that the *Porteños* are widely despised across the United or disunited Provinces of the River Plate?"

In those days Tucumán was a small town twelve blocks across. The bell towers of the four churches and the *Cabildo* could be seen from afar. The inhabitants of Tucumán, about 13,000, led a quiet life which would only liven up at midday, when the town center was suddenly crowded by carts, street vendors and people who wandered about the *pulperías* (taverns) and stores. There was always sugar for the maté and a singer willing to cheer up the people with a *zamba*.

Social gathering were held in the evenings, just like in Buenos Aires, but at ten the curfew reminded them that they lived in a war zone and that they had to seek shelter in their homes.

The first to arrive in Tucumán were the *porteño* deputies and the people from Cuyo. The remaining delegates gradually reached their destination and on the 24th of March 1816 the Congress began its sessions.

The Congress Begins

On the 24th of March – a date then lacking the infamous connotations it holds today** – 1816 the Congress began to hold meetings, presided over by Dr Pedro Medrano, who would confess to a friend: "Don't you agree with me that the task of giving a speech at the opening ceremony of the Congress is quite a drag? Tough luck! I have been thinking of something to say, but still haven't come up with anything." But eventually he must have come up with something and the sessions began. It was resolved that the

** **Translator's note:** The 24th of March 1976 is the date when the military took power and the darkest and most sinister period in Argentine history began.

presidency would change every month, and two secretaries were designated: Juan José Paso and Mariano Serrano.[5]

"So poor was the country that, like Jesus, it had nowhere to be born," said the popular couplet, and, in point of fact, the Congress began to sit at the house of Doña Francisca Bazán de Laguna – as we all know from childhood, the best cook of *empanadas* in all Tucumán – situated on Calle del Rey 151. It had been built towards the close of the 18th century and was a typical colonial house. The owner consented to some modifications being made *ad hoc*. Some walls were knocked down and a large room of 49 x 16 ft was thereby created. Governor Aráoz and the Convents of Santo Domingo and San Francisco contributed some of the furniture. When the Congress moved to Buenos Aires, Doña Francisca recovered her house. In 1869 the government bought it, but not in order to turn it into a museum, but to build a post office! In 1880, when the house was beginning to crumble down, a project of restoration was passed which took more than fifty years to be carried out.

Represented provinces:
Buenos Aires, 7 deputies; Córdoba, 5 deputies; Tucumán, 3 deputies; Catamarca, 2; Santiago del Estero, 2; Mendoza, 2; Salta, 2; La Rioja, 2; San Luis, 1; Jujuy, 1; Chuquisaca, 4 deputies; Cochabamba, 1; La Plata, 2; Chichas, 1 deputy

---

5 José Mariano Serrano came from Upper Perú. He took his doctor's degree in Charcas, which he represented at the 1813 Assembly and at the Congress of Tucumán. He was the author of the Act and Declaration of Independence. Nine years later, in 1825, he penned the Act of Independence of Bolivia, where he held legal and government posts until his death in 1851.

elected in exile (the district was controlled by the Spaniards); Mizque, 1 deputy elected in exile (the district was controlled by the Spaniards).

Members of Congress, sorted by profession and place of birth:

Priests: Antonio Sáenz, Buenos Aires; Justo Santa María de Oro, San Juan; Pedro José Miguel Aráoz, Tucumán; José Eusebio Colombres, born in Tucumán but representing Catamarca; Pedro León Gallo, Santiago del Estero; José Ignacio Thames, born in Córdoba, represented Tucumán; Pedro Ignacio Castro Barros, La Rioja; José Andrés Pacheco de Melo, born in Salta, represented Chichas; Mariano Sánchez de Loria, Chuquisaca; Cayetano José Rodríguez, Buenos Aires, editor of *El Redactor del Congreso Nacional*; Pedro Francisco de Uriarte, Santiago del Estero; Jerónimo Salguero, Córdoba.

Holding a University degree (mostly lawyers): Juan José Paso, Buenos Aires; José María Serrano, Chuquisaca; Pedro Medrano, Buenos Aires; José Darragueira, Buenos Aires; Esteban Agustín Gascón, Buenos Aires; Tomás Manuel de Anchorena; Buenos Aires; Tomás Godoy Cruz, Mendoza; Eduardo Pérez de Bulnes, Córdoba; José Antonio Cabrera, Córdoba; Teodoro Sánchez de Bustamante, Jujuy; José Antonio Olmos de Aguilera, Catamarca; José Severo Malabia, Chuquisaca; Felipe Antonio de Iriarte, La Plata (Upper Perú); Jaime Zudáñez, La Plata (Upper Perú); Pedro Ignacio Rivera, Mizque (Upper Perú); Pedro Carrasco, Cochabamba (Upper Perú); Francisco Narciso de Laprida, San Juan; Juan Agustín Maza, Mendoza; Juan Martín de Pueyrredón, San Luis.

The first matter to be addressed by the Congress was the replacement of renouncing Supreme Director Ignacio Álvarez Thomas. The deputy for San Luis, Colonel Major Juan Martín de Pueyrredón was then elected, of whom Medrano said:

"There might be more virtuous men, but no man as political. There might be wiser men, but no man as discreet. There might holier men, but not as shrewd and cunning. Out of the former qualities, Juan Martín has all the essential ones, and above all virtuous men he has diplomacy, cunning and adroitness, and, more importantly, opinion."[6] The new director was to travel to Salta right away to confirm Güemes as commander of the northern frontier after the defeat of Rondeau at Sipe-Sipe.

The next item in the agenda was the deliberation about the form of government. Most of the congress members agreed on establishing a constitutional monarchy, which was the most acceptable form of government in Restoration Europe. There was only one republic left in the world: The United States of America.

On the secret meeting that took place on the 6th of July 1816, Belgrano, who had just returned from Europe after his failed mission, proposed before the congress members of Tucumán that, instead of crowning a European prince or coming under Spanish rule, a moderate monarchy be established, ruled by an Inca prince.

Manuel Belgrano argued: "The nations of Europe are trying to monarchize it all. I believe that the form of government most befitting these provinces is monarchy; if we establish this form of government European nations will accept our independence. Furthermore, by giving the throne to a representative of the House of the Incas, justice would be done."

Belgrano received the warm support of Güemes and San Martín. Upper Perú deputies were also keen on the idea, suggesting the creation of a kingdom with its capital in

6 Academia Nacional de la Historia, *Historia de la Nación Argentina*, Buenos Aires, El Ateneo, 1961.

Cuzco; it was assumed that this would secure the support of the Indians for the revolutionary cause.

The manner in which historians have depicted Belgrano's idea is worth examining. Almost without exception they ridicule it and refer to is as exotic. They do not use the same adjective to describe the tsars, the prince of Lucca or the members of the European royalty whom the supporters of the director were attempting to crown. It seems that the only exotic monarch is the Inca – in this sense, the definition of the term given by the Dictionary of the Royal Spanish Academy is enlightening: "Exotic: foreigner, especially if coming from a faraway land."[7] Undoubtedly, for many local scriveners, an Inca, a *criollo*, or a *"cabecita negra"*[***] will always be more exotic than any parasite from a transatlantic monarchy.

For the *Porteños*, the crowning of an Inca was inadmissible and "ridiculous." The deputy for Buenos Aires, Tomás de Anchorena, claimed he would not accept "a king of the caste of the chocolate-skinned, a monarch in sandals," and suggested that, in view of the significant differences existing among the various regions, a federation be established.

Fray Justo Santa María de Oro, exhibiting his usual political cunning, claimed that before making any decisions about the form of government, the peoples throughout the territory had to be consulted, threatening to abandon the congress if that course of action were not taken. Discussions between the pro-monarchic and the republicans heated up but no agreement was reached.

---

7 *Diccionario de la Lengua Española*, Real Academia Española, Espasa, Madrid, 2002.

*** **Translator's note:** Disparaging name given to Argentine citizens whose dark complexions might evince their Indian descent, by those Argentine citizens whose fair complexions might evince their European descent.

Pueyrredón returned to Tucumán, urged the deputies to declare independence for once and for all and traveled to Buenos Aires.

A commission integrated by deputies Gascón, Sánchez de Bustamante, and Serrano wrote a memo of sorts for the congress, including the ever-postponed question of independence, a matter which made the governor of Cuyo, José de San Martín impatient, as can be inferred from the letter he sent the deputy for Cuyo, Tomás Godoy Cruz: "How long will we have to wait before independence is declared? Don't you think it is ridiculous to have our own coin, a national flag and rosette and fight the sovereign who we supposedly depend upon? On the other hand, what kind of relationship may we establish if we are still pupils? (...) Courage, my friend, for endeavors such as this one demand brave men." San Martín finished his letter expressing his cruel doubts: "The violent means to which we are committed, will they or will they not have the results expected by good Americans? Will we be able to attain them, and overcome the selfishness of the wealthy?"[8]

The Sun of the 9th Is on the Rise

On the 9th of July 1816 it did not rain, as it had on May 25 six years earlier. The day was sunny, and about two in the afternoon, the Congress began its sessions. At the request of the deputy for Jujuy, Sánchez de Bustamante, "the project of deliberation about the freedom and independence of the country" was addressed. Under the presidency of San Juan-

8 Letter from San Martín to Cuyo representative Godoy Cruz, in: Ricardo Levene, *El genio político de San Martín,* Buenos Aires, Depalma, 1950.

born Narciso Laprida,[9] the secretary Juan José Paso asked the members of congress "if they wanted the Provinces of the Union to be a free nation from the Sovereigns of Spain and their metropolis." All the deputies approved Paso's motion unanimously. Amidst the shouting of the onlookers peeping in through the windows and of those who had managed to get into the room, one by one the members of congress proceeded to sign the Act of Independence, which declared "solemnly to the face of the earth, that it is the unanimous and indubitable will of these provinces to break the ties that bind them to the Spanish sovereigns, recover the rights of which they were deprived and confer upon themselves the high title of a nation independent of the King Ferdinand VII, his successors and the metropolis."

On the session of July 19, one of the deputies for Buenos Aires, Pedro Medrano, in anticipation of the furious reaction of San Martín, who was aware of a secret plan involving some members of congress and the superior director himself, to hand over these provinces, now freed from Spain, to Portuguese or British rule, pointed out that before passing on to the army the Act of Independence and the new oath, an amendment should be made: after "his successors and the metropolis," the phrase "and from all foreign rule," was added; "to suffocate the rumor about handing the country over to the Portuguese."

The declaration was accompanied by a suggestive document that read "*end of the Revolution, commencement*

---

9 Francisco Narciso Laprida had been born in San Juan in 1786. When his work at the Congress was over, he returned to his province and was elected governor. On the *Unitario* side he fought against Quiroga and was defeated and killed in the 1829 Battle of Pilar.

of Order," in an attempt to project an image of moderation and appease European powers, which, after Napoleon's defeat, could not tolerate the word "revolution."

The commander of the English fleet informed His Majesty about the latest events as follows: "It might surprise His Majesty that the existing government (...) has chosen this particular moment to declare its independence, not only from Spain but from any other power as well. But this can be easily explained by the fact that it was necessary to placate the revolutionary zeal of those who constituted a threat, who could certainly not be informed of the true reasons. Public ceremonies were postponed until the 13th, when it became absolutely necessary to carry them out so as to allay suspicions; it was not hard to realize that the actors taking part in the ceremony were not very keen on the role they had to represent."[10]

The Infamous Treason to the Country

Medrano knew that the idea of "handing the country over to the Portuguese" was much more than a rumor. The Argentine minister in Rio de Janeiro, the ineffable and ubiquitous Manuel José García, had written to Supreme director Pueyrredón: "I believe that very soon Artigas will disappear from that province and perhaps from the whole Banda Oriental. You should begin to think of the man who will deal with General Lecor."[11]

10 Letter from the chief of the English fleet in the River Plate, Commodore William Bowles, dated Buenos Aires 16th of August 1816, in John Street, *Gran Betaña y la Independencia del Río de la Plata*, Buenos Aires, Paidós, 1967.

11 General Carlos Federico Lecor, better known as the Baron of Laguna, was the commander of the Portuguese troops.

Brazilian historian Caio Prado Junior explains the role played by the Portuguese court, to which these provinces were to be handed over: "The Portuguese monarchy was a mere puppet in the hands of England. The sovereign remained in Rio de Janeiro under the protection of a British naval division which was permanently stationed on the coast. The Spanish colonies which had made up the former viceroyalties of Perú and the River Plate would often orient themselves both commercially and politically towards Rio de Janeiro, which held the prestigious title of seat of a European throne and where the British general diplomatic and commercial headquarters were established for this part of the globe."[12]

While the Congress formally proclaimed our independence, the head of the new independent State, Juan Martín de Pueyrredón, sent commissioner Terrada to Rio with the following instructions: "The basis of negotiations should be the independence of those provinces represented in the Congress." Thus, the provinces of Entre Ríos, Corrientes, Misiones, Santa Fe and the Banda Oriental were left unprotected, that is to say, in the hands of the Portuguese. And the secret instructions Pueyrredón gave the other envoy, Miguel Irigoyen, read: "If the commissioner were told that these provinces ought to be incorporated into those of Brazil, he will categorically refuse. But, if after having exhausted all the resources of policy they were to insist, as if on his personal opinion he is to tell them that, at the most, these provinces would agree to constituting a State different from that of Brazil and recognizing its monarch as their own

12 Caio Prado Junior, *Historia económica del Brasil*, Buenos Aires, FCE, 1960.

while the court remained in the continent, but under a constitution that ought to be passed by Congress."[13]

On finding about these negotiations, the American emissary stated that "The government of these provinces is too submissive to Great Britain to be recognized by the United States as an independent power." In addition, the Secretary of State of the US wrote to the agent of that nation David Curtis Forest the following: "The measures taken by the government of Buenos Aires cast serious doubts as to whether it really was or will continue to be independent."[14]

Setting himself apart from the economic liberalism exhibited by the *Porteños*, on the 9th of September 1815 Artigas issued a Bill of Commerce establishing that: "Foreign products are to be equally laden with taxes throughout the United Provinces, specially those products which hamper our arts or factories, in order to promote industry in our territory."[15]

While the supreme director and the *porteño* landowning bourgeoisie were once again ready to commit treason against the country, on the opposite bank of the river and of history, José Gervasio Artigas implemented the most advanced agrarian law ever known in the River Plate area.

Artigas founded a farming colony that combined the communal traditions of the Abipón and the Guaycurú Indians from the province of Chaco – supporters of Artigas'

---

13 José Luis Busaniche, "Cómo fueron destruidos los pueblos de las Misiones Occidentales del Uruguay", *Boletín de la Comisión Nacional de Museos y Monumentos Históricos* N° 9, Buenos Aires, 1948.

14 A. P. Whitaker, *Los Estados Unidos y la independencia*, Buenos Aires, Eudeba, 1971.

15 J. P. Barrán y B. Nahum, *Bases económicas de la revolución artiguista*, Montevideo, Ediciones de la Banda Oriental, 1963.

ideas just like the Charrúa Indians – who had already been granted the area of Arerunguá in property for their subsistence. In addition, he had the *Cabildo* of Corrientes endow the indigenous peoples with lands, after making following claim: "Indians ought to be treated with more consideration, because it is not reasonable that while we claim our rights, we deprive them of theirs. Their ignorance and lack of civilization is not a reprehensible offense. They should, in fact, be pitied for a situation Your Excellency does not ignore who is responsible for. Are we to perpetuate this situation? Are we to be regarded as patriots when we are indifferent to such evil? For the same reason it is necessary that the magistrates endeavor to attract them, persuade them and convince them, and with deeds rather than words, show their compassion and filial love."

Less than a month after the proclamation of our independence, the previsions and wishes of Pueyrredón and envoy García were fulfilled. In a letter to the ambassador in Rio, Pueyrredón said that "the people no longer persevered in their democratic ideas and that the time had come to propose the crowning of the Infante of Brazil in the River Plate in order to dispel any doubts Spain might entertain."

A Portuguese intervention was thus given the green light. In mid-August 1816, a devastating Portuguese invasion was unleashed upon the Banda Oriental. The attack was carried out by 30,000 soldiers with modern weapons under the advice of our well-known friend, former English invader William Carr Beresford, hired by the court of Rio to reorganize the army. They were after Artigas and his people; their goal was to put an end to the most democratic and popular experience ever carried out in this part of the globe, to nip the "bad example," which they feared might spread, in the bud. Buenos Aires covered the back of the Portuguese, and its envoy García – whose diplomacy, according to Mitre, was sinister in extreme – signed with the court of Rio a treaty stipulating what follows: "The Argentine government commits itself to withdrawing the troops and ammunition it may have previously destined to assist Artigas, and to denying leave of entry to the latter and his supporters into the territory situated on the Western Band of the Uruguay River. Were he to enter, and could not be expelled, the cooperation of Portuguese troops will be requested to such effect."

Outraged, Artigas sent Pueyrredón the following letter, which revealed the hypocrisy of the supreme director: "How long does Your Excellency plan to increase our misery? Eight years of revolutions, toils, dangers, setbacks and miseries should constitute enough evidence to justify my decision and rectify the judgement of that government. On several occasions, your government has had the opportunity to verify the loyalty and dignity of the Oriental people, and it should also attest to my delicacy with regards its sacred rights. And Your Excellency dares desecrate them? Is Your Excellency determined to provoke my extreme moderation? Your Excellency should fear the mere thought of it! Following Portugal's aggression, it would be criminal to repeat the insults with which the enemies describe their enterprise as if it had already been accomplished. In vain may your government pretend to have generous feelings, they are gainsaid by the present events, which only confirm that Your Excellency is glad to make our times even harder, rather than encourage the determination and drive necessary to kindle the spirit of the free against the power of tyrants."

In another communiqué addressed to Pueyrredón, he wrote: "I have been persecuted but my feelings have never been humiliated. The freedom of America constitutes my system and to accomplish this is my only wish. Perhaps if Your Excellency was in my position and had my resources, he would have already succumbed and prostituted himself."

Artigas was wrong: Pueyrredón and his class had prostituted themselves long ago, as two English merchants poignantly observed: "Pueyrredón's Directory, sustained by the National Congress, was the source of incalculable damage to Buenos Aires. Bribery and corruption were the primary means to finance the Executive, and under his patronage, a large-scale smuggling network had been organized, large enough to dilapidate and ruin the public funds, while the pockets of the head of State were filled to the point of overflow."[16]

The massacre had begun; what follows is an account given by one of the generals of the genocidal army, the Portuguese Chagas Santos: "Having destroyed and plundered seven towns on the western bank of the Uruguay River and plundered only the towns of Apóstoles, San José and San Carlos, having abused and plundered the whole of the countryside adjoining these towns for a radius of fifty leagues, not being able to chase and attack Artigas in his own camp as I had wished, for lack of horses, on the 13th we crossed the Uruguay again and gathered in this here town of San Borja. Throughout the territory, 50 arrobas of silver were plundered and brought to our side of the river, many rich ornaments, many and excellent bells, a thousand horses, as many mares, and 130,000 pesos. In brief, the

---

16 William Parish Robertson, *Cartas de Sudamérica*, Buenos Aires, Hyspamérica, 1985. *Letters on South America; comprising travels on the banks of the Paraná and Río de la Plata*, London, J. Murray, 1843.

hostilities and damage we have caused and that we will continue to cause in this country, which is going be devastated, constitute undoubtedly the hardest blow Artigas has yet received."[17]

After reading the previous statement, the director of the invaded State, Juan Martín de Pueyrredón, wrote the invading commander, Lecor – whom he addresses "Chief of the Pacification Army" – as follows: "In the mutual interest of both governments I demand that Artigas be persecuted until he be deprived of all hopes to do mischief, to which his temperament incline him."[18]

Thus four years of resistance began, four years of combat between the Free Peoples and the Portuguese invaders supported by Buenos Aires, its landowners and merchants, who, for the time being, could breathe again, and cynically declare Artigas "Infamous Traitor to the Country."

Independing

A great step had been taken. After six years of going back and forth, of combats and violence, of heated debates between "the resolute" and "the unresolved," and many changes in the international scene, independence had been declared. We were past the ridiculous situation, as San Martín described it, of having a flag, a currency, a National Anthem, and fighting Spain while continuing to recognize its authority. Gone were the days when Belgrano was reprimanded for hoisting the flag and Castelli for "going too far." The provinces were a politically free territory, but political

17 J. L. Busaniche, *op. cit.*
18 Joaquín Pérez, *Artigas, San Martín y los proyectos monárquicos en el Río de la Plata y Chile (1818-1820)*, Buenos Aires, Misión, 1979.

independence did not guarantee economic independence. We were politically independent from "Spain and all foreign rule," but Spain had left us in a very weak economic position, and that eventually would push us into the arms of other foreign powers.

Spain had not only *not* fostered industry and trade among the various regions comprised in this vast territory; it had done everything it could to stop its American colonies from developing. Besides, the scant Spanish industrial production could not even meet the basic needs of the inhabitants of the Peninsula, and so they were forced to import most manufactured products.

Among us, incompetence, added to the lack of willpower and patriotism of the most powerful groups, doomed our country to produce raw materials and buy manufactured goods, often out of our own raw materials. Obviously, an English scarf cost much more than the Argentine wool it was made of. This entailed economic dependence to the buying and selling country, England in this case, which imposed its tastes, prices, and methods of payment. Besides, the countries which depend on the exportation of raw materials, such as grains or meat, are more prone to suffer the consequences of natural disasters such as draughts, floods or animal epidemics, and this can ruin their economy. Instead, industrialized countries are able to plan their economy without worrying whether it will be rainy, cloudy or sunny.

Independence was thus formal and exclusively political. On the economic level, we were beginning to be even more dependent on our great buyer and seller: England.

The new State, controlled ever since these foundational times by a parasitic landowning class, will hamper the progress of a nation settled in a territory which, potentially, is one of richest in the world.

Due to lack of transport and communications, the territory seemed much larger than today. In the eyes of travelers, it was a very backward area, with archaic forms of production, and with serious difficulties for the circulation of currency and products.

Provincial handicrafts were in full decline, and only investment and modernization could have transformed them into real industries, as was happening in the United States at the time. But the only ones who could have made investments were the *porteño* landowners and their embryonic national State. And none of them showed any interest in taking that step, which could have transformed our country into a world power.

Landowners in the province of Buenos Aires were too comfortable with their way of making a living to make any efforts. They were paid in gold or pounds sterling for their exports but paid their employees and native purveyors in pesos, usually devaluated. The less the currency was worth, the more they made.

As for the national State, it had just begun to take form, a process which would only be completed fifty years later. While it existed, between 1810 and 1820, it was mainly ruled by the abovementioned *porteño* cattle-raising and mercantile groups, which transferred their commercial practices onto politics.

This ruling class will be the one that will hold the reins of the country and that in 1820 will lead it almost to the brink of dissolution, the one that will prefer an association with England over any other connection with the rest of the country. Thus, a close economic dependence to England will materialize. And when one country depends economically on another country, when this other country decides what should be produced and what should not, when the prices of national manufactures are set in the "metropolis" and not in the factory, political dependence is added to economic dependence, because the autonomy and decision-making of the weaker country is almost negligible.

The main source of income for the incipient State derived from the duties paid by imports and commerce, which . negatively affected the poorer consumers in the country. Instead, the big landowners of Buenos Aires and the big merchants, particularly the English, by selling to the State, could deduct their forced loans and thus become its creditors and gain influence over its decisions.

The situation in the provinces was different. In some regions, like Cuyo, Córdoba, Corrientes and the northeast provinces, small and medium-scale industries had been developed, very rudimentary in some cases, but which nonetheless were able to supply the local markets and offer employment opportunities to its inhabitants. For the provinces, free trade meant the ruin of their regional economies, which were devastated by cheaper and better imports.

The superiority in economic and financial resources of Buenos Aires would make *porteño* influence prevail in any kind of national government. In this sense, for the provinces to escape the rule of Buenos Aires, it was essential that they obtain economic and fiscal autonomy to some extent; to accomplish this they had to obtain political autonomy and limit the power and authority of the central government. The following years of 19th century Argentine history, often very cruel and violent, will be thoroughly conditioned by this dispute.

Bibliography

General Bibliography

Abad de Santillán, Diego, *Gran enciclopedia argentina*, Buenos Aires, Ediar, 1956.

Abad de Santillán, Diego, *Historia argentina*, Buenos Aires, TEA, 1971.

Academia Nacional de la Historia, *Nueva historia de la Nación argentina*, Buenos Aires, Planeta, 2000.

Academia Nacional de la Historia, *Historia de la Nación Argentina*, Buenos Aires, El Ateneo, 1961.

Busaniche, José Luis, *Historia argentina*, Buenos Aires, Solar Hachette, 1973.

Caldas Villar, Jorge, *Nueva historia argentina*, Buenos Aires, Juan C. Granda, 1980.

Chomsky, Noam, *Política y cultura a finales del siglo XX*, Buenos Aires, Ariel, 1995.

Cutolo, Vicente Osvaldo, *Nuevo diccionario biográfico argentino*, Buenos Aires, Elche, 1971.

Di Stefano, Roberto, y Loris Zanatta, *Historia de la Iglesia argentina*, Buenos Aires, Grijalbo Mondadori, 2001.

Díaz Alejandro, C. F., *Ensayos sobre la historia económica argentina*, Buenos Aires, Amorrortu, 1975.

Dorfman, Adolfo, *Historia de la industria argentina*, Buenos Aires, Hyspamérica, Biblioteca Argentina de Historia y Política, N° 47, 1986.

Fernández López, Manuel, *Historia del pensamiento económico*, Buenos Aires, A-Z, 1998.

Ferrer, Aldo, *La economía argentina*, Buenos Aires, FCE, 1990 (2ª ed.).

Floria, Carlos, y César García Belsunce, *Historia de los argentinos*, Buenos Aires, Larousse, 1992.

Gianello, Leoncio, *Historia de las instituciones políticas y sociales argentinas*, Santa Fe, Castellvi, 1952.

González, Julio V., *Historia argentina: la era colonial*, Buenos Aires, FCE, 1957.

Kirkpatrick, F. A., *Compendio de historia argentina*, Londres, Cambridge University Press, 1931.

Levene, Ricardo, *Historia Argentina*, Buenos Aires, Lojouane, 1937.

Levene, Ricardo, *Lecciones de historia argentina*, Buenos Aires, Lojouane, 1950.

Levene, Ricardo, *Lecturas históricas argentinas*, Buenos Aires, De Belgrano, 1978.

López, Vicente Fidel, *Historia argentina*, Buenos Aires, Sopena, 1966.

Luna, Félix (dir.), Colección de la Revista *Todo es Historia*, 1967-2003.

Lynch, John, y otros, *Historia de la Argentina*, Buenos Aires, Crítica, 2002.

Palacio, Ernesto, *Historia argentina*, Buenos Aires, Hachette, 1951.

Pérez Amuchástegui, J. (dir.), *Crónica histórica argentina*, Buenos Aires, Codex, 1968.

Pigna, Felipe, *El mundo contemporáneo*, Buenos Aires, A-Z, 2000.

Pigna, Felipe, *La Argentina contemporánea*, Buenos Aires, A-Z, 2001.

Ramos Mejía, Héctor, *Historia de la Nación Argentina*, Buenos Aires, Ayacucho, 1945.

Real, Juan José, *Manual de historia argentina*, Buenos Aires, Fundamentos, 1951.

Rock, David, *Argentina 1516-1987*, Buenos Aires, Alianza, 1987.

Rodríguez Molas, Ricardo, *Historia de la tortura y el orden represivo en la Argentina*, Buenos Aires, Eudeba, 1984.

Romero, José Luis, y Luis Alberto Romero (comps.), *Buenos Aires, historia de cuatro siglos*, Buenos Aires, Altamira, 2000.

Romero, José Luis, *Breve historia de la Argentina*, Buenos Aires, Eudeba, 1965.

Romero, José Luis, *Las ideas políticas en Argentina*, Buenos Aires, FCE, 1975.

Rosa, José María, *Historia argentina*, tomo 1, Buenos Aires, Oriente, 1971.

Sáenz Quesada, María, *La Argentina, historia del país y su gente*, Buenos Aires, Sudamericana, 2001.

Sánchez Barba, Mario, "La sociedad colonial hispánica en el siglo XVIII", *Historia universal de América II*, Madrid, Guadarrama, 1961.

Sierra, Vicente, *Historia de la Argentina*, Buenos Aires, UDEL, 1957.

UNESCO, *Historia de la humanidad*, 10 tomos, Madrid, Planeta, 1982.

VV.AA., *Historia integral argentina*, Buenos Aires, CEAL, 1971.

VV.AA., *Historia universal*, Siglo XXI, México, 1975.

VV.AA., *Historia universal*, vols. XI-XVI, Barcelona, Salvat, 1985.

Wright, Ione S., y Lisa P. Nekhom, *Diccionario histórico argentino*, Buenos Aires, Emecé, 1978.

Yunque, Álvaro, *Breve historia de los argentinos*, Buenos Aires, Futuro, 1957.

Specific Bibliography

Álvarez, Juan, *Las guerras civiles argentinas*, Buenos Aires, Eudeba, 1969.

Anderson, Perry, *El Estado absolutista*, México, Siglo XX, 1992.

Andrews, George Reid, *Los afroargentinos en Buenos Aires 1800-1900*, De La Flor, Buenos Aires, 1989.

Ansaldi, Waldo, y José Luis Moreno, *Estado y sociedad en el pensamiento nacional*, Buenos Aires, Cántaro, 1996.

Ansaldi, Waldo, *Estado y sociedad en la Argentina del siglo XIX*, Col. Conflictos y procesos de la historia argentina contemporánea, CEAL, Buenos Aires, Argentina, 1988.

Aragón, Raúl, *Belgrano y la educación*, Buenos Aires, Leviatán, 2000.

Arciniegas, Germán, *Biografía del Caribe*, Buenos Aires, Sudamericana, 1973.

Assadourián, Carlos, y José Carlos Chiaramonte, *Historia argentina: de la conquista a la independencia*, vol. II, Buenos Aires, Paidós, 1996.

Assadourián, Carlos, *El sistema de la economía colonial: el mercado interior, regiones y espacio económico*, Buenos Aires, Nueva Imagen, 1986.

Azara, Félix de, *Viajes a la América meridional*, Calpe, Madrid, 1923.

Bagu, Sergio, *Estructura social de la colonia*, El Ateneo, Buenos Aires, 1952.

Barrán, J. P. y B. Nahum, *Bases económicas de la revolución artiguista*, Montevideo, Ediciones de la Banda Oriental, 1963.

Belgrano, Manuel, *Autobiografía*, Buenos Aires, Carlos Pérez, 1968.

Belgrano, Manuel, *Escritos económicos*, Buenos Aires, Hyspamérica, 1988.

Belgrano, Mario, *Belgrano*, Buenos Aires, Instituto Nacional Belgraniano, 1999.

Benarós, León, "La trata de negros en el Río de la Plata", en *Todo es Historia*, Buenos Aires, 1982.

Bernecker, Walther, y otros, *Los reyes de España*, Madrid, Siglo XXI, 1999.

Beruti, Juan Manuel, *Memorias curiosas*, Buenos Aires, Emecé, 2000.

Bethell, Leisle de, *Historia de América Latina*, Barcelona, Crítica, 1991.

Bruschera, Oscar, *Artigas*, Montevideo, Biblioteca de Marcha, 1969.

Burchardt, Jacobo, *Cultura del Renacimiento en Italia*, Losada, Buenos Aires, 1962.

Burguin, Miron, *Aspectos económicos del federalismo argentino*, Buenos Aires, Solar-Hachette, 1974.

Busaniche, José Luis, *Estampas del pasado*, Buenos Aires, Hyspamérica, 1986.

Busaniche, José Luis, "Cómo fueron destruidos los pueblos de las Misiones Occidentales del Uruguay", Boletín de la Comisión Nacional de Museos y Monumentos Históricos N° 9, Buenos Aires, 1948.

Cánepa, Luis, *El Buenos Aires de antaño*, Buenos Aires, Talleres Gráficos Linari, 1936.

Carande, Ramón, *Carlos V y sus banqueros*, 2 tomos, Barcelona, Crítica, 1983.

Carranza, Neptalí, *Oratoria argentina*, Buenos Aires, Sesé y Larrañaga Editores, 1905.

Chaunu, Pierre, *La expansión europea (siglos XIII al XV)*, Col. Nueva Clío, Barcelona, Labor, 1977.

Chaves, Julio César, *Castelli, el adalid de Mayo*, Buenos Aires, Leviatán, 1957.

Chiaramonte, José Carlos, *Ciudades, provincias, estados: orígenes de la Nación Argentina (1800-1846)*, Biblioteca del Pensamiento Argentino, tomo I, Buenos Aires, Ariel Historia, 1997.

Chiaramonte, José Carlos, *La crítica ilustrada de la realidad. Economía y sociedad en el pensamiento argentino e iberoamericano del siglo XVIII*, Buenos Aires, CEAL, 1982.

Cipolla, Carlo (ed.), *Historia económica de Europa, siglos XVI y XVII*, Barcelona, Ariel, 1979.

Cipolla, Carlo, *Conquistadores, piratas y mercaderes*, México, FCE, 1999.

Clark, George, *La Europa moderna 1450-1720*, México, FCE, 1980.

Colón, Cristóbal, *Capitulaciones. Diario de a bordo y primeras cartas sobre el descubrimiento*, Madrid, edición de facsímil, 1991.

Colón, Cristóbal, *Los cuatro viajes del Almirante y su testamento*, Madrid, Espasa-Calpe, 1977.

Colón, Hernando, *Historia del Almirante*, Buenos Aires, El Ateneo, 1944.

Corbiere, Emilio P., *El terrorismo en la Revolución de Mayo*, Buenos Aires, La Facultad, 1937.

Cordero, Héctor, *El primitivo Buenos Aires*, Buenos Aires, Plus Ultra, 1986.

Cortes Conde, Roberto, *Hispanoamérica: la apertura al comercio mundial*, Paidós, Buenos Aires, 1974.

D'ailly, Pierre, *Imago mundi*, 3 vols., París, Burón, 1930.

De Gandia, Enrique, *Conspiraciones y revoluciones de la independencia de América*, Buenos Aires, OCESA, 1960.

De Gandia, Enrique, *Historia del 25 de Mayo*, Buenos Aires, Claridad, 1960.

De Landa, Diego, *Relación de las cosas de Yucatán (1576)*, México, Garibay, 1976.

De las Casas, Bartolomé, *Historia general de las Indias*, México, FCE, 1951.

De las Casas, Bartolomé, *Relación del tercer viaje por don Cristóbal Colón*, Madrid, edición facsímil de la carta enviada a los reyes, según el texto manuscrito por el padre Bartolomé de las Casas, 1962.

De Ridder de Zemborain, Maud, "Cuando en Buenos Aires se remataban negros", *Todo es Historia* N° 393, Buenos Aires, 2000.

De Sepúlveda, Ginés, *Demócrates alter*, Buenos Aires, Indianas, 1927.

Del Techo, Nicolás, *Historia de la Provincia del Paraguay y de la Compañía de Jesús*, tomo II, Madrid, Regium, 1879.

Durnhofer, Eduardo, *Mariano Moreno inédito*, Buenos Aires, Plus Ultra, 1972.

Elliot, John, *La España imperial (1469-1716)*, Madrid, Vicens Vives, 1965.

Elliot, John, *Poder y sociedad en la España de los Austrias*, Crítica, Barcelona, 1982.

Facultad de Filosofía y Letras, Universidad de Buenos Aires, Instituto de Investigaciones Históricas Doctor Emilio Ravignani, "Advertencia y Prólogo de Ricardo Callet Bois", *Mayo documental*, Buenos Aires, 1961.

Facultad de Filosofía y Letras, Universidad de Buenos Aires, Sección de Historia, *Documentos relativos a los antecedentes de la independencia de la República Argentina*, Buenos Aires, 1912.

Fernández de Oviedo, Gonzalo, *Historia general y natural de las Indias*, Madrid, Oriente, 1917.

Ferns, H. S., *La Argentina*, Buenos Aires, Sudamericana, 1973.

Ferns, H. S., *Gran Bretaña y la Argentina en el siglo XIX*, Buenos Aires, Solar, 1977.

Ferro, Marc, *La colonización, una historial gobal*, México, Siglo XXI, 1994.

Figuerola, José Francisco, *¿Por qué Hernandarias?*, Buenos Aires, Plus Ultra, 1981.

Fitte, Ernesto J., "Castelli y Monteagudo", en *Revista Historia*, Buenos Aires, Theoría, 1960.

Garavaglia, Juan Carlos, "Notas para una historia rural pampeana un poco menos mítica", en Bjerg, Mónica, y Andrea Reguera, *Problemas de la historia agraria*, Tandil, 1995.

García, Juan Agustín, *La ciudad indiana*, Buenos Aires, Jackson, 1957.

Gelman, Jorge, "El mundo rural en transición", en Goldman, Noemí, *Nueva historia argentina*, Buenos Aires, Sudamericana, 1998.

Gerbi, Antonello, *La naturaleza de las Indias Nuevas. De Cristóbal Colón a Gonzalo Fernández de Oviedo*, México, FCE, 1978.

Giberti, Horacio, *Historia económica de la ganadería argentina*, Buenos Aires, Hyspamérica, Biblioteca Argentina de Historia y Política N° 12, 1970.

Gillespie, Alejandro, *Buenos Aires y el interior*, Buenos Aires, A. Zeta, 1994.

Goldberg, Marta Beatriz, "Nuestros negros, ¿desaparecidos o ignorados?", *Todo es Historia* N° 393, Buenos Aires, 2000.

González Arzac, Alberto, "La esclavitud en la Argentina", en *Polémica*, Buenos Aires, CEAL, 1972.

Guido, Tomás, "Reseña histórica de los sucesos de Mayo", en *Los sucesos de Mayo contados por sus autores*, prólogo de Ricardo Levene, Buenos Aires, El Ateneo, 1928.

Guzmán, Florencia, "Vida de esclavos en el antiguo Tucumán", *Todo es Historia* N° 393, Buenos Aires, 2000.

Irazusta, Julio, *Breve historia argentina*, Buenos Aires, Independencia, 1982.

Hall, John A., y John Ikeberry, *El Estado*, Madrid, Alianza, 1993.

Halperin Donghi, Tulio, "La expansión ganadera de la campaña de Buenos Aires", en Di Tella, Torcuato, y Tulio Halperin Donghi, *Los fragmentos del poder de la oligarquía a la poliarquía argentina*, Buenos Aires, Jorge Álvarez, 1969.

Halperin Donghi, Tulio, *Revolución y guerra*, Buenos Aires, Siglo XXI, 1972.

Halperin Donghi, Tulio, *Historia contemporánea de América Latina*, Madrid, Alianza, 1974.

Halperin Donghi, Tulio, *De la Revolución de Mayo a la organización nacional*, Buenos Aires, Paidós, 2000.

Hamilton, Earl, *El tesoro americano y la revolución de los precios en España (1501-1650)*, Barcelona, Ariel, 1983 (1ª ed. 1934).

Haring, Clarence, *El imperio hispánico en América*, Buenos Aires, Solar-Hachette, 1996.

Heers, Jacques, *Occidente durante los siglos XIV y XV*, Barcelona, Col. Nueva Clío, Labor, 1968.

Hidalgo de Cisneros, Baltasar, "Informe dando cuenta al rey de España de las ocurrencias de su gobierno, Buenos Aires, 1810", en *Memorias de los virreyes del Río de la Plata*, Buenos Aires, Bajel, 1945.

Hobsbawm, Eric, *Las revoluciones burguesas*, Madrid, Guadarrama, 1978.

Hora, Roy, *Los terratenientes de la pampa gringa*, Buenos Aires, Siglo XXI, 2003.

Huizinga, Johann, *El otoño de la Edad Media*, Madrid, Revista de Occidente, 1973.

Ianni, Octavio, *Esclavitud y capitalismo*, México, Siglo XXI, 1976.

Johnson, Paul, *Historia del cristianismo*, Buenos Aires, Javier Vergara, 1989.

Lafont, Julio B., *Historia de la Constitución Argentina*, Buenos Aires, El Ateneo, 1935.

Lafuente Machain, Ricardo, *Buenos Aires en el siglo XVII*, Buenos Aires, Municipalidad de la Ciudad de Buenos Aires, 1980.

Lanuza, José Luis, *Morenada, una historia de la raza africana en el Río de la Plata*, s./d.

Larriqueta, Enrique, *La Argentina renegada*, Buenos Aires, Sudamericana, 1992.

León Portilla, Miguel, *Visión de los vencidos*, México, Dastin, 2000.

Levene, Gustavo Gabriel, *Breve historia de la independencia argentina*, Buenos Aires, Eudeba, 1966.

Levene, Ricardo, *Ensayo histórico sobre la Revolución de Mayo y Mariano Moreno*, Apéndice, Buenos Aires, El Ateneo, 1961.

Levene, Ricardo, *El genio político de San Martín*, Buenos Aires, Depalma, 1950.

Levene, Ricardo, *El pensamiento vivo de Mariano Moreno*, Buenos Aires, Losada, 1942.

Lewin, Boleslao, *La rebelión de Túpac Amaru*, Buenos Aires, SELA, 1957.

Lewin, Boleslao, *Rousseau y la independencia americana*, Buenos Aires, Eudeba, 1965.

Litter, Manuel, *Farmacología*, Buenos Aires, El Ateneo, 1961.

López de Gómara, *Historia general de las Indias*, Madrid, Oriente, 1902.

Lopreto, Gladys, *Que vivo en esta conquista. Textos del Río de la Plata (siglo XVI)*, Buenos Aires, Universidad de La Plata, 1996.

Lozano, P., *Historia del Paraguay*, Buenos Aires, Ediciones Porteñas, 1916.

Madero, Eduardo, *Historia del puerto de Buenos Aires*, Buenos Aires, La Nación, 1902.

Maquiavelo, Nicolás, *El príncipe*, Madrid, Sarpe, 1983, págs. 108-109.

Martínez Sarasola, Carlos, *Nuestros paisanos los indios*, Buenos Aires, Emecé, 1998.

Matheu, Domingo, *Memorias*, tomo II, Buenos Aires, Biblioteca de Mayo, 1966.

Mauro, Federic, *La expansión europea*, Col. Nueva Clío, Labor, Barcelona, 1979.

Mellafe, Rolando: *La esclavitud en Hispanoamérica*, Buenos Aires, Eudeba, 1964.

Mesonero Romanos, Ramón de, *Memorias de un setentón*, 2 vols., Madrid, Oficinas de la Ilustración Española y Americana, 1881.

Mitre, Bartolomé, *Historia de Belgrano y de la independencia argentina*, Buenos Aires, Lojouane, 1887.

Mitre, Bartolomé, *Historia de San Martín*, Buenos Aires, Eudeba, 1971.

Molinari, Diego Luis, *Buenos Aires cuatro siglos*, Buenos Aires, TEA, 1984.

Monteagudo, Bernardo de, *Escritos políticos*, Buenos Aires, La Cultura Argentina, 1916.

Monteagudo, Bernardo de, "Ensayo sobre la Revolución del Río de la Plata desde el 25 de Mayo de 1809", *Mártir o libre*, Buenos Aires, 1812.

Morales Padrón, F., *Historia del descubrimiento y conquista de América*, Madrid, Editora Nacional, 1981.

Moreno, Manuel, *Vida y memorias del Dr. Mariano Moreno*, Buenos Aires, Eudeba, 1972.

Moreno, Mariano, *Escritos políticos*, Buenos Aires, La Cultura Argentina, 1915.

Moreno, Mariano, *Escritos*, Buenos Aires, Estrada, 1943.

Moreno, Mariano, *Plan revolucionario de operaciones*, Buenos Aires, Plus Ultra, 1973.

Morison, Samuel Eliot, *El almirante de la Mar Océano. Vida de Cristóbal Colón*, México, FCE, 1991.

Moutoukias, Zacarías, *Contrabando y control colonial en el siglo XVII*, Buenos Aires, CEAL, 1988.

Moutoukias, Zacarías, "Burocracia, contrabando y autotransformación de las elites. Buenos Aires en el siglo XVII", Tandil, *Anuario IEHS*, III, 1988.

Núñez, Ignacio, *Noticias históricas*, Buenos Aires, Jackson, 1957.

O'Gorman, Edmundo, *La invención de América*, México, FCE, 1958.

Oszlak, Oscar, *La formación del Estado argentino*, Buenos Aires, Planeta, 1997.

Panettieri, José, y María Minellono, *Argentina, propósitos y frustraciones de un país periférico*, La Plata, Al Margen, 2002.

Parish Robertson, Guillermo, *Cartas de Sudamérica*, Buenos Aires, Hyspamérica, 1985.

Parry, J. H., *Época de los descubrimientos geográficos*, Madrid, Guadarrama, 1964.

Parry, J. H., *Europa y la expansión del mundo*, México, FCE, 1971.

Pelliza, Mariano A., *Monteagudo, su vida y sus escritos*, Buenos Aires, Lojouane, 1880.

Peña, Milcíades, *Antes de Mayo*, Buenos Aires, Fichas, 1973.

Peña, Milcíades, *Masas, caudillos y elites*, Buenos Aires, Fichas, 1973.

Pérez, Joaquín, *Artigas, San Martín y los proyectos monárquicos en el Río de la Plata y Chile (1818-1820)*, Buenos Aires, Misión, 1979.

Pérez, Joseph, *Isabel y Fernando. Los Reyes Católicos*, Madrid, Editorial Nerea, 1991.

Pérez Galdós, Benito, "La corte de Carlos IV", en *Episodios nacionales*, Madrid, Alianza, 1971.

Pigafetta, Antonio, *Primer viaje en torno del globo*, Buenos Aires, Espasa Calpe, 1946.

Prado Junior, Caio, *Historia económica del Brasil*, Buenos Aires, FCE, 1960.

Prestigiacomo, Raquel, y Fabián Ucello, *La pequeña aldea*, Buenos Aires, Eudeba, 1999.

Pueyrredón, Carlos Alberto, *1810. La Revolución de Mayo*, Buenos Aires, Peuser, 1953.

Puigross, Rodolfo, *Historia económica del Río de la Plata*, Buenos Aires, Peña y Lillo, 1973.

Puigross, Rodolfo, *La época de Mariano Moreno*, Buenos Aires, Sophos, 1960.

Quesada, Vicente, *Escenas de la vida colonial*, Buenos Aires, BEA, 1945.

Quiroga, Marcial, *Manuel Moreno*, Buenos Aires, Eudeba, 1972.

Rato de Sambucetti, Susana, *La Revolución de Mayo*, Buenos Aires, Siglo XX, 1983.

Ribeiro, Darcy (1985), *Las Américas y la civilización: procesos de formación y causas del desarrollo desigual de los pueblos americanos*, Buenos Aires, CEAL, 1971.

Rodríguez, Martín, *Memorias*, Biblioteca de Mayo, Senado de la Nación, 1962.

Rodríguez Molas, Ricardo, *Historia social del gaucho*, Buenos Aires, CEAL, 1982.

Romano, Ruggiero, *Coyunturas opuestas. La crisis del siglo XVII en Europa e Hispanoamérica*, México, FCE, 1993.

Romero, José Luis, *Las ciudades y las ideas*, Buenos Aires, FCE, 1971.

Rosenblat, Ángel, *La población indígena y mestizaje en América*, 2 vols., Buenos Aires, Nova, 1954.

Rousseau, Jean Jacques, *El contrato social*, Buenos Aires, Losada, 1998.

Ruiz Guiñazú, Enrique, *Epifanía de la libertad, documentos secretos de la Revolución de Mayo*, Buenos Aires, Nova, 1952.

Saavedra, Cornelio, *Memoria autógrafa*, Buenos Aires, Biblioteca de Mayo, tomo II, 1966.

Saguí, Francisco, *Los últimos cuatro años de la dominación española en el antiguo Virreynato del Río de la Plata, desde 26 de junio de 1806 hasta 25 de mayo de 1810. Memoria histórica familiar*, Buenos Aires, Imprenta Americana, 1874, Senado de la Nación, Biblioteca de Mayo, 1960.

Salas, Alberto, y Andrés Vázquez, *Relación varia de hechos, hombres y cosas de estas indias meridionales*, Buenos Aires, Losada, 1963.

Salas, Alberto, *Crónica florida del mestizaje de las Indias*, Buenos Aires, Losada, 1960.

Salas, Alberto, *Diario de Buenos Aires 1806-1807*, Buenos Aires, Sudamericana, 1981.

Sánchez Albornoz, Nicolás, *La población de América, desde los tiempos precolombinos al año 2000*, Madrid, Alianza, 1977.

Santisteban Ochoa, Julián, *Documentos para la historia del Cuzco*, Cuzco, Archivos del Cuzco, 1963.

Scenna, Miguel Ángel, "Jesuitas y bandeirantes", Buenos Aires, *Todo es Historia* N° 76, 1973.

Schmidl, Ulrico, *Viaje al Río de la Plata*, Buenos Aires, Emecé, 2000.

Schvarzer, Jorge, *La industria que supimos conseguir. Una historia político-social de la industria argentina*, Buenos Aires, Planeta, 1996.

Segreti, Carlos, *Temas de historia colonial (comercio e interferencia extranjera)*, Buenos Aires, Academia Nacional de la Historia, 1987.

Sejourne, Laurette, "Antiguas culturas precolombinas", en *Historia universal*, México, Siglo XXI, 1975.

Sierra, Vicente, *Historia de la Argentina*, Buenos Aires, UDEL, 1957.

Smith, Adam, *La riqueza de las naciones*, Buenos Aires, Distal, 2002.

Solorzano Pereyra, Juan de, *Política indiana*, México, Porrúa, 1980.

Street, John, *Gran Bretaña y la independencia del Río de la Plata*, Buenos Aires, Paidós, 1967.

Tenenti, Alberto, y Ruggiero Romano, *Los fundamentos del mundo moderno*, México, Siglo XXI, 1985.

Tenenti, Alberto, *La formación del mundo moderno*, Barcelona, Crítica, 1985.

Todorov, Tzvetan, *La conquista de América, el problema del otro*, México, Siglo XXI, 1992.

Torre Revello, José, "Sociedad colonial", en *Historia de la Nación Argentina*, vol. IV, 1ª sec., Buenos Aires, 1940.

Udaondo, E., *Las invasiones inglesas y la villa de Luján*, Buenos Aires, Raigal, 1928.

Valcárcel, Daniel, *Rebeliones coloniales sudamericanas*, México, FCE, 1982.

Varela, C., y J. Gil, *Cristóbal Colón. Textos y documentos completos. Nuevas cartas*. Madrid, Alianza, 1997.

Vespucio, Américo, *El Nuevo Mundo*, Buenos Aires, Nova, 1951.

Vigo, Juan M., "Hernandarias entre contrabandistas y judíos", *Todo es Historia* N° 51, Buenos Aires, 1971.

Villalobos, Sergio, *Comercio y contrabando en el Río de la Plata y Chile*, Buenos Aires, Eudeba, 1965.

Villalta, Blanco, *Historia de la conquista del Río de la Plata*, Buenos Aires, Atlántida, 1946.

Viñas, David, *Indios, ejército y fronteras*, Buenos Aires, Siglo XXI, 1982.

Vitoria, Francisco de, *Relaciones sobre los indios y el derecho de guerra*, Madrid, Col. Austral, Espasa Calpe, 1975.

VV.AA., *25 de mayo, testimonios, juicios y documentos*, Buenos Aires, Eudeba, 1968.

Wast, Hugo, *El año X*, Buenos Aires, Peuser, 1947.

Watchel, Nathan, *Los Vencidos*, Madrid, Alianza, 1971.

Webster, C. K., *Gran Bretaña y la independencia de América Latina*, Buenos Aires, Paidós, 1971.

Whitaker, A. P., *Los Estados Unidos y la independencia*, Buenos Aires, Eudeba, 1971.

Williams Álzaga, Enrique, *Cartas que nunca llegaron*, Buenos Aires, Emecé, 1967.

Williams Álzaga, Enrique, *Dos revoluciones, 1º de enero de 1809 y 25 de mayo de 1810*, Buenos Aires, Emecé, 1963.

Zapata Gollán, Agustín, *La conquista criolla*, Santa Fe, edición del autor, 1938.

Zapata Gollán, Agustín, *Los precursores*, Santa Fe, Colmegna, 1980.

Zavala, Silvio, *Las instituciones jurídicas de la conquista de América*, México, Porrúa, 1978.

Zavala, Silvio, *Historia de América en la época colonial*, México, Instituto Mexicano de Geografía e Historia, 1961.

Zynn, Howard, *La otra historia de los EE.UU.*, México, Siglo XXI, 1999.